T0366751

A GREAT REVOLUTIONARY WAVE

WOMEN'S SUFFRAGE AND THE STRUGGLE FOR DEMOCRACY

SERIES EDITOR: VERONICA STRONG-BOAG

The story of women's struggles and victories in the pursuit of political equality is not just a matter of the past: it has the value of informing current debate about the health of democracy in our country.

This series of short, insightful books presents a history of the vote, with vivid accounts of famous and unsung suffragists and overdue explanations of why some women were banned from the ballot box until the 1940s and 1960s. More than a celebration of women's achievements in the political realm, this series provides deeper understanding of Canadian society and politics, serving as a well-timed reminder never to take political rights for granted.

Books in the series:

One Hundred Years of Struggle: The History of Women and the Vote in Canada,
    by Joan Sangster

Our Voices Must Be Heard: Women and the Vote in Ontario,
    by Tarah Brookfield

To Be Equals in Our Own Country: Women and the Vote in Quebec,
    by Denyse Baillargeon

A Great Revolutionary Wave: Women and the Vote in British Columbia,
    by Lara Campbell

Ours by Every Law of Right and Justice: Women and the Vote in the Prairie Provinces, by Sarah Carter

We Shall Persist: Women and the Vote in the Atlantic Provinces,
    by Heidi MacDonald

Working Tirelessly for Change: Indigenous Women and the Vote in Canada,
    by Lianne Leddy

LARA CAMPBELL

A GREAT
REVOLUTIONARY
WAVE

Women and the Vote
in British Columbia

UBCPress

VANCOUVER & TORONTO

28 27 26 25 24 23 22 21 20   5 4 3 2 1

Printed in Canada on FSC-certified ancient-forest-free paper
(100% post-consumer recycled) that is processed chlorine- and acid-free.

Library and Archives Canada Cataloguing in Publication

Title: A great revolutionary wave: women and the vote in British Columbia /
Lara Campbell.
Names: Campbell, Lara, 1970- author.
Series: Women's suffrage and the struggle for democracy; v. 4.

Description: Series statement: Women's suffrage and the struggle for
democracy; v. 4 | Includes bibliographical references and index.

Identifiers: Canadiana (print) 20200219871 | Canadiana (ebook) 20200219901 |
ISBN 9780774863223 (hardcover) | ISBN 9780774863230 (softcover) |
ISBN 9780774863247 (PDF) | ISBN 9780774863254 (EPUB) |
ISBN 9780774863261 (Kindle)

Subjects: LCSH: Women – Suffrage – British Columbia – History. |
LCSH: Suffrage – British Columbia – History. | LCSH: Women – Legal status,
laws, etc. – British Columbia – History. | LCSH: Women – British Columbia –
Social conditions. | LCSH: Suffragists – British Columbia – History. |
LCSH: Voting – British Columbia – History.

Classification: LCC JL192 .C36 2020 | DDC 324.6/2309711 – dc23

Canadä

UBC Press gratefully acknowledges the financial support for our publishing
program of the Government of Canada (through the Canada Book Fund),
the Canada Council for the Arts, and the British Columbia Arts Council.

Printed and bound in Canada by Friesens
Set in Gill Sans and Tundra by Artegraphica Design Co. Ltd.
Copy editor: Deborah Kerr
Proofreader: Kristy Hankewitz
Indexer: Judy Dunlop
Cover and series design: Jessica Sullivan

UBC Press
The University of British Columbia
2029 West Mall
Vancouver, BC V6T 1Z2
www.ubcpress.ca

CONTENTS

IN 1912, VICTORIA suffragists Maria Pollard Grant and Dorothy Davis published the first issue of the *Champion*. The only Canadian suffrage journal whose copies survive, the *Champion* was the official periodical of the BC Political Equality League, and it holds a unique place in the history of Canadian print culture. During its short two-year run (ended by the outbreak of the First World War), it published reports from British Columbia and around the world, as well as political satire and writing by famous American suffragists and British suffragettes.

During its first few months, the cover of the *Champion* borrowed an image that had appeared in the *Vote*, a British suffrage journal. Its central figure of Justice – embodied in the form of a woman – was a classic symbol of democracy for both British and North American suffrage movements. This particular interpretation (called "The Appeal of Womanhood") was designed by Louise Jacobs, a member of the London-based Artists' Suffrage League. But someone at the BC Political Equality League reworked the cover for a provincial audience. The revised version featured Justice standing before the official shield of British Columbia: a tripartite image composed of the Union Jack (representing Canada's relationship to the British Empire), waves (representing the Pacific Ocean), and the rays of the sun. At the bottom, the artist added a laurel wreath, a traditional symbol of victory and honour. The cover of the *Champion* conveys a British Columbia movement both immersed in local culture and connected to global suffrage activism. Though most of its members would never leave their city or their province, they saw themselves as part of what labour

Published in Victoria by the BC Political Equality League
between 1912 and 1914, the *Champion* was initially co-edited
by Maria Grant and Dorothy Davis. It featured local, national,
and international news about the suffrage movement, as
well as original poems, satire, and commentary.

organizer and suffragist Helena Gutteridge called "a great revolutionary wave," a demand for social justice and equality that was sweeping the modern world.

The evocative images and aspirational rhetoric of the suffrage movement reflect the profound desire of many women for political equality. But they also remind us, over one hundred years later, that although this dream was visionary and empowering for many women, it was enmeshed in the deepest exclusions of its time. After forty years of activism, a public referendum in 1916, and legislation in April 1917, the franchise was extended to the majority of settler women in British Columbia. But another thirty-two years would elapse before the provincial government allowed First Nations, Japanese, Chinese, and South Asian Canadian women *and* men to vote.

The women's (or woman) suffrage movement was an international phenomenon that made up one component of first-wave feminism. Suffrage rested on multiple arguments for women's right to political participation, including maternalism or maternal feminism (that mothers should influence legislation to protect the home and the family) and the ideals of justice and equal rights. Although its priorities fluctuated over time, the movement remained connected to nineteenth-century social reform politics and the desire to improve the situation of women in the workplace, the home, and public life. By 1910, suffragists had become focused on winning the vote, hoping it would allow them to influence legislation and help implement legal reforms.

The history of women's suffrage challenges a simple story of steady progress toward ever greater equality and inclusion. Enfranchisement in British Columbia – and elsewhere in Canada – is understood as a continuum rather than a clearly defined right that was won at a specific time. The ability to vote was grounded in property restrictions, length of residency, job and military status, religion, race, national origin and date of naturalization, marital status, and gender. By 1876, five years after British Columbia entered Confederation, male British subjects who were twenty-one or older and who met the residential requirements were allowed to vote. The property requirement was dropped at the provincial but not the municipal level. But as increasing numbers of settler men were added to the provincial electorate, racialized disenfranchisement was codified. Men of Chinese heritage were disenfranchised between 1874 and 1947, First Nations people with Indian status between 1874 and 1949, men of Japanese heritage between 1895 and 1949, and men of South Asian heritage (often called "Hindus") between 1907 and 1947. Because of their faith-based opposition to military service, both Mennonites and Doukhobors were provincially and federally disenfranchised at various times between 1917 and 1952. Voting rights existed in a web of complex and ever-changing sets of restrictions that differed across the country.

The rallying cry of provincial, national, and international suffrage movements was political equality for women on the "same terms as men." This phrase highlighted the injustice of sex discrimination but accepted existing race- and property-based exclusions. By the time suffrage opponent Richard McBride resigned as premier and Conservative Party leader in 1915, support for women's suffrage had become more respectable. Preparing for the 1916 election, McBride's replacement, William Bowser, promised to introduce an enfranchisement bill if a majority of the electorate voted for it in a referendum. Although the Bowser Conservatives lost the election, the referendum passed, but the legislation was delayed in the transition to the new Liberal government and by delays in counting the overseas soldier vote. The Liberals finally amended the Provincial Elections Act, and provincial suffrage for (most) women was officially proclaimed on 5 April 1917. But the legislation did not establish universal suffrage for all British Columbians, and because the provincial electoral list affected the right to vote federally, racial restrictions extended to the federal franchise.

The most prominent suffrage organizations and leaders were in central Canada or the Prairies, and it is they who have been most frequently commemorated. No suffragist in British Columbia held the same national platform as Winnipegger Nellie McClung, who travelled extensively across North America. And the emergence of the first Canadian suffrage organization in Toronto, the Canadian Women's Suffrage Association (1883), often overshadows efforts in other provinces. This tendency to focus on Ontario and the Prairies excludes the diverse histories of other regions and the long political careers of reformers Maria Pollard Grant and Cecilia Spofford, labour activist Helena Gutteridge, and socialist Bertha Merrill Burns. This lack of attention has led some historians to assume that British Columbia was backward or insular in comparison to other Canadian provinces. In fact, its suffragists were active

Maria Pollard Grant (1854–1937). The best-known BC suffragist Maria Grant was a member of the Victoria middle class and daughter of a Methodist minister. With a property gift from her father, William Pollard, she was one of the first married women in the province to meet municipal property qualifications for the vote. Her activism began in the 1870s and spanned more than forty years. In 1883, she became a founding member of the BC chapter of the Woman's Christian Temperance Union, the province's pre-eminent suffrage and reform vehicle. Grant also established its first suffrage organizations (the Victoria Political Equality League in 1910 and the BC Political Equality League in 1911) and the Victoria Local Council of Women. In 1895, she became the first elected female school trustee in the province. Initially a devout Methodist, she later joined the Unity Church.

and connected to national and international women's movements by the early 1880s.

The history of women's suffrage in British Columbia shares similarities with that of other regions, and with the national story documented by Joan Sangster's book in this series, *One Hundred Years of Struggle: The History of Women and the Vote in Canada*. The most prominent early suffrage leaders in British Columbia had much in common with those in other parts of English-speaking Canada: generally of British descent (mainly English and Scots), Christian and largely Protestant (mainly Methodist, Presbyterian, and Anglican), they had deep connections to temperance and Christian social reform organizations. The BC branch of the Woman's Christian Temperance Union (WCTU) declared support for female enfranchisement on its founding day in 1883. The development of a network of women's groups in the 1890s allowed women to co-operate on a range of projects related to improving their political and legal status, and to securing the vote at the municipal and school board level.

Although women had acquired limited voting rights at the local level before the turn of the century, suffragists grew increasingly frustrated at the slow pace of change and the stubbornness of Premier Richard McBride, who opposed enfranchisement. They were convinced that only by founding suffrage-focused and female-led organizations could they win the provincial vote. In 1910, Victoria's leading suffragists founded the Political Equality League; one month later, a Vancouver branch was established. After this, suffragists dedicated their energy to extending the campaign beyond the two major cities, creating a wide network of branches across the Lower Mainland and the interior in places such as Kelowna, Revelstoke, and Summerland. This distribution reflected the demographic pattern of the province, as the vast majority of the white settler population lived in either Victoria or Vancouver and their adjacent municipalities. The Vancouver branch soon declared its independence and became the Pioneer

Political Equality League, with an Evening Work Committee dedicated to working women. Vancouver also boasted numerous neighbourhood-based groups, as well as the BC Woman's Suffrage League (WSL), whose purpose was to forge connections with the labour movement. Breakaway associations formed along other lines: the Victoria-based Go-Aheads accepted enfranchisement that was restricted by age and marital status, whereas the BC Equal Franchise Association rejected confrontational campaigning. The leagues and their sister organizations flourished and grew more disciplined as they focused on winning the provincial vote.

Most Canadian suffragists shared an arsenal of tactics designed to win the vote within the system of parliamentary democracy. They concentrated on public education, rhetorical persuasion (writing many newspaper columns and letters to the editor), petitioning, and lobbying the government. At the same time, most firmly believed that the acquisition of the franchise was only one way of bettering women's status. They also sought improvements to women's property rights, access to higher education and professional training, child guardianship rights for mothers, and workplace reforms such as a minimum wage and equal pay. Suffragists acted strategically, lobbying all levels of government (municipal, provincial, and federal) for changes in legislation that would give women the right to vote for school board trustees, municipal councillors, and candidates for provincial and federal office.

Arguments for and against enfranchisement in British Columbia resembled those made elsewhere in North America. Claims about women's equality were rooted in a rich tapestry of political, intellectual, and philosophical traditions. The feminist humanism of Mary Wollstonecraft's *A Vindication of the Rights of Woman* (1792) linked women's freedom to emerging ideas about self-determination and democracy and asserted that women's inequality was not natural but created by institutions of religion and education. Early-nineteenth-century socialists believed that marriage oppressed women by turning them into property to be owned by men. Echoes of these earlier ideas resonated in mainstream suffrage arguments that gender inequality was destructive to men, women, and harmonious human relations, that women's subordination to men was a form of slavery, and that freedom lay in the opportunity to achieve one's full potential. Nineteenth-century feminist liberals fought to remove barriers to economic and individual autonomy, and emphasized the importance of legal equality and women's capacity to reason. Progressive Christian suffragists evoked powerful Biblical ideals of justice and spiritual equality. And socialist and labour suffragists argued that the concentration of wealth under capitalism exploited women's labour. Later, many suffragists espoused what scholars often call the "new liberalism" because they imagined that regulation of the economy and state social welfare programs might minimize the worst effects of capitalism.

Suffragists also situated the development of women's rights within ideas about progress and global modernity. They drew on popular ideas in the natural and social sciences that societies and cultures progressed from the savage, or primitive (characterized by life in a state of nature), to the most civilized (characterized by reason and law). These ideas about progress were connected to assumptions about race and racial hierarchy, in which the most civilized and superior societies were held to be northern European and British, and the least civilized were subject to colonial rule. These concepts emerged as European societies grappled with the impact of revolutions in France and America (which overthrew monarchical rule), industrialization (which introduced rapid technological development and a separation between the workplace and the home), and colonial expansion (which sought to justify rule over Indigenous and non-European nations).

Progress and civilization, however, could be interpreted in differing ways. Those who rejected expansive definitions of democracy justified the exclusion of women from politics by arguing that the most civilized societies should protect them from the roughness of public life. Anti-suffrage men and women believed that both God and nature had established fundamental differences between men and women. This "separate spheres" framework portrayed women as naturally suited to the private sphere of the home (children and domestic life) and men as naturally suited for the public sphere of politics and breadwinning. The concept assumed that women had little interest in politics and that enfranchised women would upset a divinely ordained hierarchy in which men, as household heads, were responsible for protecting dependent women and children. Women could influence their husbands informally but should remain content in their role as "Guardian Angels" of the home.

Many suffragists subverted the separate spheres argument by claiming that women's domestic responsibilities gave them a special mandate to shape laws and policy that affected motherhood and the family. Maternal feminists believed that women's difference from men, and their superior skills of domestic organization, would clean up the corrupt world of politics and balance men's point of view. This reasoning was sometimes presented as if women had an inherently more refined morality than men. But it was also rooted in the belief that women's primary responsibility for children and domestic work gave them the right to a voice in matters related to family life.

But maternalism was just one line of argument for enfranchisement. Suffragists also used ideas of justice and equality to contend that women and men shared a fundamental humanity, intelligence, and ability to reason. As one half of the population, women had the right to legislative representation and to a voice in making the laws that governed them. Victoria's Agnes Deans Cameron, whose photograph graces the cover of this book, voiced what she called "simple justice" in her arguments: "Woman should have the right of suffrage because she is judged by the law ... Since I am man's equal *under* the law, then surely I should

A Very Good Idea

Mrs Vancouver – Just give me that brush, Captain, and you will not have half
the trouble with your clothes in future.

This *Vancouver Sun* cartoon of 1913 illustrates the maternal
feminist argument for enfranchisement. If "Mrs. Vancouver" wins
the vote, she will clean up the political dirt and corruption that
accumulate when men hoard political power.

Agnes Deans Cameron (1863–1912) was born in Victoria, trained as a teacher, and taught in Vancouver and on Vancouver Island. She was the first woman in the province to teach high school (1891) and the first female principal of a public school (1894). A journalist and travel writer, she travelled throughout the West and the North and worked for the Western Canada Immigration Association. She was active in the Victoria Teachers' Association, the Local Council of Women, the Women's Press Club, and the YWCA. When suffragette Emmeline Pankhurst lectured in Victoria in 1911, Cameron sat on the stage. She died in 1912 of an infection from an appendectomy.

be his equal *before* the law." And most suffragists interpreted ideas about progress and civilization in emancipatory ways in relation to gender equality. In particular, the ideas of French socialist Charles Fourier – that a society could be judged on the basis of its treatment of women – became a common tenet in suffragist thought. It was Fourier who suggested that "the extension of the privileges of women is the fundamental cause of all progress." In other words, the more a society moved toward greater liberty and emancipation for women, the more civilized it became.

Some historians have assumed that maternal feminists were more traditional than those who championed women's political equality on the basis of justice. But most suffragists – whether liberal, conservative, religious, secular, or socialist – accepted gender differences between women and men, believed that women had a special role in the political sphere as wives and mothers, and rarely imagined a world beyond heterosexual family life. They hoped to widen the public sphere to include more women, but very few in Canada challenged mainstream beliefs about gender and sexuality. In making their case, most cited maternalism, justice, humanity, modernity, and citizenship rights. This refusal to adopt a single message might seem confusing, but it was a pragmatic way of bringing people with diverse views into one "big tent" of political activism.

But pragmatism is not the only reason that suffragists held multiple perspectives. Like feminists today, they struggled to understand the reasons for women's subordination and debated how best to counter it. Most recognized that women's legal, economic, and political inequality contributed to their oppression, but they were unwilling to deny the value of motherhood and did not assume that men and women must be treated in the same way if women were to achieve equality. This tension between difference and sameness – and how to address inequities arising from gender – troubles feminist politics to this day.

Yet, most suffragists did not extend the ideals of justice, humanity, and equality to Asian and First Nations men and women, none of whom could vote in provincial elections until the late 1940s. By the late nineteenth century, suffragists had joined political leaders in British Columbia in the confident belief that white settler population growth and economic development would lead to a prosperous future. This vision was built on permanent white settlement and the implementation of British laws and institutions in an established Euro-Canadian society. The suffrage movement developed in concert with settler colonialism, anti-immigrant xenophobia, and anti-Asian racism, and its members prioritized the concerns of white settler women and took British superiority for granted. These values played out in a province where white and British-born colonists were a demographic minority until the mid-1880s and in which politicians, labour leaders, and citizens proclaimed their desire to build "a white man's province." But assumptions about cultural superiority were slowly challenged after 1900 by the discovery that women in non-British nation-states were demanding and achieving political equality. Like all social movements past and present, the campaign for female enfranchisement was steeped in the larger values of its time, even as it defied some of them.

If suffrage history in British Columbia echoes that of other provinces, the United States, and Great Britain, why should historians tell regional stories? The suffrage movement is regionally diverse – or "decentralized" as Joan Sangster explains – in part because of Canada's federal political structure. Provinces had the authority to establish their own voting eligibility criteria on any basis, including race and gender. These criteria also affected the ability to vote federally, and many battles were fought over which level of government would control federal voting qualifications. Prime Minister John A. Macdonald proposed to extend the right to vote to widows and unmarried women in the 1885 Electoral Franchise Act. But after extensive debate, in which most MPs made their opposition clear, the plan was dropped. After the federal Liberal government introduced new voting legislation in 1898, removing racial restrictions, British Columbia responded in 1901 by instituting a literacy requirement that had the effect of disenfranchising many Chinese and Japanese residents. The Dominion Elections Act of 1920 made the provincial electoral list the basis of the federal vote: as a result, anyone who could not vote provincially was also excluded from voting federally. Furthermore, the constitutional division of powers in the British North America Act gave provinces the responsibility to legislate on family law, labour standards, and education. In a large and geographically dispersed federal nation-state, achieving such reforms necessitated a provincial focus.

The women's suffrage movement and later campaigns for postwar enfranchisement emerged from and responded to specific conditions in a region that historian Adele Perry calls the "edge of empire." As the former Colony of British Columbia, which was created by the merger of two British colonies on the mainland and Vancouver Island in 1866, the province existed within regional, national, and transnational networks. The province's late (1871) entry into Confederation, its early years as a small and male-dominated white settler community and majority Indigenous population, its geographic distance from the centre of federal power in Eastern Canada, its primary resource extraction economy (fur, coal, minerals, lumber, and fish) and economic roots in the gold rush and the fur trade, and its trans-Pacific economic and population ties to Asia, especially China, often render it peripheral in Canada's national story. Political, economic, and labour historians of British Columbia have rectified this exclusion, but few have paid attention to women's political activism.

British Columbia's economic, political, and cultural conditions shaped the tactics and priorities of provincial suffrage organizations. Despite similarities to other Canadian suffrage stories, the BC history is noteworthy in particular ways. The first attempt in Canada to pass a provincial women's suffrage bill came from elected politicians in British Columbia in 1875 as they debated the meaning of responsible government in the new province. British Columbia was the first province to officially extend municipal voting rights to property-owning women regardless of their marital status (1873–74), although propertied women had voted in some pre-Confederation colonies until they were formally excluded in the late 1840s. The BC Political Equality League formed later than similar organizations in Ontario, but the BC Woman's Christian Temperance Union seems to have been the first branch in the country to officially endorse female suffrage and to create a Franchise Department to lobby for the vote. Canada's only successful dedicated suffrage movement periodical (the *Champion*) was published in Victoria by the Political Equality League. And though a number of Ontario municipalities held local referendums on the franchise, British Columbia was the only province to put provincial voting rights to a public referendum, in the fall of 1916.

Whereas most suffrage organizations across the country saw themselves as part of a global movement, transnational politics took a unique shape in Canada's westernmost province. BC suffragists often employed a discourse of Western progressivism in their claims for political equality. Linking themselves to suffragists in the Canadian Prairies, the American West, and the Pacific Coast, they contended that the "frontier" spirit of an emerging white settler society had created a distinctively independent woman whose work ethic proved that she deserved the vote. And though suffragists were attuned to these Western movements, they were heavily influenced by developments in Great Britain. In a province with a large British immigrant population, they felt stronger connections to the militant suffragettes of the British Women's Social and Political Union (WSPU) than most others in Canada. They assured the public that they would not adopt the confrontational and increasingly violent tactics of the WSPU, but provincial suffrage leagues were the only ones in Canada to adopt the WSPU colours of purple, white, and green, and Victoria suffragists organized a short-lived WSPU-affiliated branch.

Finally, the class makeup of the BC suffrage leagues was more diverse than elsewhere in Canada. The movement's early years were dominated by middle-class and elite women who did not work for pay and who lived primarily in Victoria and New Westminster. But its supporters were more diverse than their best-known leaders. At times, women's organizations in British Columbia included small numbers of black women, Jewish women, and Catholic women. They also included the descendants of Indigenous women and former colonial officials and Hudson's Bay traders of British background, and who therefore did not hold Indian status under the federal Indian Act. But what makes the province particularly distinctive is the important role that white working-class women played in suffrage leagues after the turn of the century, especially

Born in England, Helena Gutteridge (1879–1960) apprenticed as a cutter and was a WSPU member. After arriving in Vancouver in 1911, she joined the Vancouver Political Equality League, became vice-president of the Journeyman Tailors' Association, and was the first woman to serve as secretary of the Vancouver Trades and Labour Council. In 1913, she formed Vancouver's first working-class suffrage organizations: the Evening Work Committee and, shortly after, the BC Woman's Suffrage League. Gutteridge edited a regular suffrage column in the B.C. Federationist, *joined the Co-operative Commonwealth Federation, and was the first woman elected to Vancouver City Council, in 1937.*

as leadership shifted to Vancouver. Some had connections to the major socialist parties, including the Socialist Party of British Columbia (which merged with the Canadian Socialist League in 1904 to become the Socialist Party of Canada) and the Social Democratic Party, as well as to the labour movement. Vancouver was the only Canadian city that had an independent suffrage association founded by a working-class woman (Helena Gutteridge) and designed specifically to reach working women. The BC Woman's Suffrage League emphasized the dual impact of unregulated capitalism and political disenfranchisement on working women's lives.

A Great Revolutionary Wave follows the story of the women's suffrage movement from 1871, the year that British Columbia entered Confederation, through the development of women's movements in the 1880s and 1890s and the birth of an independent suffrage movement in 1910, to the enfranchisement referendum of fall 1916. It extends the question of political citizenship into the 1940s, as racialized groups and First Nations drew on years of community activism to end their exclusion from the franchise. The chapters follow suffragists as they sought both enfranchisement and legal reforms to improve the lives of women and children. To achieve change in the face of powerful resistance, they worked within existing political structures and cultivated sympathetic male allies, but they also built dynamic associations led by women and developed a vibrant culture of non-partisan dissent and debate. They understood the importance of local and provincial organizing while connecting to global networks across North America and the British Empire, and of staying attuned to worldwide trends in women's rights.

Like the other books in this series, *A Great Revolutionary Wave* rethinks the legacy of the suffrage movement. The books ask us to value the courage and creativity of the suffrage movement without characterizing its leaders and members as uncomplicated heroines and champions of equality. The motivations of people in the past are often messy and difficult to understand from the perspective of the present. Like all of us today, suffragists made choices within a larger system not of their own making and in the context of what they imagined possible at the time. Sometimes, those feminist futures challenged fundamental beliefs about gender and human equality, but sometimes they did not. The stories of their successes but also of their limitations, failures, and exclusions – and what those stories mean to understanding the past and the future of movements for equality, freedom, and liberation – lie at the heart of this book.

If in the purpose of the ages, this woman's movement has been called into existence to teach the world the value of human life and human freedom then it is well worth while – for that is the greatest lesson we need in this age.

– FLORENCE HALL,

CHAMPION, SEPTEMBER 1913, 14–15.

It sounds so shallow for a man to tell us that motherhood is the crowning glory; for when the first opportunity affords, the man-made laws cause this crowning glory to become a crowning sorrow ... Nice, isn't it?

– SUSIE LANE CLARK,

VANCOUVER DAILY WORLD, 24 NOVEMBER 1913, 11.

ONE

SUFFRAGE
AND REFORM

Cecilia McNaughton Spofford (1859–1938). Born into a
Nova Scotia Baptist family, Cecilia McNaughton worked as
a teacher prior to her 1883 marriage to William Spofford.
In Victoria, she was president of both the Woman's Christian
Temperance Union and the Local Council of Women. Elected a
school trustee in 1919, she lobbied for female enfranchisement,
supported progressive legislation, and ran twice for provincial
office, once as an Independent and again as a Liberal.

AT THE TURN of the twentieth century, British Columbians were told that they lived in a modern province whose future was one of unlimited progress and economic growth. With Richard McBride and the Conservative Party at the helm of government (1903–15), the province experienced rapid population expansion and economic development. The white settler community increased eight-fold in just thirty years: from 50,000 in 1881 to 400,000 in 1911. But although settlers and politicians embraced the promise of economic prosperity, they could not ignore the effects of unregulated capitalism. As elsewhere in North America, concerns deepened about the impact of unfettered industrial growth, rapid urbanization, and non-British immigration. And as women increasingly worked for pay and middle-class women demanded higher education, the public role of women in modern Canada was up for debate.

A growing number of women's groups pointed to the problems associated with unregulated capitalism, including unemployment, low wages, and unsafe working conditions. Between the 1870s and the 1920s, they mobilized across the country – and globally – to address these concerns. Historian Joan Sangster refers to these associations as a "women's movement," which encompassed educational clubs, professional organizations, missionary societies, and religious and philanthropic groups. They brought women together to provide social services during an era that lacked adequate welfare and to advocate for reforms that would improve the status of women and children.

But suffragists and reformers did not always agree about how to solve these problems. Some hoped to make change mainly at the individual level, though increasing numbers sought state intervention to prohibit alcohol consumption, restrict immigration, and regulate capitalism through protective labour legislation. Others called for state-funded social welfare programs to redistribute wealth and address poverty. Most were convinced that politically active women of British background would improve society. And though some groups were not explicitly sectarian (that is, they did not advocate a particular Christian denominational ideology), most believed in both the spiritual superiority of Christianity and the cultural superiority of Britishness.

Most women's associations gradually concluded that gaining the vote was essential for wielding political influence. By the 1890s, almost all of them supported municipal and school board suffrage, legal reforms to restrict a husband's authority over wives and children, and a living wage to allow economic independence from men. By the 1910s, it was rare to find a women's organization that opposed enfranchisement, and most shared resources with the suffrage movement to achieve both the vote and the reforms that were necessary for equality.

RELIGION, REFORM, AND THE SOCIAL GOSPEL

The rise of the suffrage movement was intimately connected to Christian social reform, even though white settlers in the province – especially in the male-dominated mining towns of the interior – had the highest Canadian rates of what historian Lynne Marks calls "irreligion." Predictably, the churches were concerned about the morality of BC men. Working- and middle-class settler women made up the majority of congregations in the three largest denominations (Anglican, Presbyterian, and Methodist), and as their numbers increased, they played an important role in developing reform organizations. Religious groups gave women an authoritative language to criticize male power while still remaining respectable. And although only men could join the clergy, some Protestant denominations supported suffrage for maternalist reasons. For example, Anglican William Perrin, the bishop of British Columbia (1893–1911), believed that women's suffrage could improve society; in later years, Anglican reverend Henry Edwards was an active member of the Vancouver Political Equality League. On an institutional level, BC Baptists endorsed suffrage in 1912, and the Methodist Conference did the same in 1913, stating that it was a matter of justice that would "greatly aid in the moral uplift of social and political affairs for which we are all working."

Who were Christian reformers, and how were they connected to the suffrage movement? They believed that individuals suffered under exploitative economic conditions and agreed that prostitution, poverty, and dangerous working situations were problems of modern capitalism. But reformers differed widely about how (or whether) the state should respond. Some felt that charity, hard work, modest sexual behaviour, and conversion to Christianity would solve social and economic problems, but by the end of the nineteenth century, an increasing number believed that the authority of the state should be harnessed to produce a greater social good. The most active nineteenth-century suffragists were shaped by this faith in the power of social reform. Methodist Maria Grant participated in numerous women's organizations along with her mother and sister, and her contemporary Cecilia Spofford was a Baptist temperance activist who attended the same church as future Liberal leader and premier Harlan Brewster.

The social gospel tradition, which interpreted the Gospels with an eye toward social justice and not solely individual salvation, became increasingly prevalent among Protestant denominations (mainly Methodists) in the years leading up to the First World War. Social gospellers supported a range of policies that promised to address injustice and build the Kingdom of Heaven on Earth – which they imagined as a more egalitarian world, based on the values of co-operation and compassion rather than competition and private profit. The social gospel emphasized spiritual equality before God and offered a feminist reading of the Gospels that called for an end to the legal and economic exploitation of women.

This Christian commitment to justice and feminist spirituality was outlined in Florence Hall's columns in the *Western Methodist Recorder*. Her "Suffragette Sermons" argued that "man and woman were made in the image of God, both stood on equal ground when the Creator placed them in this world." Hall extended the idea of spiritual equality to everyday life, writing that a man and a woman were "mates, companions, not master and slave ... She was as fully equipped a human being as the man, and therefore destined to share equally in all pertaining to human rights and human life, and this prerogative is still hers, for it is founded on eternal justice." Both Hall and her husband, William Lashley Hall, were deeply concerned about poverty and believed that capitalism cheapened humanity because it valued profit more than "precious lives."

Reformers and suffragists shared a belief that the universe was gradually moving toward greater equality. This force was described in spiritual terms, though it was not always understood as emanating from an interventionist Christian God. Popular British suffragette Barbara Wylie informed a Vancouver audience that the suffrage movement was a powerful "fight of spiritual against physical force and spiritual always wins ... A spirit is above force. The victory is bound to be on our side." Quaker suffragist Helen Sturge visited from Bristol in 1913 to speak on the "necessity of spiritual force and concentration of mind power toward obtaining the great end for which all intelligent women are working." Similarly, American Charlotte Perkins Gilman told her Vancouver audience that the "world mind" would be moved forward by suffrage activism.

Christian suffragists such as Florence Hall imagined Wylie's spiritual force as a "great propeller" powered by God. But a few

Florence Sarah Hussey Hall (1864–1917). Florence Hussey (or Huzzey) was born in Newland, Gloucestershire, England. Prior to her marriage to Methodist minister William Lashley Hall, she worked as a teacher in Wales and England, and with Sisters of the People, a Methodist urban mission located in London, England. Together, the Halls served the Methodist Church throughout British Columbia. He became president of the BC Methodist Conference in 1913. She was the founding president of the Vancouver Political Equality League and a member of the WCTU and the Women's Missionary Society. In 1912, she became a paid organizer for the BC Political Equality League, touring the province to help set up local branches. She died in North Vancouver in 1917. William remarried and died in 1947.

suffragists participated in non-traditional spiritual systems, such as Theosophy, which saw the universe as alive and divine, emphasized the truth in all religions, and promoted the values of human equality regardless of gender, race, or caste. Though it had few official adherents, Theosophy attracted leading Canadian suffragists such as Augusta Stowe-Gullen and Flora MacDonald Denison. Leading Theosophists lectured to packed audiences through the auspices of the Vancouver Theosophical Society, and the Vancouver Political Equality League held its founding meeting in the Theosophical Hall. Helena Gutteridge was involved with Theosophy before moving to Vancouver. Socialist Bertha Merrill Burns was raised Baptist and identified as agnostic but was influenced by Theosophical thought. She was deeply critical of the Christian Church and its followers, who claimed to love God while simultaneously seeking profit and power. She suggested that Jesus himself would have been "despised and forsaken" by most Christians and that only socialism could create the conditions that would enable humans to "love one another as we ought to do." But Burns spoke in the language of justice and compassion, and her writing rang with a spiritual certainty that would not have been out of place in a rousing social gospel sermon. In 1903, her Thanksgiving column in the *Western Clarion* reminded readers that true prosperity would prevail for women and men when economic justice was achieved:

> Some day there will be a real thanksgiving in the land. It will be when Greed shall have been dethroned from among the lives of men and when Justice shall have apportioned to each a share in the means of life; when "prosperity" that blesses the few at the expense of the many shall have been repudiated by the nations of the earth ... when, in fact the dead Christ of a crucified Manhood shall have arisen to a new life of fraternity and fellowship that will leave no son or daughter of humanity sadly wondering what they can be thankful for.

Victoria suffragist Maria Grant was raised Methodist but later joined the Unity Church, which took a universalist approach to religion and focused on the potential within all humans to harness the power of the mind to solve social problems. Grant's particular spiritual journey was unique, but her life shows how spirituality complemented the suffrage view of women's political enfranchisement as modern and forward thinking. For Grant, attaining the vote was "the outcome of an internal process of unfoldment and development in harmony with the law of Life. This growth experiences itself in the demand for liberty and equality." She saw women's desire for equality as a transformative process, with women gradually "freeing themselves" and realizing their full potential through the "annihilation of all that hinders the upward and onward winging of their way." References to "being awake" resonated across belief systems. Those who were asleep were unattuned to the light of God or the movement of the universe, whereas those who were in the process of awakening were growing toward greater compassion and equality. This belief in forward movement and progress drew together suffragists with a range of beliefs: Methodists, Baptists, Theosophists, liberals, and socialists all had faith that individuals *and* the social order could be perfected. Overlapping interests in spirituality and reform are sometimes seen as less radical than a sole focus on women's political equality. But many suffragists first found their political voice in religious or reform movements, which were important incubators of women's political activism in North America.

"DO EVERYTHING": THE WOMAN'S CHRISTIAN TEMPERANCE UNION

The most influential women's reform organization of this period was the Woman's Christian Temperance Union (WCTU), which was founded in the United States in 1874 and led by Frances Willard, a Methodist. Local, provincial, national, and transnational branches made the WCTU a driving force in women's activism. Not all Christian reformers agreed that the sale and consumption of alcohol should be strictly prohibited, but many believed that men's intemperance damaged the larger social fabric, contributed to poverty and violence, and harmed the economic security of women and children.

Willard was an inspirational international figure known for her charismatic presence and oratory. A contemporary described her as magnetic and as "possessing that occult force which all leaders must have." In 1883, Willard was invited by Victoria's Pandora Street Methodist Church to help organize a provincial branch of the WCTU and to hold a convention for the "Ladies of this Province." Her hour-long speech provoked both tears and outbursts of applause as she spoke about the devastating effects of

The well-known leader of the WCTU, Frances Willard was
welcomed to Victoria in 1883 by local clergy, politicians, and
their wives and daughters. She delivered a public address at the
Pandora Street Methodist Church, which is pictured here on
the occasion of her visit, dramatically decorated with flowers,
banners, the Stars and Stripes, and the British Ensign.

alcohol on women's lives. The following day, she met with Maria
Pollard and her daughters Annie and Maria (Grant), Cecilia
Spofford, and Margaret Jenkins, who quickly set up a provincial
and local Victoria WCTU branch and endorsed female suffrage
with a classic maternal feminist argument: "As woman is the natural conservator of the home, she should be endowed with the
use of the ballot as a means of protection of her home." With this,
the WCTU became the first temperance group in Canada to formally support suffrage, and it remained the primary vehicle for
suffrage activism until the establishment of the BC Political
Equality League in 1910.

The WCTU's first task was to lobby the provincial government for legislation on prohibition and suffrage. It moved quickly. By June 1884, it had formed a Committee on Petitions, headed by Maria Grant and two others who announced they were planning to petition the Legislative Assembly "to grant to woman the privilege of the ballot box." Grant and Margaret Jenkins were nominated to "call on the legislators and solicit their influence on behalf" of the bill. The provincial body and local WCTU branches established lobbying subcommittees, which they called Departments of Legislation, Petition, and Franchise. Vancouver, Victoria, New Westminster, and Chilliwack all boasted these departments by 1888. By April 1885, the WCTU had circulated its first petition and convinced two MLAs, Montague Tyrwhitt-Drake and James Cunningham, to present it to the legislature. Tyrwhitt-Drake introduced a private member's bill that same year to extend the franchise to women.

Middle- and upper-class Protestant women dominated the WCTU executive, but the organization attracted women across the boundaries of class, denomination, and occasionally race. The 1885 petition, signed by more than nine hundred people, demonstrates the support that the WCTU had amassed during its first two years. The signatories included clergy, reformers, former Hudson's Bay Company officials, and the children of their marriages with women of Indigenous descent, including multiple generations from the Finlayson, McNeill Moffatt, and Tolmie families. Unlike the Ontario branches, the BC WCTU did not have racially segregated local unions, and numerous black women and their husbands signed the petition. Most WCTU members were Protestants, but a few Jewish women also joined, and at least one Jewish woman and man from Victoria – Mrs. (Sophia) Gustav Leiser and Frank Sylvester – signed this first petition.

By the 1880s, the WCTU had become a global organization, with missions on six continents and travelling speakers from the United States, Britain, Australia, and New Zealand. It sent women to establish branches throughout the province, and by 1908, it had expanded outside of Victoria and New Westminster to create at least twenty-four new locals in the Lower Mainland, Vancouver Island, and the interior. Women travelled widely to give speeches and attend conventions, where they met with members from across the country and the world. Maria Grant spent a month journeying to Toronto for the world WCTU convention in 1897, where she met international delegates and spent time with Frances Willard. Her updates were published in the *Daily Colonist,* allowing locals to stay abreast of events.

The WCTU hoped for prohibition but it embraced other causes, including government-subsidized homes for elderly women, a minimum wage, and female factory inspectors. Recognition of women's economic vulnerability made the WCTU a frequent ally of organized labour on projects including a living wage for women. When the provincial branch was formed, Willard was developing her powerful "do everything" approach – an assertion that all social issues were interconnected. She supported women's suffrage, higher education, the labour movement, and the socialist Fabian Society. Many of her followers were deeply inspired by her expansive approach to reform. Maria Grant took on a range of causes and named her youngest daughter Frances Willard in her honour. Mary Ann Cunningham, married to Liberal politician James Cunningham, was active in both suffrage and the WCTU. She echoed Willard and Grant in her determination to link temperance and enfranchisement, telling women that the "WCTU woman must possess all the rights of the franchise, and exercise them; it is useless to pray 'Thy Kingdom Come' and vote contra or stay away from the polls." But she believed that women deserved the vote not just because they were mothers who might enact temperance but because they were intelligent beings who had "the right to express their opinions as decidedly as their husbands do."

Why did nineteenth-century women find the WCTU so attractive? Some historians suggest that middle-class women saw it as a

Mary Ann Woodman Cunningham (1841–1930). Born in St. Thomas, Ontario, Mary Ann taught for two years at the St. Thomas Central School. A devout Methodist, she also supported prohibition. She married Irish-born James Cunningham in 1865 and lived in New Westminster, where he co-owned a hardware store. James supported the Liberals and was elected an MP (1874–78), an MLA (1884–86), and mayor of New Westminster (1873). Mary Ann sat on the executives of the WCTU, Ladies' Aid, the Missionary Society, the Local Council of Women, the YWCA, and the Political Equality League. She voted municipally in New Westminster from 1894 onward and was an active member of the Franchise Department of the New Westminster WCTU.

tool through which to control the behaviour of poor, working-class, and European immigrant men, who were often portrayed as irrational and irresponsible. Other historians argue that temperance activism is best understood as what Sharon Cook calls a "constellation" issue. In other words, it safely challenged men's economic and cultural power at a time when even the most privileged women were legally subordinate to men. Temperance invested household and domestic responsibilities with a sense of moral righteousness. Contrasting women's respectable behaviour with the irresponsible economic and social behaviour of men who drank (or who profited from the sale of alcohol) allowed temperance supporters to refute arguments that women were too irrational to vote intelligently. Grant believed that enfranchised women would balance the votes of "irresponsible men, who are so often led by the saloon owners and who have not one noble idea or high interest in life."

But alcohol use was a contentious issue in the nineteenth century. Temperance women were outraged that men could spend the household income on anything they wished, including liquor. However, tavern owners earned high profits from male labourers, and many male workers enjoyed drinking and resented attempts to limit their consumption. The Vancouver Island and Kootenay mining communities from which socialist politicians drew their support did not favour temperance and had reputations for heavy drinking. The Socialist Party of Canada maintained that temperance was a restriction on working men's leisure and independence. But though socialist suffragist Bertha Merrill Burns was critical of the WCTU's narrow focus, she was perhaps shaped by her Baptist upbringing. She believed that male alcohol consumption was harmful, and that "beer and tobacco are the narcotics which capital has used to deaden [men's] senses."

The WCTU never lost interest in enfranchisement even as dedicated suffrage leagues grew more prominent by the 1910s. But its power declined after women won the vote and prohibition failed. Support for prohibition peaked during the First World War, and the majority of the BC electorate voted for it in a 1916 referendum, but it was difficult to enforce. In 1921, British Columbia became the first English Canadian province to repeal prohibition, and social reformers shifted their focus to other issues.

WOMEN'S CLUBS AND PROFESSIONAL ASSOCIATIONS

By the 1880s, secular women's clubs were proliferating across Canada, as white middle-class women accessed university education and professions such as teaching. Most clubs were reluctant to fully endorse suffrage, though they approved of the New Woman of the late nineteenth century. A reflection of women's greater public presence, the New Woman was educated, trained in a profession or skill, and interested in current affairs, though she was still expected to marry and become a mother. To be a New Woman was to reject old-fashioned limitations on women's public role. It is "the woman's age," argued the Victoria Local Council of Women (LCW) in 1895, in which "custom is the enemy of progress." But the New Woman would not enter the modern era alone. She was ideally accompanied by a husband of good "manly character." Such men were worthy of respect not because they were authoritarian patriarchs but because they were willing to help improve women's status. Many BC suffragists were married to New Men, who signed petitions, attended public talks, and joined suffrage leagues. Laura Jamieson's husband, Jack, who studied theology at the University of Toronto before becoming a lawyer, was inspired by progressive theologians who emphasized women's equality, and he helped educate women's groups on family law. The English-born Liberal MLA, Fabian Society supporter, and newspaper editor John Sedgwick Cowper spoke in the language of the New Man when he pointed out that suffrage was not a favour to be granted by chivalrous men to deserving women. "Knight errants and such heroics have gone out of fashion," he argued. Rather, suffrage should be granted "on the grounds of simple justice."

In addition to joining the WCTU, many leading women in British Columbia and across the country also joined the National Council of Women of Canada. In 1894, its founder, Lady Aberdeen, arrived in the province to help establish the Vancouver and Victoria Local Councils of Women, with New Westminster (1898), Vernon (1895), and Nelson (1900) soon following. The LCWs were designed to be non-sectarian and to bridge Protestant, Jewish, and Catholic divides. By 1914, for example, the Vancouver LCW enjoyed representation from a small but growing Jewish community, and one of its affiliated committees included the Ladies' Auxiliary of the Temple Emanu-El, a semi-reform congregation established in 1894. LCWs were a research hub on the status of women and children in the family and in the workplace, and they pressed for everything from factory regulations to better treatment of women in the criminal justice system.

The National Council of Women of Canada was established in Toronto in 1893 by Lady Ishbel Aberdeen, wife of the newly appointed governor general. Both she and her husband were supporters of liberal reform causes, such as broader suffrage rights, labour rights, and non-sectarian politics. LCWs soon formed across Ontario and the country. The national council was connected to the International Council of Women, which was founded in 1888 as an international umbrella organization for a wide range of women's groups that were interested in improving the status of women.

Dominated by middle-class and elite women, the LCWs initially had an ambivalent relationship to the suffrage movement. In Canada, the Victoria LCW became the first to endorse suffrage in 1908, followed by Vancouver in 1909, and the national council in 1910. This early reluctance did not extend to the municipal and school board franchise, however, and LCWs petitioned for an expanded local franchise. They also worked to nominate women for the position of school trustee, which was the only elected office that women were allowed to hold prior to 1917. Many club members hoped that women's involvement in local politics would reform corrupt political structures and build better schools, towns, and cities.

The small but growing cohort of middle-class women with university degrees and professional training founded more exclusive associations. Reflecting the increasing number of university-educated women, the University Women's Clubs (UWCs) were established in Vancouver (1907) and in Victoria (1908). Their members undertook research, hosted talks, and sponsored legal reforms.

Members were often married to influential men, and though they were passionately committed to women's higher education, their class and race status meant that most withdrew from paid labour upon marriage and were heavily involved in voluntary work. A founding member and first president of the Vancouver UWC, Evlyn Fenwick Farris held degrees from Acadia and was married to lawyer J. Wallace de Becque Farris, a prominent Liberal and future attorney general. Farris helped the Victoria UWC organize in the spring of 1908. The club also offered the small number of female doctors a place to connect. Drs. Helen E. Reynolds Ryan, Etta Paterson-Devon, and Belle Wilson were all UWC members who were also active in the suffrage movement.

One of the first campaigns undertaken by Farris and the Vancouver UWC was support for Mabel French, a New Brunswick-trained lawyer who was refused admission to the Law Society of British Columbia in 1910. The UWC successfully lobbied the provincial government to amend the Professions Act to allow women to practise law and campaigned to force the newly established University of British Columbia to allow women to sit on its Senate. Farris eventually came to favour suffrage, although unlike her fellow club members Helen Gregory MacGill, Mary Ellen Smith, Laura Jamieson, and Mary McConkey, she never formally joined the movement.

As increasing numbers of women wrote for newspapers and periodicals, their keen observational skills and ability to harness the power of print culture played a key role in spreading suffrage propaganda. Canada had few professional female journalists: according to historian Marjory Lang, only about thirty-eight worked in British Columba in 1921, though census numbers do not capture those who worked part-time or freelance. The Vancouver Women's Press Club (1909) did not officially endorse enfranchisement, but its membership of writers and journalists often overlapped with that of the suffrage movement. Prominent members included Sara McLagan, owner of the *Vancouver Daily World,* and PEL members Helen Gregory MacGill, who had worked as a journalist in California, and concert promoter, journalist, and editor Lily Laverock.

Although higher education had become more accessible by the beginning of the twentieth century, it remained out of reach for the vast majority of women. But by the end of the nineteenth century, caregiving was understood as a profession that required education and training in modern techniques of housework, cooking, and child care. Advocates of this new "domestic science" hoped to convince women that marriage and motherhood was a serious profession. The home economics or domestic science courses offered in public schools and universities were intended to modernize domestic labour and allow women to raise healthier families. Victoria suffragist Margaret Jenkins, also an elected school trustee, organized the first domestic science curriculum in the province in 1903. Not all suffragists agreed that domestic science was the best avenue for women's education; both Farris and teacher Agnes Deans Cameron, for example, preferred intellectual rather than practical education for girls and young women.

The domestic science trend found a home in the women's movement through the Women's Institutes (WIS), which were founded in 1897 by Ontarian Adelaide Hoodless. After her infant son's death, believed to be caused by drinking unpasteurized milk, Hoodless championed the modernization of housekeeping. The BC WIS were established in 1909, housed within the Department of Agriculture, and focused on bringing household science to rural women. Institutes viewed white settler families as the heart of the modern province and wished to work with the government to make the lives of rural families healthier and more productive. Hoodless was decidedly not in favour of suffrage, and the WIS did not officially endorse it. But many of their members did. The institutes recommended that members educate themselves about unequal laws, organized lectures by prominent suffragists such as Laura Jamieson, and encouraged women to run for school trustee.

Born Margaret Robertson in Collingwood, Ontario, Madge Watt (1868–1948) was a professional writer, teacher, and suffrage and women's rights supporter. Watt held a master's degree from the University of Toronto, was a member of the UWC and the International Council of Women, and was appointed to the University of British Columbia Senate in 1912. Passionate about domestic science, she helped organize the BC WIs and was appointed to their advisory board. After 1913, she introduced the WI model to Britain. Upon returning to Canada in 1919, she founded an international rural women's group, the Associated Countrywomen of the World (1933) and served as its president between 1933 and 1947.

REFORMING THE LAWS ON WOMEN AND CHILDREN

By 1900, BC women's groups were enthusiastically researching women's legal status. What they discovered was not heartening: women were subordinate to men in property and inheritance rights, marriage and divorce, and guardianship of children. Despite some minimal protections, men held legal authority as head of the household. The ideal family model was a lifelong union in which women and children were economically supported by men, and fathers had sole authority over dependent children. Suffragists did not criticize the principle of marriage, but they did believe that couples should live together in companionate relationships, and they deplored the fact that women were forced to rely on marriage for economic security yet had little remedy against an abusive or neglectful husband. As British suffragist Emmeline Pankhurst argued, women's marital life was dependent on "getting a good ticket in the lottery."

Suffragists were horrified by the laws that governed women and children. Under British common law, husbands retained control over family property until the mid-nineteenth century. In Ontario, slow legislative changes began to increase married women's property rights in the 1850s, and similar developments occurred in British Columbia during the 1870s and 1880s. The Deserted Wives Maintenance Act established minimum obligations of economic support in cases of desertion, and the Married Women's Property Act offered legal protection to women who owned property in their name. But reforms remained limited. Married women in British Columbia did not have the protection of a dower law (use of one-third of a husband's estate after his death), unlike women in a number of other provinces. Unless a wife held property in her own name, her husband could sell it without her consent. If he died without a will, she could lose family property to a male relative. Even into the 1970s, women had no legal right to the property they had helped build during marriage, an issue that deeply affected the unpaid labour of farming women. Legal protections remained minimal because legislators worried that economic independence would encourage women to remain unmarried or to divorce their husbands and because they saw wealth and property as a male prerogative.

The research undertaken in the 1890s by LCW and WCTU subcommittees discovered such deep inequities that they published a series of reports and began a concerted educational campaign about women's legal subordination. In 1908, the Vancouver University Women's Club (UWC) invited local lawyer and judge A.E. Bull to speak on the legal status of women, inspiring Helen Gregory MacGill – who had received legal training in California – to create a Committee for Better Laws for Women and Children. In 1909, the LCW and the UWC petitioned the provincial government to revise inheritance laws and give equal guardianship rights to mothers. Legal reform had widespread support because it addressed not just women's status as individuals but their position as mothers and wives.

But numerous failed lobbying campaigns made it clear that women's informal influence would never produce change. A limited 1911 dower law barely passed in the legislature, and though it promised a wife one-third of her husband's property after his death, he could still dispose of it without her consent during their marriage. As a result, legal issues came to dominate public talks given by suffrage leagues, which used them to raise women's consciousness about the importance of the vote. The leagues relied heavily on their male allies in these public campaigns. John Stuart (Jack) Jamieson, the husband of suffragist Laura Jamieson, was a lawyer and judge who worked with LCWs to educate women on family law. Socialist lawyer R.B. Kerr spoke about women's lack of property rights and argued that the law forced them to stay in "brutal" and violent marriages for fear of losing their children.

Organizations also disseminated information through pamphlets and newspapers. The first publication released by the BC

Helen Gregory MacGill (1864–1947) was born in Hamilton,
Ontario, earned a master's degree at Trinity College, Toronto, and
moved to California with her first husband, where she co-owned
and edited a newspaper with her mother, Emma. In 1902, she
moved to Vancouver with her second husband, James MacGill,
and was appointed a Juvenile Court judge in 1917. She stands at
the far right, during the May 1926 cornerstone-laying ceremony
for the Vancouver Women's Building, which provided meeting
space for women's groups throughout the city.

Political Equality League, a pamphlet on women's legal status, was written by novelist Alice Ashworth Townley and was widely shared by provincial suffrage groups. The unequal status of women under a British-based legal system was a bitter pill for those who saw British culture as the highest achievement of civilization. Townley resolved this contradiction by arguing that though British law was the "best and fairest" in the world, provincial laws had not adequately evolved in "an age of progress." She also drew on anti-immigration rhetoric to highlight the unfair treatment of settler women of British background. They had stood by their men as they built homes in their new country but did not have the same political rights as European immigrant men, whom she described as "ignorant foreigners."

Inequitable laws relating to intimate family relationships were perhaps most deeply felt. Discrimination was built into the divorce law until 1925. For example, though both parties could sue for divorce, a husband merely had to prove that his wife was unfaithful, whereas a wife had to show "aggravated adultery," such as desertion or cruelty, by her husband. But most contentious were the laws related to the guardianship of children. Suffragists railed at the hypocrisy of a system in which motherhood was glorified yet women had no rights to their children. Fathers were the sole legal guardians of their children, and they controlled their wages, schooling, living arrangements, and bodies. In British Columbia, fathers had the sole right to approve the marriage of minor children. Bertha Merrill Burns argued that these laws forced women to "barter" for their children by exchanging economic support in return for custody. Male authority over children was a sore spot, given the cultural weight attached to motherhood. This paradox helps explain the suffrage tendency to compare the status of women with that of children: in legal terms, a married woman was not dissimilar to a dependent child.

These were not just abstract arguments for suffragists: many had a personal experience of vulnerability under family law. Marriage

Born in California, Susie Lane Clark (1875–1956) became involved in American suffrage politics. A teacher, she emigrated to Vancouver in 1906 with her husband, John Allen Clark, a printer, where she joined the LCW and the Vancouver Political Equality League. She wrote and edited the "Suffrage Movement News" column for the Vancouver Daily World *and contributed regularly to the* B.C. Federationist. *After women won the vote, she organized and became president of the New Era League. Divorced during the 1920s, she ran for the school board under the banner of the Independent Labor Party. She later joined the Co-operative Commonwealth Federation and was elected to the Vancouver Park Board in 1937.*

was supposed to be lifelong and companionate, but it did not always live up to this ideal. Vancouver suffragist Rose (Mrs. Roy M.) Taylor was pregnant as a teenager before marriage, twice divorced, and had several children under her care. Although there is no record of her relationship with the fathers of her children, she warned women that they had no legal right to custody of their children and bitterly noted the chasm between the idealization and reality of motherhood. "Mother" was the "sweetest word in the English language," she stated, "yet how little that word means in British Columbia, where mothers are not even entitled to their own children." Other leading Vancouver suffragists, including Ida Douglas-Fearn and Susie Lane Clark, were also divorced and raising dependent children. Theirs was a relatively rare status in a country where divorce was both expensive and difficult to get.

But the argument that all women were subordinated on the basis of sex glossed over significant differences of class and race.

Many women – and men – had little property to share in the case of divorce or death. This was especially true for immigrants who worked in low-paying jobs and were banned from employment in better-paid positions. Suffragists drew on liberal traditions to suggest that it was undemocratic and dehumanizing for one portion of the citizenry to make laws for the other and that women were rational citizens who should not be subject to laws they had no voice in making. But this reasoning never acknowledged how governments regulated the lives of immigrant and Indigenous men and women. Asian men were not allowed to work in certain industries or the professions, and discriminatory legislation prohibited them from bringing their families to Canada. The lives of Indigenous women were governed by the federal Indian Act, which stripped them and their descendants of Indian status if they married non-Indigenous men, preventing many women and their children from living with their communities on-reserve. The act also excluded Indigenous women from participating in band council elections and coerced residential schooling for children. Suffragists neither acknowledged nor addressed these profound legal harms.

THE SEXUAL DOUBLE STANDARD

By the end of the nineteenth century, suffragists had become increasingly concerned with what they called the sexual double standard – the expectation that women would remain sexually pure before and during marriage. The same standard did not apply to men. This seemed to be an extension of female subordination in the home, the workplace, and politics. Most suffragists supported monogamous and heterosexual marriage, especially at a time when birth control was illegal and unreliable. But they encouraged a "single standard of morals for men and women – both socially and before the law."

The most visible outcome of the double standard was the prevalence of prostitution. Reformers across North America referred to sex work as a vice or a "social evil" and condemned it as immoral because it involved sex outside of marriage. But nineteenth-century reformers increasingly understood it as rooted in external factors rather than individual sin. The popular term "white slavery" came from exposés written by muckraking British journalist W.T. Stead, who portrayed prostitution as coerced sexual labour where economically vulnerable young women were "kidnapped" by procurers to satisfy a global sex trade. This belief was grafted onto racist ideas that white women were vulnerable to exploitation by Chinese men and that Chinese sex workers were in desperate need of rescue by respectable white women. Coercion no doubt existed, but women were not kidnapped on a global scale. And even though small numbers of Chinese and Japanese women were brought to the province to work in the sex trade – in the cities or mining towns – they were vastly outnumbered by white women. The Victoria Methodist Woman's Missionary Society founded the Chinese Rescue Home in 1888 to "rescue" Chinese sex workers, but they used the home for their own needs: to leave situations of domestic violence, for example, or to access the medical treatments they could not otherwise afford.

Women's organizations and suffrage groups gathered statistics, researched municipal policies, and wrote newspaper columns on the impact of sex work on women. In most BC towns and cities during this period, red light districts were tolerated, but suffragists had faith that female voters would shut them down – and convince legislators to prosecute male clients. They did not see sex work as a job or listen to worker concerns about their safety. But the language of coercion allowed them to emphasize factors such as low wages and the double standard. As Reverend Charles M. Sheldon told parishioners of the Wesleyan Methodist Church in Vancouver during a guest sermon, "it was not by choice that girls live immoral lives, but from the fact that they cannot in many stores in the cities earn a living wage." Helena Gutteridge agreed that sex work resulted from low wages and capitalism, and pondered why the men who bought sexual services were not arrested. The shift from the language of "white slavery" to "traffic in women" in 1909 was initiated by the International Council of Women, and it reflected a growing sense that women opted for prostitution largely due to economic coercion.

Differences among socialists, reformers, and suffragists regarding sex work were a matter of degree rather than kind. Socialists argued that capitalism was its primary cause: men could not afford to marry, and women's wages were so low that they were compelled to choose between "starvation or shame." This assumption fit well with mainstream beliefs that men had a right to sexual relationships and to a dependent wife. Socialists also used sex work as a metaphor for exploitation, seeing it as just one way in which working people sold their bodies to survive. An editorial in the socialist *Western Clarion* contended that "every merchant on earth today is trafficking in human life in some form or other." But the emphasis on exploitation elided the fact that some sex workers earned a good living. Historian Patrick Dunae used the 1901 census to show that the mainly young white women who worked in brothels could make almost $1,000 a year. By comparison, the annual wage for female store clerks ranged between $300 and $500, and it was even lower for domestic workers. Suffragists refused to acknowledge this reality, however, choosing instead to stress exploitation and to lobby governments to eradicate red light districts. There is little evidence that these tactics were effective, and many feminists argue that they actually made the industry more dangerous for sex workers.

The women's movement spanned the nineteenth and twentieth centuries, retaining a focus on improving the lives of women even as its priorities shifted over time. Shaped by widespread cultural beliefs about the important roles that women played as wives and mothers, it also called for economic and legal equality between white settler men and women. Some women's groups were initially reluctant to embrace suffrage as the main vehicle for achieving that equality, but most eventually agreed that women could only improve the social order if they were enfranchised. The vote mattered, and women throughout the province increasingly dedicated their time and energy to building a movement that prioritized winning it on the same terms as men.

C stands for "Champion," the paper that's new
H stands for "help," which is wanted from you
A stands for "ability," which we do not lack
M stands for "money" – that we never send back!
P stands for "prejudice," the enemy of the cause
I for "independence," greater than the laws
O for "opposition" – listen to it rave!
N is for our "newspaper," fearless, true and brave.

– D.H.H.C., *CHAMPION*, OCTOBER 1912, 11.

Co-operate, agitate, educate, vote, legislate.

– MRS. R.L. (NELLIE) CRAIG,
PIONEER POLITICAL EQUALITY LEAGUE,
VANCOUVER DAILY WORLD, 24 NOVEMBER 1913, 11.

TWO

BUILDING
A MOVEMENT

Members of the Victoria LCW on the steps of the Legislative
Assembly in either 1895 or 1897. The photo probably
commemorates one of the many delegations that presented
suffrage petitions and lobbied politicians to pass legislation.
The names of the women are not recorded, but it's likely that
Maria Grant, Cecilia Spofford, Margaret Jenkins, and
Constance Langford Davie are among them.

IN MARCH 1907, Baptist temperance activist and suffragist Cecilia Spofford addressed a two-hundred-person crowd in downtown Victoria. This public meeting had been called by the LCW and the WCTU to protest the recent actions of the Conservative provincial government. Just one year earlier, it had amended the Municipal Elections Act, inadvertently conferring the municipal franchise on a wide group of non-propertied women. Excited by this prospect, many Victoria women had signed up to the voters' list. The government then claimed that the wording of the legislation had been unintentional and pledged to undo it as soon as possible.

At the meeting, Spofford seized the opportunity to explain why women should vote at all levels of government. Expressing maternalist claims that they had a "stronger moral character" than men, she stated that women would exert a "refining" and "purifying" influence on local governments. But Spofford was also convinced by humanist reasoning that women's subordination to men was "degrading" and by liberal arguments that those subject to the law "should be granted some say in the making of the laws of the country." She asserted that women had a unique role to play in building the province. "We are inclined to forget that the only end of this human existence is not the laying up of material wealth," she told her enthusiastic audience. "The production of soul wealth for the nation is a higher and more worthy aim." The solitary male listener who suggested that women were not ready for suffrage encountered such derision that he was "quite overcome by the storm which he had aroused." A disconcerted *Colonist* reporter described the behaviour of the boisterous and largely female crowd as characterized by "indignant shrieks of protest" and "hisses like the escape of steam from a boiler with the safety valve tied down."

The municipal voting controversy of 1906–08 illustrates that suffragists called for female enfranchisement at all levels of government in British Columbia. The first rumblings of support had emerged in the 1870s, as a handful of politicians debated the possibility of extending the vote to women. Women were organizing on their own behalf by the 1880s, but they also built alliances with sympathetic male allies, with whom they worked to introduce private members' bills. With the rise of suffrage leagues across the province, they created dedicated organizations that worked tirelessly to educate the public and win broad support. By the 1910s, the sheer quantity of suffrage groups and extensive media coverage made the struggle for the vote impossible to ignore.

MALE ALLIES

Suffragists initially found a few allies in the provincial legislature. The issue of the franchise occupied politicians in the 1870s as they debated responsible government and the question of who should vote in Canada's newest province. Some of these politicians adopted emerging ideas about women's potential for political citizenship, and although they believed that women's responsibilities lay mainly within the home, they also felt that women and children deserved some protection from male power. Likewise, they were influenced by humanist liberal ideas that linked women's political liberty to autonomy and representative democracy in a modern society.

Male sympathizers in the 1870s and 1880s held a range of views regarding gender and women, but many fell into what historian Robert A.J. McDonald calls a general "opposition group" of politicians; they were small-business owners, lawyers, merchants, newspaper editors or proprietors, and former prospectors and gold miners. All shared the settler desire for wealth and property, but unlike the colonial elite, they believed in the importance of representative government and an enlarged franchise for the white settler population. They supported non-sectarian and state-funded public schools and a professional civil service. Many favoured the single tax, an idea developed by American reformer Henry George, who held that the government should raise revenue by heavily taxing land in the public interest. They marshalled a range of arguments to make their case: maternal feminism; a Christian emphasis on improving the social order; and liberal humanism, which saw gender inequality as uncivilized and drew on the idea that progressive societies should not be bound to the past. These ideas were given a unique spin in BC settler society, which acknowledged the role of white women in building a prosperous province. They are reflected in the political careers of William Fraser Tolmie, James Cunningham, John Cunningham Brown, Montague Tyrwhitt-Drake, Simeon Duck, and Charles Semlin, all of whom supported legislation in favour of women's rights. Another ally, John Robson, had become a highly influential politician by the 1880s (he was premier between 1889 and 1892), and his support for suffrage was rooted in his Christian faith and commitment to both temperance and representative government.

Like other women's organizations, the suffrage movement believed in non-partisanship, choosing to work with allies across ideological differences. Because British Columbia had no political parties prior to the turn of the century, suffragists approached powerful men to whom they were connected through kinship, the reform movement, or religious groups. And though most elected politicians remained opposed to votes for women, suffragists held out hope that they could gradually build on these connections to influence legislation.

THE MUNICIPAL FRANCHISE

The earliest debates about the female franchise centred on local voting rights, and women first achieved a limited franchise at the municipal and school board levels. Although the rules differed from province to province, enfranchisement was generally restricted by race, age, property, and, for women, marital status. After 1876, men were no longer required to own property to vote provincially in British Columbia, but municipal voting was still confined to property holders on the assumption that they had the highest stake in the community. The rules differed by municipality, but voters generally had to own property, possess a certain amount in savings, or pay rent on a home that was valued at a pre-determined sum.

Vigorous debates about who was entitled to vote arose as the new legislature contemplated whether propertied women should vote municipally. The first attempt to extend the municipal franchise failed in 1872, but a second attempt succeeded in 1873. Both debates centred on whether women desired to vote and whether a truly representative government should include them. Thomas B. Humphreys, the Liverpool-born MLA for Lillooet who had worked as a gold miner and auctioneer, made the first motion in 1872, stating that property-owning women deserved representation because they paid taxes. Horrified by his stance, the *Colonist* wrote that it was "tantamount to an assertion that he is in favour of 'Woman's Rights.'" The motion was defeated by fifteen to five.

But a motion the following year by Charles Semlin succeeded after a forceful debate. Semlin proposed that "female" be inserted into the Municipality Act, and another MLA suggested that references to gender should be replaced by "person." Both ideas provoked laughter and typical anti-suffrage objections: women did not want the vote; those who did cast a ballot would "upend" the social order; and women's refined femininity would be harmed by the rowdiness of the polls. The debate turned on issues of property, race, and the right to run for office. First, the legislature had no intention of enfranchising women who did not satisfy the property requirements. Second, John Robson, who was not yet a suffrage supporter, worried about a racial slippery slope because

"Indian and Chinese" residents might wish to vote. Finally, he and others feared that women might want to run for municipal council or become mayors, a spectre greeted by bursts of laughter. Only George Walkem, a lawyer who had immigrated from Northern Ireland to the Cariboo during the gold rush, thought that running for office was a favourable job "for the ladies." The amendment carried by one vote after the Speaker broke a tie, and probably only because it excluded women from holding municipal office.

The 1873 amendment set out conditions that enfranchised any *feme sole* (unmarried or widowed woman) who met the property qualifications (as a freeholder, householder, free miner, or long-term leaseholder). Furthermore, after the first municipal election, the voting base was expanded to include any qualified "male or female" regardless of marital status who was at least twenty-one years old. The result was an uneven set of requirements. In Victoria and Nanaimo, married women who met the racial, property, and residency qualifications could vote. But in Vancouver and New Westminster, only unmarried or widowed women were initially allowed to vote municipally. The New Westminster Act was amended in 1892 to include married women who satisfied the property qualifications, but married women in Vancouver had to wait until 1910. The exclusion of women from the right to run for municipal office lasted longer, despite efforts in 1889 to allow them to run on the basis of their competency and taxpaying status.

Although legislation in the 1870s gave property-holding women some of the most expansive municipal voting rights in the country, most women did not hold enough property (including business licences and rent assessed at a certain value) in their own name to qualify. In the hotly contested Victoria municipal election of January 1874, only 3 of the 1,211 people on the voters' list were female. Despite this tiny number, the *Colonist* reported that "public expectation was on tiptoe" leading up to the election, but "at the last minute it was announced that the ladies had decided not to vote, and thus was the contest robbed of its fairest feature." The following January, however, the first three recorded female voters in the province voted for mayor. The media response to the election results reveals the city's divides of gender and race. The *Colonist,* which had endorsed the losing candidate, blamed political corruption for the victory of John Drummond, a local merchant who had secured the support of Chinese men. At this time, Chinese men could still vote municipally, and the editors were outraged because ninety-two of them had cast their ballots, presumably for Drummond. Their votes, along with those of the three women, spurred the paper to condemn the "swarms of Chinamen or, for the matter of that, women, who cannot be properly accounted residents of Victoria," who had been "brought in" to defeat the "legitimate candidate."

The promise of the municipal vote led women's organizations to campaign for broader terms of enfranchisement in the 1880s and 1890s. But these demands were hotly contested and limited by race, residency, marital status, and property. Multiple amendments to the Municipal Elections Act and the School Board Act meant that suffragists waged a constant battle to achieve, expand, and protect local voting rights. Municipal and school board voting rights were extended and retracted numerous times between the 1870s and 1916. Sometimes, even city officials themselves seemed unclear on who was entitled to cast a ballot.

Not all women's groups supported provincial suffrage, but they recognized that local politics had a direct impact on domestic life. Under the terms of the British North America Act, municipal governments were responsible for health inspections, policing red light districts, and handling urban waste and garbage disposal, all of which affected the health and well-being of families and children. Similarly, though the provinces were responsible for public education, school board trustees were nominated or elected at the local level, and they influenced school budgets and curriculums.

Maternal feminism fit comfortably with the demand for the municipal franchise, imagining the home as "woman's domain" but creatively interpreting that to extend outward to the "schools [and] the streets." Victoria suffragist Constance Langford Davie argued in 1895 that women should understand every detail about their city: how the roads were paved, the streetcars regulated, sewage systems constructed, police functioned, and water purified. These concerns remained relevant into the 1910s and drew together conservative, liberal, and socialist supporters. Socialist Louisa Parr suggested that though women might not be interested in "big national or provincial issues," they felt that municipal voting would bring a "refining influence" to city council. Women could "watch" over city politics and every decision related to the well-being of their families.

In Vancouver, the campaign for the municipal vote developed after the city was incorporated in 1886. Under the city charter, a small group of property-holding widows and unmarried women could vote, but married women could not. The charter also explicitly prevented Asian, South Asian, and First Nations city residents from voting regardless of property status. Not until 1910 did the LCW, the University Women's Club, and the WCTU petition city council to include married women among municipal voters. They found a supporter in Mayor L.D. Taylor, who also owned the *Vancouver Daily World.* The LCW argued that married women voters would improve urban conditions and had an important role to play in the "enlightened world." Suffragists Janet Kemp and Alice Ashworth Townley addressed city council in November 1910, and a motion to amend the city charter and extend the vote to property-holding married women passed with no apparent debate. But Susie Lane Clark pointed out in 1913 that a property-based municipal franchise was hardly democratic, and she criticized a system that "places property values ahead of life." The working-class BC Woman's Suffrage League kept the issue alive by declaring that property should not determine voting rights for either men or women. "Let us learn to be truly a democracy," argued a male member of the league, and "register the person and not the property." But property restrictions would not be abolished in Vancouver until 1954.

After propertied married women won the municipal vote in Vancouver, a new educational group was soon created. The Women's Forum was founded in 1910 by seven Vancouver women, most of whom were suffragists, including Janet Kemp (later president of the BC Political Equality League), Helen Gregory MacGill, Mary McConkey, and Mary Ellen Smith. By 1913, it represented approximately 1,700 female municipal franchise holders in the city. By 1915, there were four additional branches in the Vancouver suburbs and one in each of Vancouver's eight city wards. Another was established in Revelstoke in 1916. A non-partisan body, the forum focused on women's political education and supported a minimum wage, equal pay, and mothers' pensions. It encouraged women to run for school trustee and nominated them for municipal boards. The Burnaby branch, headed by suffragist Laura Jamieson, launched a campaign for shorter store working hours and held events on how to vote municipally. But provincial enfranchisement seems to have deflated its purpose, and it faded out by the early 1920s.

Victoria women were visible in early campaigns for the municipal vote, and for a brief period between 1906 and 1908, it seemed that their rights would expand significantly. When the Municipal Elections Act was amended in 1906, the voting base of propertied women had been enlarged when the definition of "householder" was expanded to include anyone who had paid at least two dollars a year or more in municipal taxes or fees (such as for a dog licence) in the current year. The intent was to ensure that militia men were able to vote, but the amendment also inadvertently extended the vote to unpropertied, tax-paying women. This amendment did not apply in Vancouver, but it did in Victoria, where it stirred up intense opposition. The Licensed Victuallers' Association feared that women would vote to restrict the consumption and sale of alcohol. The Property Owners Association was concerned that the presence of "immoral women" at the polls, meaning those who owned brothels, would bring the democratic process into disrepute. Even the eminently respectable Cecilia Spofford ridiculed the morality argument. As she told a mass meeting in 1907, there "seems to have been some fear that the extension of the franchise in this city would have put undue power in the hands of immoral women." But then, she added, should not "we have the right to demand that only moral men vote[?]"

Attorney General William Bowser and Premier Richard McBride took steps to rescind the expansion of the franchise. The WCTU and the LCW immediately protested, and the March 1907 meeting that opened this chapter passed a motion asking the government to retain the 1906 legislation. But it refused, and the battle soon moved to the courts. The Property Owners Association won a ruling from the Magistrates' Court that ordered the removal of 486 women from the voters' list. Women's groups then won an injunction from the Supreme Court of British Columbia, which allowed them to vote in the 1908 election. The WCTU and the LCW followed up with a thousand-name petition and more public meetings, and they warned McBride that if he did not abide by suffrage demands, "the members of the government will know what to expect." Maria Grant and Margaret Jenkins peppered McBride with arguments by letter and in person, even providing him with a draft of potential legislation. But the Conservatives stood firm. The suffragists had lost the battle for an expanded municipal franchise, and their deep disappointment contributed to an increased focus on gaining the provincial vote.

THE SCHOOL BOARD FRANCHISE

Many suffragists felt that they could win the right to vote for school trustee because children's education was a crucial area of concern for mothers, especially after the Public Schools Act of 1872 mandated free common schools and enforced attendance. Furthermore, teaching, especially at the elementary level, was the most accessible profession for unmarried women. The attempt to gain the school board vote and later, to run for the office of trustee, enabled suffragists to flex their political muscle at the local level.

But winning the school board franchise was not easy, and successive provincial governments expanded and contracted the right to vote. In 1884, the province enfranchised propertied, unmarried, urban women; a year later, the wives of male householders and freeholders who met property qualifications joined their ranks. Rural women would have to wait longer – until 1897 – because rural trustees were appointed rather than elected. But even such limited rights were awarded only after extensive debate in which politicians insisted that women had no wish to be "dragged" into voting. As soon as the first bill passed in 1884, Margaret Jenkins and Cecilia Spofford began canvassing door to door, urging women to exercise their rights to prove "they are deeply interested in public affairs, and that they are prepared for further privileges." In June 1884, 269 women voted for the first time in school board elections. Suffragists saw this as evidence that voting women would retain their "dignity" and "womanliness." However, female voters experienced harassment from two male candidates at the polls, whom suffragists reported as "rude and ungentlemanly," and unable to "control both tongue and temper." More than a decade would pass before even these limited concessions were firmly in place. As late as 1892, the provincial government redefined "voter" to encompass landholders and freeholders without including the phrase "wife of," unintentionally disenfranchising married women. Apparently, some women simply continued to vote, even as the WCTU began a campaign to repeal the amendment.

As soon as they were allowed to vote at the school board level, suffragists lobbied for the right to run as trustees. John Robson moved an amendment to the School Act in 1889 that allowed urban women to run for trustee. But this too was contested. A series of amendments between 1889 and 1895 replaced elected positions with appointments but later reinstated elections, all of which precluded women from standing for office. Women's groups spent the first half of the 1890s pushing the provincial government to clarify and expand these rights. The newly formed LCW took up the cause, noting at an 1895 meeting that women "were more directly concerned than men in the education of children, and for this reason, if no other, women should have their place on the trustee boards." The first president of the Victoria LCW was Louise Baker, wife of Minister of Education Colonel James Baker.

With his support and the backing of an LCW-organized petition, the province finally introduced an amendment confirming that women could run for school board trustee.

But the amendment did not apply in Vancouver, as the Vancouver LCW discovered in 1895 when it met to propose a nomination for trustee. The LCW duly launched an extensive campaign, invoking the "progressive cities" of Victoria and Seattle. By the winter of 1897, it had achieved its goal and soon turned to nominating female candidates. At this time, it was not controversial for women's organizations to support women for the office of school trustee. As the Vancouver LCW put it, every school board should include at least "one or two sensible, educated women." Female candidates had a fair degree of success in Victoria, Vancouver, and New Westminster.

The day after women secured the right to run for trustee, the Victoria LCW nominated Cecilia Spofford. But she was married to a carpenter and did not meet the property qualifications. She was replaced by Maria Grant, who became the first woman elected to any office in the province. But when two women – Maria Grant and Helen Grant – ran in 1896, it appeared to be too much for the electorate. Maria Grant lost and afterward claimed that a man had stood outside the polling booth, instructing voters, "Don't vote for the ladies." In Vancouver, the first female trustee was elected in 1898, after several failed attempts by women's groups to find a candidate, but the city waited twelve years for the next. In Victoria, however, at least one woman was elected every year between 1895 and 1919. Over these twenty-four years, the positions were held by four prominent women: Maria Grant, Helen Grant, Margaret Jenkins, and Agnes Deans Cameron. By 1905, five women were serving on rural Vancouver Island school boards as trustees. Not surprisingly, however, the position was unpaid. And rights to municipal and school board voting were uneven across the province, and were subject to restrictive property requirements.

THE PROVINCIAL VOTE

Suffragists expended a great deal of energy on local enfranchisement but were also determined to lobby the legislature for the
provincial vote. The first attempt to change the relevant legislation came from MLA Dr. William Fraser Tolmie, who introduced
a motion in April 1875 to include the words "every person male or
female" in the Qualification and Registration of Voters Act. Tolmie
believed that the "endeavor to emancipate Woman from electoral
disabilities is as good and holy a cause as Man ever strove for." He
was convinced that women wanted to vote, that men had a duty to
support them, and that female enfranchisement was a modern
inevitability for "a young country yet in the gristle, uninterested
in old-time prejudice." His name and those of four of his twelve
children (including at least one of his daughters, May Fraser
Tolmie) appeared on the suffrage petition presented to the legislature in 1885.

One of the earliest attempts in Canada to enact female suffrage, Tolmie's initiative remained unique in the province during
the 1870s. It generated considerable debate between the three
MLAs in support – W.A. Robertson, Simeon Duck, and Tolmie himself – and their opponents. Drawing on ancient precedent from
East Indian proverbs, Greek and Roman history, trends in British
women's co-education, and women's rights in Wyoming, Tolmie
declared that suffrage would improve the world and make
British Columbia appealing to the white female settlers whom
the provincial government desired to attract. Far from degrading
women, it would elevate the tone of politics. Robertson agreed,
stating that women were equal to men in judgment and that anti-
suffrage arguments were shameful. Tolmie's bill sparked debate
in the *Colonist*. "Transforthanus" wrote three letters to the editor,
pointing out that suffrage was an international movement and
suggesting that its "narrow-minded" opponents were unreasonable people who stood against "change and improvement." But

William Fraser Tolmie (1812–86) immigrated to North America
from Scotland in 1833 to work as a clerk and medical officer for
the Hudson's Bay Company. In 1850, he married Jane Work, a
woman of maternal Indigenous descent. Tolmie enjoyed a long
career as an MLA, was influenced by reformist trends including
liberalism and the ideas of Robert Owen, a utopian socialist, and
supported non-sectarian schooling and temperance. This 1878
photo shows the Tolmie family at their Victoria home.

suffrage supporters were greatly outnumbered by those who insisted that women did not belong in politics.

As the population of white women grew, collaboration would
strengthen between women's groups and sympathetic male politicians. Throughout the 1880s and 1890s, suffragists courted male
legislators and attempted to convince them to introduce private
members' bills. After 1903, they continued to work with sympathetic

MLAs and directly lobbied the Conservative government. Between 1875 and 1916, MLAs introduced sixteen bills to amend existing legislation, many of which progressed to second reading before being defeated.

Most of these suffrage bills originated with a persistent group of MLAs, many of whom had close ties – through church, reform organizations, or marriage – to women in the LCWs or the WCTU. After initially resisting suffrage, John Robson became one of its foremost proponents, influenced by his religious background and close connection to the women of the WCTU, whose founding meeting he had attended. Lawyer Montague Tyrwhitt-Drake and newspaper owner John Cunningham Brown were staunch allies, moving a total of seven bills between 1883 and 1893. Tyrwhitt-Drake, a cousin by marriage to Tolmie, presented numerous suffrage petitions and introduced bills in 1883, 1884, and 1885.

The increasing number of private members' bills in the 1890s reflects the growing influence of feminist arguments. Regardless of political affiliation, men's support generally echoed that of women's organizations: suffrage would protect the family, be a mark of progress, and acknowledge women's humanity. As elected officials who had witnessed the worst of the political system, they argued that political incivility was the fault of male voters. Voting would not degrade women; instead, their refining influence would elevate the entire system. Indeed, as MLA Joseph Martin remarked in 1902, "there was no possibility of women making a worse mess of politics than men had done." As provincial boosters and promoters of colonialism, politicians claimed that female enfranchisement would benefit British Columbia and counter the votes of European immigrant men. And though most male supporters accepted maternal feminist arguments, they also held humanist and liberal views about women's ability to reason and emphasized the importance of representative government in what they perceived as a democratic province.

A breakdown of votes on the suffrage bills, as recorded in the *Journals of the Legislative Assembly,* shows that support for enfranchisement peaked between 1899 and 1902, with some 45 to 47 percent of MLAs in favour. This development was tied to a number of political and economic factors. Due to rapid economic expansion, industrialization, and class conflict in the 1890s, record numbers of labour, socialist, and reform supporters were elected to the legislature between 1898 and 1903. This support reached a height during the 1903 election, when what historian Jean Barman terms "left-identified" parties won 15.4 percent of the vote. Although not all labour and reform politicians supported suffrage, there was a general overlap of interests that seemed to suggest the tide was turning.

None of the private members' bills passed, but some were defeated by slim margins, as was the case in 1899, when a bill proposed by Liberal-Labour politician Ralph Smith lost by only two votes (seventeen to fifteen). Smith believed that anti-suffrage thought was founded on the "ancient prejudice that women should be kept subservient to man." He attempted to convince his colleagues that, since women were subject to the law, "governments had no right to determine, without regard to her, the state of the law under which she should suffer." Shortly afterward, MLA Richard Hall admitted that he had intended to vote in favour of the motion but had accidentally voted against it. Had this error not occurred, the result would have been a tie broken by the Speaker, William Thomas Forster, who favoured suffrage. The women of British Columbia had been only one mistakenly cast vote away from success. This close result caught both pro- and anti-suffragists off guard and inspired an outpouring of public opinion on both sides of the question. The *Colonist* published extensive commentary, but an editorial concluded that the current system was legitimate and that any attempt to change it was "revolutionary."

THE PRINCIPLE OF NON-PARTISANSHIP

This slowly building consensus of the 1890s might have resulted in majority support for female suffrage, but it was halted by the emergence of party politics. Unstable political coalitions in a rapidly expanding province led to increasing pressure for a party-based system. Prior to this period, MLAs could vote on the basis of their individual beliefs. But after 1903, it was difficult to take a position that contradicted the vocally anti-suffrage premier, Richard McBride. Records of the Legislative Assembly show that the majority of pro-suffrage MLAs from 1904 onward belonged either to the Liberal or to one of the socialist parties. Every private member's bill from 1904 on came from a Socialist or Social Democratic MLA. Socialist MLA James Hawthornthwaite thought that women's rights would counter the exploitation of working-class women, especially as more of them entered the paid labour force. Social Democrat Jack Place was a reliable supporter who introduced private member's bills in 1913, 1914, and 1916.

The government's stance on suffrage after 1903 was overwhelmingly dismissive and condescending. In response, some supporters turned to the reformist Liberal Party, especially after it adopted a suffrage platform. In 1913, suffragists were invited to address the provincial Liberal convention in Revelstoke, where suffrage supporter and Baptist reformer Harlan Brewster was re-elected as Liberal leader, and where delegates serenaded them with a rendition of "For They Are Jolly Good Fellows." This sort of enthusiastic reception went a long way in gaining suffrage support. Several members of the Revelstoke Political Equality League, along with BC league president Janet Kemp, thanked the party for adopting suffrage and openly criticized the Conservatives. Prominent women, including Helen Gregory MacGill, Evlyn Farris, Mary Ellen Smith, and Mary McConkey, created the Liberal Women's Association in 1915, working within the party to advance the cause.

But not all suffragists were comfortable with supporting the Liberals. A significant minority identified as Conservative, such as

Bertha Merrill Burns (1864–1917). Bertha Merrill was born into a Baptist family in southwestern Ontario. After her father's death, she helped support her mother by teaching and working as a journalist at the Brantford Expositor. *Between 1891 and 1901, she and her mother moved to Nelson, British Columbia, where they opened a lodging home. By 1902, she was writing regular columns for the socialist press. A member of the Socialist Party of British Columbia, she married Birmingham-born labour organizer Ernest Burns. They lived in Vancouver, where Bertha worked for the* Western Clarion. *She and Ernest separated from the Socialist Party of Canada and helped found the Social Democratic Party of BC in 1907.*

Alice Ashworth Townley, or leaned left or socialist, such as Helena Gutteridge, Bertha Merrill Burns, and Susie Lane Clark. Some feared that Liberal support for enfranchisement was not genuine and would not survive an election victory. Much of this suspicion sprang from the Liberal Party's dealings with suffragettes in Britain. Two British-born critics – Ida Douglas-Fearn and Helena Gutteridge – felt that the Liberals could not be trusted. "All planks are not meant to stand on," claimed Ida Douglas-Fearn. "Some are merely ornamental." In her view, the British Liberal Party had offered activists a history of "rotten" planks.

Even partisan suffragists, however, continued to work with sympathetic politicians from a range of parties. And non-partisanship did not stop some from pointing out that women might feel loyal to the party that enfranchised them. Dorothy Davis played on Premier McBride's concerns about socialist electoral success when she noted that MLAs such as Jack Place favoured suffrage and were

"keenly interested in the question." "There is throughout the country a considerable volume of what one might call fluid political
feeling, especially among the women, and the voting newcomers,"
Davis warned McBride. "If the Government were now to *refuse* a
Suffrage Bill, the readiness of the Socialists to further it would
certainly turn this tide in their favour."

THE POLITICAL EQUALITY LEAGUE AND
SUFFRAGE SOCIETIES

By 1910, suffragists had been active for close to thirty years, but
the limit of their political influence was clear. A national plebis-
cite on prohibition had passed in 1898, but Ottawa refused to
implement it because the turnout of electors had been low and
because Quebec voters had rejected it. The Canada Temperance
Act (1878) allowed prohibition on the basis of local plebiscites,
but these failed to pass with the required majority in most provinces. Suffragists worked in vain for reform of domestic and
property laws. And multiple private members' bills had failed repeatedly in the legislature.

Women had secured the municipal and school board franchise
and could now run for school trustee, but these rights had been
won only after much resistance and remained limited by race, nationality, residency, property, and marital status. The fallout from
the accidental expansion of the municipal vote prompted Cecilia
Spofford to wonder whether she had been mistaken in believing
"that the present is an age of most wonderful progression." With
their faith in education, modernity, and evolutionary improvements to woman's status, suffragists were immensely frustrated
by these multiple disappointments.

These failures sparked the development of the Political Equality League (PEL), founded in December 1910 by Maria Grant, with
the aid of the Victoria LCW and a monetary contribution from
a group of anonymous American suffragists. Grant was elected
president, and the interim recording secretary was Frieda Roberts,

a visiting British suffragette. At the founding meeting, the crowd of seventy-five supporters included Victoria's reform elite, working women, mothers with infants, and future Liberal premier Harlan Brewster. Grant opened the meeting with a call to political freedom for BC women. To applause and cheers, women and men testified to women's responsible voting record in municipal affairs and their right to representation as citizens and mothers. Martha Douglas Harris, daughter of James Douglas, British Columbia's first governor, "amused" the audience with a humorous speech that mocked anti-suffragists. "Men say we are better than they are," Harris told her listeners. "Of course we are!" Spofford claimed that the "state was simply a great home, where both men and women should rule together." Brewster avowed that suffrage was unstoppable, a "movement now in Canada that will sweep it, as it will everywhere." Mr. A.B. McNeil, a Victoria school trustee, made the motion to create the PEL, whose purpose would be to "remove the disabilities which rest on woman as a voter and citizen and to secure her political enfranchisement." After all, McNeil added, "one section of the community should not rule another without their consent."

Inspired by the success in Victoria, Grant helped Florence Hall form a Vancouver PEL in January 1911. Vancouver suffragists had already been meeting to read John Stuart Mill and to discuss poor working conditions for women. The two cities provided the core of the BC Political Equality League (1911–17), which set about establishing affiliated chapters in as many regions of the province as possible. During the early years, the Victoria and Vancouver leagues shared information and personnel, and suffragists regularly made the five-hour ferry trip across the Georgia Strait to discuss strategy and speak on enfranchisement at women's organizations and clubs.

PEL membership was open to women and men, but leadership and executive positions were reserved for women. As organizers, they were no amateurs. The league was run by confident and outspoken activists who had already acquired political experience in women's groups. The rights and responsibilities of PEL membership were outlined in the constitution and by-laws, which stated that the organization's main goal was "establishment of the Political, Social and Industrial Rights of Women and Men." The PEL hired organizers to travel the province, published the *Champion* every month, and advanced the petition work previously undertaken by the WCTU. In January 1913, it held a one-day petition drive at the legislature on opening day, handing out literature, offering question-and-answer sessions to curious onlookers, and serving food and coffee.

This period saw wide support for suffrage develop beyond the urban centres of Vancouver Island and the Lower Mainland. By 1911, a substantial minority of British Columbians – about 25 percent – lived in towns and small cities throughout the southern interior. The PEL raised money and sent Florence Hall and Dorothy Davis to tour the interior and the Fraser Valley. Suffragists in Kelowna did not wait for them to arrive, however; socialist Dora

British-born Dorothy Marian Davis (1876–1949) immigrated to Canada in 1911 under the employ of the Colonial Intelligence League. A British organization, the league promoted settlement and found work for educated unmarried women in the colonies, largely in farming. Davis attempted to farm with a female friend in the Okanagan but then moved to Victoria, where she joined the PEL. She co-edited the Champion, *helped organize the mass 1913 suffrage petition, and joined many delegations to the legislature. She married Richard Bishop in 1913 and founded the Women's Freedom Union (or the Go-Aheads).*

Forster Kerr had taken the initiative and formed the Equal Franchise League in March 1911. It was particularly active, with weekly meetings hosted by Kerr and her husband.

By all accounts, the tours of Hall and Davis were highly successful, with Davis's trip lasting for three months. By 1914, branches had been established in Kelowna, Cranbrook, Creston, Penticton, Ashcroft, Agassiz, Enderby, Fernie, Golden, Greenwood, Mission, Kaslo, Kamloops, Revelstoke, Rossland, and Vernon. Although the PEL envisioned an equal network of local leagues, some branches were more active than others. Some complained of too much emphasis on activities in Victoria. There is no doubt that the league struggled, in a time before easy communication, to get the desired feedback from local members.

As Hall and Davis travelled the province, they relied on their political contacts to reach a wide range of people. Chairs of founding meetings were usually prestigious male lawyers, politicians, board of trade members, and clergy. The Enderby PEL enjoyed the organizational skill of former English suffragist Mrs. Grossman,

Born in England, Dora Forster (1864–1935) married Scottish barrister Robert B. Kerr in 1895 and moved to British Columbia, living for many years in Kelowna. Non-sectarian freethinkers and members of the Socialist Party of Canada, the Kerrs supported suffrage and wrote columns for the American-based anarchist journal Lucifer. *Dora wrote articles on women's work, feminism, and socialism for socialist papers, including* Cotton's Weekly *and the* Western Clarion.

Members of the Revelstoke Women's Canadian Club in 1920.
Established after 1909, women's Canadian clubs held talks on
politics, literature, and current events. In many communities,
their membership significantly overlapped with that of the local
Political Equality League. Helen Sturdy, one of Revelstoke's most
active suffragists, is at the far left in the middle row. She was also
a member of the Political Equality League and the Women's Forum.

whereas the Kelowna branch quickly got off the ground due to the
combined forces of socialists Dora and R.B. Kerr and several veterans of the British suffrage movement, including the married couple
James and Rose McCready. In Vernon, the WCTU had initiated a
meeting on suffrage in 1909, and its newly established PEL took
up the call, with most of the organizational effort handled by two
unmarried working women, Alys Evans and Miss Parkhurst. The
Revelstoke PEL was particularly active, holding monthly meetings, scheduling debates in churches and community organizations, sponsoring films, hosting visiting speakers Cecilia Spofford,
Nellie McClung, and Emmeline Pankhurst, and sending delegates
to PEL conventions and political meetings in Victoria. The branch
was no doubt strengthened by the presence of Florence Hall, after
her husband became the minister of the local Methodist church.

Davis returned to Victoria and recounted the details of her tour to public acclaim. The PEL was invested in portraying the tours as successful, but newspaper coverage corroborates that the enthusiasm was genuine. A group of Vernon lawyers had staged a public suffrage debate; Revelstoke had held three large public meetings; and supporters in Greenwood had organized a meeting, a suffrage play, and a petition signing all in under five days, prompting an excited male supporter to shout during a meeting, "Give the long-haired darlings a chance!"

Throughout 1913, local PELs called meetings, drew up resolutions, and mailed their demands to the premier. As Rose Winstead from Kaslo reminded McBride, "the Government needs the viewpoint of the women in the lawmaking department much more than the women need the Government." The PEL created a generic form for branches to record the meeting dates, number of people in attendance, and statements of support. This tactic allowed the league to flood the premier's office with letters and telegrams from hundreds of citizens, associations, and trade unions. Some PEL meetings were attended by almost two hundred people, and all pro-suffrage resolutions passed, though supporters diligently recorded the occasional "dissident" who spoke in opposition, such as the "bank boys giggling in the gallery" during an Enderby meeting.

As Vancouver grew in size and power, friction arose between the Victoria and Vancouver PELs, which the *Champion* editors described as "sore feeling and rivalry." As a result, the Vancouver branch declared its independence in 1913 and renamed itself the Pioneer Political Equality League. The split reflected Vancouver's rise to demographic dominance and a shift in much of the suffrage leadership away from Victoria. It may also have been grounded in class tensions and generational differences. Increasing numbers of Vancouver suffragists were working-class or professional working women. The Victoria suffrage scene was dominated by Maria Grant and Cecilia Spofford, both of whom were devout evangelical Christians with temperance connections. Born during the 1850s, they were a decade or more older than the younger leaders. At its 1913 convention, the PEL attempted to heal the rift by electing suffragists from outside the capital to the provincial executive. Grant was replaced as president by Vancouver's Janet Kemp, a forty-eight-year-old Ontario-born mother of three who was married to a carpenter. But a report in the *Champion* showed that the tension had not disappeared. During her acceptance speech, Kemp promised that Vancouver suffragists would take on additional "responsibility" for the movement. But the editors of the *Champion* sarcastically suggested that her remark had more to do with a desire for increased "status" than with a commitment to the duties of leadership.

Anyone who chose to join the suffrage movement at this time had a wide range of options, particularly in the Lower Mainland. Political Equality Leagues were founded in Port Coquitlam, New Westminster, and North Vancouver. Vancouver boasted Canada's only suffrage league that was designed for working-class women, and neighbourhood-based associations flourished in Mount Pleasant, Grandview, South Vancouver (including Cedar Cottage), Kerrisdale, and Point Grey. But not all suffragists shared the same perspective and goals. The period saw splintering along ideological and political lines. For instance, the BC Equal Franchise Association, led by Alice Ashworth Townley, was formed in 1912 with an emphasis on more restrained and less public campaigning. In Victoria, Dorothy Davis left the PEL in 1913 to set up the Women's Freedom Union. Known as the Go-Aheads, its members were willing to accept restrictions on the franchise (married women over age twenty-one would be permitted to vote, but unmarried women would have to wait until they turned twenty-six). In 1911, Victoria suffragists also toyed briefly with a breakaway militant local affiliated with the Women's Social and Political Union.

With so many suffrage groups, there was a flurry of meetings, debates, public talks, dances, parties, and fundraisers. Events reached a peak in 1913. During two and a half weeks in the fall of that year, for example, Vancouver suffrage associations held two public debates, five public meetings, and a dance/whist fundraiser. The emergence of so many new organizations prompted Maria Grant to write a column titled "Suffrage Vitality," in which she argued that multiple associations and viewpoints did not reflect "dissension, much less rivalry." She believed that the new branches were healthy signs of "vigorous growth," proof that the movement was "broad enough to contain legions." Perhaps Grant was right to encourage increased diversity. Newspaper accounts of events and delegations reveal that several thousand people were keenly interested in the progress of suffrage during the first decades of the twentieth century. All this activity, and the fact that thousands of people signed pro-suffrage petitions, indicates that interest in the movement was deeper and more widespread than historians have imagined.

The suffrage movement in British Columbia began in earnest during the 1880s and gradually became more popular and organized. Drawing on male allies in the legislature and the work of women's groups, suffragists built support for the municipal and school board vote. The support of well-known politicians and the explosion of new suffrage organizations and events seemed to bode well for the cause. But the advent of the First World War slowed activism until Premier McBride's 1915 resignation and a looming referendum on enfranchisement rejuvenated the campaign in the summer of 1916.

We do not question for a moment the ability of women to grasp the abstract principles underlying the British system of government ... but the average woman does not take a deep interest in public affairs. She does not read the reports of the proceedings of the city council, of the legislature or of parliament. She seems out of her element at public meetings. We do not blame woman for any of these things. On the contrary we consider her happy in her position of isolation.

– EDITORIAL, *VICTORIA DAILY TIMES*,
30 JANUARY 1908, 4.

In the absolutely brutal struggle which must follow any organization of society based upon equality between the sexes, the finest traits of feminine character inevitably disappear as women cannot continue to possess all the privileges of their own sex, whilst greedily and mistakenly grasping for the cares and responsibilities shouldered by men.

– EDITORIAL, *REVELSTOKE MAIL-HERALD*,
30 NOVEMBER 1912, 2.

THE
ANTI-SUFFRAGISTS

"*Too Proud to Speak*"

HAUGHTY

It Is Assumed That Premier McBride Is Not in Favor of Woman Suffrage.

This *Vancouver Sun* cartoon of a "haughty" Richard McBride
reflects the general contempt and frustration that many
suffragists felt for the premier. It was published shortly after
McBride formally rejected a ten-thousand-name suffrage petition
organized by the BC Political Equality League in February 1913.

IN MARCH 1913, members of the Legislative Assembly were presented with a private member's bill in support of female suffrage. A number of MLAs spoke against it, but A.E. McPhillips gave the most dramatic anti-suffrage speech of the session. Citing examples from world history and the British suffragette movement, he argued that female enfranchisement would not improve society and might even make it worse. As proof, he pointed to women in the French Revolution, who had marched

> through the streets, on the barricades, at that pitch when all idea of morality, and of propriety had been lost. They had been perhaps the principal factors in bringing about a condition in the fair country of France of infidelity, of atheism, of lawlessness. That event showed that there might be some reason for drawing a conclusion that women as a controlling body, were an unsafe body.

Midway through his speech, McPhillips warned MLAs that "the vote must mean the expression of the power of government. If you give votes to women you must carry your mind on to the time when the prime minister will be a woman." At that moment, a lone voice piped up from the visitors' gallery: "And why not?" This interjection did not change McPhillips's mind (and neither, apparently, did his wife, who was a member of the Political Equality League). His words expressed deep and long-standing fears that female suffrage was a dangerous threat to both the family and the stability of the nation-state.

Unlike the United States and Great Britain, British Columbia had no formal organization whose purpose was to oppose suffrage. But resolutely anti-suffragist men held positions of power and influence in politics, the church, and the media throughout the province and the country. Among them were humorist Stephen Leacock, politician and writer Goldwin Smith, and scientist Sir Andrew Macphail. The "antis," as they were called, advanced a range of arguments that were common across North America and the British Empire. At best, suffrage was unnecessary and irrelevant. At worst, it was a direct threat to God's ordained hierarchy of male authority in the family, the workplace, and the political sphere. These views would hold sway among the majority of elected politicians in British Columbia until 1916.

ANTI-SUFFRAGE SENTIMENT

Although the idea of female enfranchisement became increasingly popular and respectable during the early twentieth century, its supporters constantly fought against anti-suffrage sentiment. Most people who did not favour votes for women expressed their opinions through editorials, speeches in the legislature, letters to the editor, and sermons. They also retained the majority in the legislature. Between 60 and 80 percent of MLAs consistently voted against suffrage bills, and even as the movement became more respectable in Canada and around the world, opposition intensified in the legislature. In 1913, 71 percent of BC MLAs voted against suffrage, and a full 80 percent followed suit as late as 1916.

Such politicians dominated the legislature from the 1870s onward, where they spoke about the decline of the family and the nation that would occur were women permitted to vote. Records of debates in the *Journals of the Legislative Assembly* and in local newspapers reveal that suffrage aroused amusement, contempt, and fear. MLAs joked about women's attempts to gain the franchise, prompting even suffrage skeptic William Smithe to scold them for treating such a serious matter "with so much levity." But suffragists battled the longest with Richard McBride, Conservative Party leader and premier between 1903 and 1915, who remained opposed to suffrage throughout his political career. The battle with McBride echoes the one between Manitoba suffragists and Premier Rodmond Roblin, whose Conservative government (1900–15) stubbornly resisted suffrage. Roblin was convinced that enfranchisement led to high rates of divorce and that "politics is no sphere in which woman should exercise herself. I have never found women of Canada expressing any particular desire for a vote and, as a matter of fact, I believe they think more of themselves."

The antis shared a set of core beliefs about gender, women, and the family that rested on the idea of separate spheres. They felt strongly that women were designed by both God and biology to remain in the private realm of the family. Women's sole responsibility was to run a household and provide a comfortable space for their husbands and children. Men were intended to provide for and protect women and children. As household heads, they alone had the right to represent their wives at the polls. But this strict division of responsibility rarely corresponded with reality. Only comfortably well-off families could rely on a sole male breadwinner, and many women had worked for pay to contribute to the family finances. But the normative family unit was a powerful ideal, and the dream of women as homemakers and men as breadwinners was accepted by clergy, politicians, labour leaders, and socialists – all of whom believed that men were entitled to a job whose "family wage" was high enough to support a dependent wife and children. The call for female suffrage disrupted this ideal by suggesting that women might have a direct relationship to the state. To antis, enfranchisement signalled disorder in the home, the family, and the nation. They feared that it would inspire women to abandon marriage and children, compete with men for paid positions, or even engage in sexually immoral behaviour. The rough world of politics would cheapen femininity and masculinize women. And most antis insisted that women would either simply not bother to vote or would be incapable of doing so responsibly.

HOME AND FAMILY

Anti-suffragists across the country feared that blurring the lines between the public and the private would create disorder in both the family and the social order. A common anti argument was that enfranchised women would abandon their God-given responsibilities to marriage, housework, and children. If women refused to marry and raise children, how could the human race survive? Suffragists fought this assertion well into the twentieth century, pointing out that they themselves were often happily married mothers with children and were not "soured old spinster[s]."

Opponents of suffrage were equally disturbed by how enfranchisement would affect men. If married women shirked their traditional responsibilities, men would be obliged to shoulder such "unmanly" tasks as child care and housework. The word "desex" captured this fear about masculinized women and emasculated men. Anti-suffrage propaganda often showed men stuck at home, cooking, cleaning, and changing diapers, while their wives waltzed off to the polling booths. Being forced to do the laundry seemed to arouse great discomfort and was often employed to mock suffragists and warn men of their fate should they support enfranchisement. Men were both horrified and amused by the prospect of doing "women's work." In 1875, MLA Henry Holbrook triggered robust laughter in the legislature when he joked that enfranchised women would force men to stay home and wash the clothes, but this trope remained consistent for almost forty years. After a public debate held by the Liberal Party in 1911, a number of men apparently expressed "serious doubts of the results to family life if the women generally took too kindly to politics and many amusing instances were given of the position man must take in rearing the little ones, instead of the mother."

Similarly, some women felt that enfranchisement would upset gender roles. A letter to McBride, written by "A Woman Who Admires Manly Gentlemen, and Womanly Women," suggested that instead of seeking the vote, women should perfect their housewifery skills, such as early rising and the "preparation of meals without scramble," which would bring "happiness to every one and all."

Anti-suffragists feared that enfranchised and opinionated women could destroy family harmony by introducing political disagreements or "acrimonies" into the home. MLA A.R. Robertson, for example, asserted that suffrage would "disarrange the whole fabric of society." Such political quarrels probably occurred between husbands and wives (and extended family members), though the fabric of society remained intact. For instance, A.E.B. Davie, MLA and premier from 1887 to 1889, repeatedly voted against suffrage, whereas his wife, Constance Langford Davie, wrote pro-suffrage articles for the *Colonist* after his death. One of their daughters, Emily Sophia, was an active member of the PEL but was married to A.E. McPhillips, the prominent Conservative who voted against extending suffrage to women.

In the absence of public opinion polls, it is difficult to know the age and gender breakdown of British Columbians who opposed suffrage. McBride received a few letters from anti-suffrage women, but these were dwarfed by the volume of letters and petitions in support. Many elite women who enjoyed high status worried that political equality would undermine men's responsibility to look after their families. And they were nervous about engaging in what they perceived as a divisive or unfeminine debate. Due to such concerns, the national and local councils of women, and patriotic groups such as the Imperial Order Daughters of the Empire (IODE), were initially reluctant to endorse suffrage. The sense of trepidation helps account for the refusal of elite women such as Evlyn Farris and Julia Henshaw to embrace the movement until it had become more respectable. However, they saw no contradiction in taking on leadership roles in prominent organizations, as long as they were not challenging men for political power. Vancouver socialite Julia Henshaw claimed in 1909 that she would "sooner put my hand into a hornet's nest" than support the movement. But this did not prevent her from joining women's clubs, accepting paid employment as a journalist, publishing several novels, and becoming a remunerated speaker on alpine botany. In December 1909, when the Victoria Women's Canadian Club hosted a talk by Ralph Bond, who belonged to the British Men's League for Opposing Woman Suffrage, its members were divided. The club refused to take a position but listened as Bond asserted his belief that voting women would create "anarchy" in British politics and social life. Club member and pillar of Victoria society Margaret Rocke Robertson, who also belonged to the LCW, the Ladies' Hospital Auxiliary, and the IODE, agreed that women did not need the vote, though she did not concur that they were "feeble-minded." The sixty-five-year-old widow of former judge and politician Alexander Rocke Robertson voiced the anti-suffrage faith that "men were strong," and "for that reason she was satisfied to let them legislate for her."

Unlike in Great Britain and some American states, however, no powerful anti-suffrage organizing occurred in British Columbia. In Vancouver, a handful of women founded an anti-suffrage club in 1914, but it seems to have been unique in the province. With a tiny membership of about twelve, the Dulce Donum club seemed to exert little influence and soon folded. Most of its members were young married women. But the club had to address the role of New Women, arguing that even women opposed to suffrage

are no less public spirited than their suffrage sisters, yet they feel that the interests of their sex, and the entire race, may be best served by the advancement of home and home interests ... They are not altogether sure that political equality would work to that end. They believe that the majority of

women could not enter the political field without neglect-
ing their far more important work of home and motherhood.

DEGRADING AND DESEXING WOMEN

The claim that exposure to the corrupt and boisterous world of
politics would desex women and rob them of their feminine deli-
cacy arose partly from the rough reality of voting in the nineteenth century. Elections did not use the secret ballot before 1873,
candidate nominations were generally by show of hand, and voters were not infrequently intimidated at the polls. But an environ-
ment of public disagreement sat comfortably with ideas about
masculinity where men were understood as tough, strong, and determined. MLA Charles Pooley argued in 1884 that women should
not be involved in the "noticeable turmoil" of politics. "The contentions of elections," stated an anonymous letter to the *Colonist,*
"have a masculine character ill harmonizing with women mixing
up in them." Anti-suffragists raised the spectre that politicians
might harass or annoy women by soliciting their votes. Pooley
claimed that he had "too much respect for woman to vote for a
measure to bring her forward into the coarser phases of life –
their better feelings would be blunted by such privilege." His
fellow MLA Theodore Davie concurred: women's "effeminacy"
would be destroyed by being "dragged into politics." Antis believed that voting would be "repugnant" to women's personalities
and force them to "leave their homes and record their votes
amidst the excitement of a contested election." The agitation of
electoral politics, MLA Henry Holbrook warned the legislature,
might cause "strong minded women" to "throw up their bonnets
in applause of some candidate" or get into a "free fight" outside
the polls. John Robson was so offended by these kinds of remarks
that he accused Davie and his supporters of being "fossilized"
old "fogies" who held on to prejudices imported from England.
Suffragists also contested this argument by suggesting that if
male-dominated politics were corrupt, women might provide a

civilizing effect. In fact, the movement went to great lengths to cultivate a culture of open debate, demonstrating that women's sensibilities were not too delicate for vigorous political disagreement. The earliest women who went to the municipal polls in 1870s Victoria did face resistance, but they proved much tougher than most men had imagined.

Antis also feared that enfranchised women would compete with men for jobs, higher education, and political power. Not content merely to win the vote, women would soon wish to be "lawyers, soldiers, sailors, doctors. Etc." They might want to run for office or become jury members. Enfranchisement was the first step on a slippery slope to educational and employment equality, and the end of men's stranglehold on well-paid work, education, and political power. Even politicians who favoured suffrage were disturbed by this possibility. John Robson felt compelled to assure his fellow MLAs in 1884 that though he supported female enfranchisement, he did not feel that women should run for office: they should "merely [have] the power to choose for themselves those persons whom they thought fit." Premier McBride warned a group of suffragists in 1913 that enfranchised women would not only neglect their homes but would possibly form a "Woman's Party" and attempt to "run the affairs of the country." This anxiety that women might steal men's power and employment was not confined to elite men, however – it was shared by the leadership of organized labour, which feared female competition for male jobs.

The opponents of suffrage drew from nature, science, and religion to buttress their points. Many maintained that nature had designed women to stay out of public life. Not only were they physically and intellectually weaker than men and therefore not qualified to vote, but their participation in the public sphere could also cause them mental and physical harm. In 1898, MLA Major James Mutter claimed that he "had too much respect for women to want to see them in politics" and asserted it was a "scientific fact ... that the brain of a woman was two ounces lighter than that of a man." Both women's emotional sensibilities and bodies, "too refined and delicate," were at risk from being exposed to voting. This was supported by the fact of pregnancy, which was understood as a weakness that prevented women from participating in politics: how, asked a letter writer in 1871, could a woman "get on with legislative and political duties while in the condition in which ladies who love their lords are said to delight to be?"

Voting was an unnatural attempt to interfere with the design of both God and nature to place women in the home and men in public life. Father William O'Boyle, a Catholic anti-suffragist, argued that a woman's only job was to raise children and gently improve the morality of the home and the family. Any woman who became "mixed up in political questions and agitations" made herself "useless in the role God has designed for her." Even pro-suffragists who relied heavily on maternalist arguments were often mocked. John Robson believed that women should vote because their moral influence would improve politics and protect the family. But when he repeated the standard maternal argument that "the woman made the man," he was greeted with "great laughter" from his fellow MLAs in the legislature. According to the antis, as the rightful head of the family unit, a husband and father represented the political interests of his female family members. A.E. McPhillips summed up his feelings on the matter in 1913, telling the legislature that "parliament was but a development of the family idea, the family organization. In the family there must be one head – and the father was always looked up to in that regard. The same reasoning applied to the government of the state."

If casting a ballot were unnatural for women, then so too were those women who wished to vote. This supposed abnormality, along with fears of women being desexed, helps account for the unflattering descriptions of suffragists as ugly and "Amazonian." Propaganda portrayed suffragists' bodies as ungainly, masculine, and dirty. They were pictured with gaping mouths and long tongues, disarrayed clothing, and red noses and faces. One hostile observer

MORE TROUBLE FOR R. L.

In 1912, Prime Minister Robert Borden visited London, where a
group of militant WSPU members, including Mrs. Tuckwell (of
the New Westminster Political Equality League), confronted him
about female enfranchisement. The unflattering image of the
suffragette – with her homely features, unkempt appearance, and
umbrella – was commonly used to highlight political women's
lack of reason and femininity.

remarked that the suffragists in the visitors' gallery of the legislature had "faces like the engraving in Fox's *Book of Martyrs*." Newspapers commented on the appearance of suffragists, expressing
surprise if they looked diminutive or conventionally feminine.
When Barbara Wylie of the militant Women's Social and Political
Union (WSPU) visited Vancouver in 1913, the press freely discussed
her demeanour and appearance. The *Vancouver Daily World* noted

that her actions were "unladylike" and that she was tall, thin, and "sharp looking," with an "aquiline nose." The *New Westminster News* disagreed, stating that she was "stylish and good looking" – the "very opposite of the Amazonian individual that one would naturally expect to see when her record is taken into account."

WHY WOMEN DON'T NEED THE VOTE

One long-standing anti-suffragist argument was that women did not need the vote, because they were already politically represented and economically supported by their fathers and husbands. Good men were chivalrous, and they naturally desired to protect good women. As long as both men and women followed these rules, women had no need for political, economic, or legal equality. In fact, some anti-suffragists contended that allowing them to vote was undemocratic. Since they were already represented by their father or their husband, giving them the vote would supposedly double their political clout. And if they followed their husband's advice in casting their ballots, men's political voice would be unfairly amplified. The opponents of enfranchisement claimed that most women were content with male representation and were unable to vote responsibly. Elenor W. Johnson of New Westminster commended McBride on his "excellent decision" to stand against suffrage. Although Johnson saw herself as an educated woman and was even entitled to vote in her city, she felt that the typical woman voted "blindly for everything or carries the ballot paper home with her. When women do not educate themselves to use intelligently what they already have it is hardly policy to give them more."

A slightly softer version of this stance suggested that women were not yet ready for the vote and must show the government that they desired it. Their premature enfranchisement would be wasteful, dangerous, and unnecessary. This was more readily believable to politicians in the 1870s and the early 1880s, before women's organizations had been founded and the first of many suffrage petitions presented to the legislature. Theodore Davie forecast that women in "all progressive countries" would eventually acquire the franchise but that BC women were not yet ready. Without strong evidence that they wanted the vote, enfranchisement would be unfairly thrust upon them by the male electorate.

This reasoning conveniently ignored extensive suffrage activity in the United States, Britain, and other Canadian provinces. But to suffragists, it seemed to promise that women could attain political citizenship if they demonstrated that they truly wanted it, which set the stage for decades of push and pull. Suffragists took their opponents at their word: if proof were required, they would collect and present it. And so, between 1885 and 1916, they amassed endorsements from labour, clergy, and prominent individuals, as well as numerous petitions signed by ordinary British Columbians. However, each piece of proof encountered resistance and outright refusal to believe that women's desire to vote was authentic. The very first petition in 1885 was met with disbelief from sitting politicians, who insisted that it must be fraudulent. Charles Pooley dismissed it by stating that the women who signed it had no idea of the responsibilities that voting entailed or of the harassment they would endure at the polls. Theodore Davie opined not just that the signatories were poorly informed, but also that the petition itself was fraudulent and had been signed by children under the age of eighteen. Decades later, anti-suffragists were still in denial, regardless of the evidence placed before them. In May 1916, Conservative MLA Samuel Cawley told the legislature that he "opposed the granting of suffrage to women because he thought, and thinks still, that a very small proportion of the women desired the franchise, and he was more in favour of restricting the franchise than of extending it." Women were "dumb as oysters," claimed an anonymous "Elector" in 1899, and indeed throughout this entire period, anti-suffragists repeatedly insisted that they had no interest at all in politics or even in public life.

MISS DEBUTANTE WILL VOTE THIS YEAR

The claim that female voters were empty-headed and emotional
is captured in this 1921 *Vancouver Daily World* cartoon, which
shows newly enfranchised women swooning over the candidates
in the upcoming federal election.

Anti-suffragists maintained that women did not need to vote,
because their "special" place in the home had already imbued
them with power and influence. Good wives could exert indirect
moral suasion over their husbands. But if women attempted to
exchange this informal influence for formal political power, they
risked "lowering" their status in men's estimation. They would no
longer enjoy the respect and chivalry owed to proper women. In
1886, the anonymous "Publicola" was so offended by women's
support for the franchise bill that he stated, "I have more respect
for them than they appear ... to have for themselves." As the anti-

suffrage Dulce Donum club declared in 1914, a woman's indirect influence in the home was the most powerful tool she possessed. A woman "who can't subdue a few men without the use of dynamite was something of a failure." Anti-suffragists believed that in the natural order of the universe, women were treated with favour and set high upon a pedestal. Their only "shackles" were those "composed of silks and velvets" rather than chains. The argument that women neither wanted nor needed the vote spanned many points of view. Many antis were middle-class or elite men who believed their class status should protect their wives and daughters from entering the public world of work and politics. But the Socialist Party of Canada also held that enfranchising women was unnecessary, because injustice sprang from capitalism, not from gender inequality. However, the party never suggested that voting for its own candidates was a pointless exercise.

Anti-suffrage opinion prevailed in the nineteenth century, though it gradually weakened as increasing numbers of men and women, religious bodies, labour organizations, and political parties came to see women's political citizenship as both a democratic right and a potentially positive influence on society. Still, the arguments voiced by the antis set the tone for many debates. As they spoke, pontificated, and wrote editorials and letters to the newspaper, they invented a stereotypical image of suffragists as emotionally manipulative, using their feminine wiles and "seductive arguments" to trick men into giving up political power. But suffragists were also angry and unfeminine – loud, annoying, and obnoxious. They nagged and hissed and steamed and shrieked. They were erratic and irrational, like barnyard birds, or were "shrewish mischiefmakers." According to Father William O'Boyle, they were like "magpies" – "all plumage and chatter." The stereotype was strengthened by the surge of militancy in England, as suffragettes heckled politicians, marched in the streets, threw rocks, and smashed windows. Their detractors charged them with hysteria, attempting to discredit women's anger and passionate commitment to protest. Anti-suffragists were repelled by the suffragettes and found them "disgusting," their behaviour seeming proof that political participation would destroy women's femininity.

Suffragists and their supporters resisted such stereotypes. However, because these stereotypes were championed by the powerful, suffragists constantly had to "prove" that extending the franchise would have no negative impact. Far from destroying the family, suffrage would strengthen it through women's desire to protect the home. Nor would women flood male-dominated jobs and careers; they might wish to access education or employment, but they would always make a husband and children their first priority. The roughness of political life would not degrade them; rather, their care and kindness – the qualities that set them apart from men – would improve politics. But the vast majority of suffragists never unequivocally accepted the logic of maternal feminism. Even in the 1880s, they spoke of women as intelligent and rational human beings who were fundamentally equal to men and who deserved equal rights on the basis of their humanity. They had the right to argue in public, confront politicians, and dissent passionately with men in positions of authority. Nonetheless, suffragists had to guard against making any statement that would seem too radical or unnerving. In later years, they made a point of rejecting militancy, yet they were deeply sympathetic to the suffragettes, whom they saw as courageous and self-sacrificing.

However, the ongoing demand that women prove their desire to vote eventually became a tiresome and unresolvable burden. The process of collecting the required evidence was exhausting, but BC suffragists were trapped within this cycle and remained there until 1916. Many of them were displeased by the referendum, not solely because it undemocratically excluded them from the decision, but also because it propelled them into yet another campaign to convince British Columbians that they deserved the vote. They also knew that if the referendum failed, their opponents would seize on this as proof that women were still not ready to take on the political responsibilities of the franchise.

Perhaps the greatest anti-suffrage fear of all was that female enfranchisement would not democratize or widen the public sphere, but instead destroy men's hold on power, as encoded in their position as head of the household, their monopoly on the highest-paid jobs, and their exclusive right to political representation. When an 1899 private member's bill proposed by Ralph Smith almost succeeded, the editors of the *Colonist* were horrified, calling the government "unfit" and accusing the fifteen MLAs who had supported the bill of planning to "deprive the men of British Columbia of the control of its political affairs." A letter to the editor agreed, bluntly stating that suffrage entailed taking "political power from the hands of men and placing it in the hands of a new, irresponsible, emotional, and erratic element." To those who opposed suffrage, the consequences were obvious: if women gained political power, men would inevitably lose it.

Suffragists built a movement in the face of provincial and national opposition. Even as this movement grew in size and scope and drew members from across the province, politicians in British Columbia persistently argued that women did not want or need the vote, that politics would degrade their gentle feminine spirit, and that politically active women would overturn divinely ordained male authority in the home and the nation. The battle between suffragists and politicians, particularly with Premier McBride and the Conservative Party after 1903, was a source of frustration to suffrage activists. But it sharpened their organizational skills as they adopted a range of tactics designed to shame, persuade, and win over politicians and the electorate.

We should like those who read our column to come to our meetings as well. There are several leagues in town, so that the most fastidious should be able to find something to suit. Then we should prefer to have our friend, the enemy, present – for there is not much use wasting ammunition on those already for us.

– SUSIE LANE CLARK,
VANCOUVER DAILY WORLD, 24 JUNE 1913, 13.

Woman's place is in the home and every woman should have one. It is her business to get one. They can all find some kind of man to make a home for. Anyway, the more I see of the men God put into the world, the more convinced I am that God did not intend us women to be too particular.

– "VERBATIM REPORT OF AN ANTI-SUFFRAGE SPEECH
BY MRS. HOMAN CHILDE," *CHAMPION*, OCTOBER 1913, 9.

FOUR

PERFORMING POLITICS

Mary Ellen Spear Smith (1861–1933). Born in England, Mary Ellen Spear trained as a teacher. After she married Ralph Smith, the couple moved to Nanaimo in 1891, where he worked as a coal miner before becoming involved in labour politics. She joined many women's groups, co-founded the Liberal Women's Association, and became the province's first elected female MLA in 1918. She was appointed a cabinet minister, making her the first woman to hold that position in Canada and the British Empire.

IN NOVEMBER 1913, suffragist Mary Ellen Smith took the stage at the Labor Temple in downtown Vancouver to debate Father William O'Boyle. That summer, O'Boyle had delivered a rousing sermon at Vancouver's Church of Our Lady of the Holy Rosary in which he denounced suffrage as destroying womanhood. He claimed that the modern woman should aspire to be like the Virgin Mary, who was obedient and content to be "supreme in the care of the house." Challenged to defend his ideas in public, O'Boyle joked that he was "the villain of the piece tonight ... the guilty party who put the 'man' in emancipation." Socialists and suffragists, he told the packed hall, were equally dangerous:

> Industrial slavery has given rise to evils which governments seem unable to amend. Socialists say "take away the government, destroy the system!" The suffragettes say the same thing in another way ... The Socialists say that the machine is out of order. Suffragettes say that the men are out of date ... Women's duty is not to remodel the representation but to redeem the character of the representatives and they can best do that by home influence.

Mary Ellen Smith informed O'Boyle that his opposition to suffrage was pointless: "You will notice that this unrest is the only unrest that is worldwide and we don't propose to stop until we are free." Drawing on examples from law, history, and the Bible, she wondered why "we hear of the Pilgrim Fathers, the Revolutionary Fathers, the Confederation Fathers and the Civic Fathers, but what about the women? I think the nations have been fathered to death and the country now needs a little mothering."

The debate between Smith and O'Boyle was one of hundreds of public suffrage events hosted in British Columbia after the turn of the century. Suffragists worked within the system of parliamentary democracy, but they also backed up political lobbying with public actions that were intended to sway the electorate and to create a visible presence. Suffragists used every available resource to advance their cause, including petitions, meetings with politicians, and events such as fairs, speaking tours, and debates. They harnessed the power of print and wrote newspaper columns, pamphlets, and letters to the editor. Every word and action countered the claims of their opponents, educated the public, and nurtured a sense of solidarity. This growing community contributed to an intense feeling that suffrage would usher in a new era of political equality.

Suffrage organizations embraced non-partisanship, with an ideal – not always achieved – of a movement that was open to everyone regardless of class, religion, or political affiliation. Instead of insisting on partisan unity, they attempted to build a cooperative coalition that focused on gaining enfranchisement on the same terms as men. As a result, suffragist culture welcomed disagreement, confrontation, and debate, and contributed to a sense of comradeship throughout the province.

DEPUTATIONS AND PETITIONS

BC suffragists did not stage visually spectacular mass protests like those in England and the United States, but they did initiate other kinds of political action. Most popular were the annual visits, or deputations, to the legislature to meet with politicians, present petitions, and press for amendments to legislation. After 1884, Maria Grant headed such a delegation almost every year. After the province-wide Political Equality Leagues were founded in 1912, delegations were joined by members from Kaslo, Revelstoke, Kamloops, and the Fraser Valley. A kind of political theatre, they generated press coverage, demonstrated the strength of the cause, and were often timed to correspond with the introduction of private members' bills. When the bills were debated, suffragists sat in the visitors' gallery to watch – and occasionally cheer, comment, and applaud. Adding to the theatricality, Grant carried a model of the ship of state when she headed up delegations. In Plato's *Republic,* the ship of state was a metaphor for stable and responsible democratic governance. Like ships, states had to be steered by wise and respectable men. By appropriating this powerful symbol, suffragists were performing their faith in democracy but also asserting that women were capable of being knowledgeable, responsible, and capable governors. Helen Gregory MacGill later remembered the atmosphere as celebratory and enthusiastic, as the women travelling to Victoria together shared staterooms on the ferry, along with "babies and children" and pets.

Most delegations backed up their demands with petitions, a long-time mainstay of the disenfranchised. Petitions provided critical evidence that women wanted the vote and refuted claims that they were not interested in enfranchisement. As the movement grew, so too did the size and scope of its petitions, from 900 signatures in 1885 to over 2,500 in 1899. The "monster" petition organized by the BC PEL in 1913 topped 10,000 names. As late as 1912, the editors of the *Champion* were still hoping that petitions would win over the Conservative government:

> It is the intention of the women to prove to the Government that the people of British Columbia are very much in earnest in their request and it is confidently asserted by some of the leaders in this movement that the Government are sufficiently broad minded to grant the vote to women as soon as they show that a large number demand it.

However, the *Champion* was doomed to disappointment. In 1912, McBride complimented women's dedication to charitable work yet told a delegation that he believed that women were "quite content" to allow men to make political decisions on their behalf. In 1913, Maria Grant organized and led a deputation of over seventy women from across the province. They presented the monster petition to McBride and met with him, various cabinet ministers, and a selection of MLAs at the legislature. The petition itself was bound in a purple, white, and green ribbon, the suffragette colours. It contained every argument for enfranchisement that had been used since the 1880s: citizenship rights, the interests of children and family, and protection from European male immigrant voters. Grant carefully selected a group of speakers to present the suffrage case, and she herself urged McBride to catch up with other progressive states on the Pacific coast. Vancouver's Janet Kemp suggested that enfranchising white settler women would counter the votes of male immigrants. But the appeal fell on stony ground. McBride had continually asked suffragists to provide proof of their desire to vote, but when they did so, he simply confirmed his intransigence by stating that it was not "in the public interest to bring down proposals of the character asked for."

Unsurprisingly, suffragists became increasingly vocal in their condemnation of the Conservative Party. Nonetheless, they tried again that winter. In December, a twelve-woman delegation from the United Suffrage Societies led by Mary McConkey travelled from Vancouver to Victoria and attempted to convince McBride that the province was falling behind the rest of the civilized world. McBride raised the possibility of a referendum but maintained that enfranchised women would neglect their homes. In 1914, after the failure of yet another suffrage bill, a writer for the *Champion*, most likely Maria Grant, offered a small ray of comfort: "Some of these members are going to die – therein is hope." Although their unproductive dealings with the Conservative

Party demonstrated the limits of working solely within the system, suffragists never gave up on parliamentary democracy. Even so, they were tired of asking for the vote and were increasingly willing to demand it.

THE PERFORMANCE OF POLITICS

Canadian suffragists avoided sensational tactics, but they found ways to capture media attention and press their arguments. Rather than simply censuring their opponents, they developed a culture of open debate. Their commitment to dialogue, disagreement, and occasional confrontation suggests that stereotypes about quiet and respectable suffrage campaigners are inaccurate. By the twentieth century, BC suffragists were loudly expressing their opinions at rousing public lectures, debates, Mock Parliaments, open-air fairs, and conventions. These events combined serious discussion and education with entertainment and theatre. This style of engagement characterizes what literary scholar Mary Chapman calls the modernist "noise" of suffrage culture. Boisterous public debates in front of large and enthusiastic audiences were designed to attract attention and bring suffrage to the public eye. But they also helped suffragists throughout the province to build ties and develop a sense of solidarity throughout the province, which in turn strengthened their resolve.

Mock or Model Parliaments were popular styles of political entertainment and debate. Suffragists could choose from two types: the gender-bending Mock Parliament (sometimes called a Women's Parliament), most famously staged by the Political Equality League at Winnipeg's Walker Theatre in 1914, and the educational Model Parliaments that were held regularly across the province. The Mock Parliament, in which women played the roles of legislators who denied the vote to men, was the least common but the most entertaining. They were collaboratively written affairs that incorporated local issues and featured well-known suffrage leaders and their children. At least thirteen were performed in Canada, beginning in Winnipeg in 1893. In British Columbia, there were at least two. One was hosted at the King Edward School in March 1914 by the Vancouver University Women's Club, which borrowed the script from the Winnipeg PEL but adapted it to the local context. The other was staged by the Victoria Local Council of Women in 1910 and directed by Martha Douglas Harris, with the lieutenant governor and McBride in the audience. Suffragists and their children played the roles of male politicians in what they called the "Land of the Happy Parallel" or what the *Colonist* termed "Vice Versa, the Shoe on the Other Foot, or It's a Poor Rule That Won't Work Both Ways." The performers used humour to address a range of injustices: disenfranchisement, unfair guardianship laws, and poor working conditions. Impressed, the *Colonist* complimented the "stateswoman" grasp of the performances of Lilla Day (playing the premier) and Helen Grant (playing the speaker). But it condescendingly added that the politicians in the audience might learn "new ways of evading embarrassing questions and of dealing with determined suffragists" and that the suffrage opposition was "skilled in all the time-honoured ways of making itself obnoxious."

More common were educational Model Parliaments where club members played roles as legislators to explore current issues. Their purpose was to educate participants and observers on parliamentary process and debate. In early versions, men took all the parts. The numerous Model Parliaments held in the Fraser Valley town of Chilliwack in 1903 (and later) show that local communities were committed to learning about parliamentary process. Playing the role of parliamentarians and cabinet ministers, the male actors introduced bills ranging from city incorporation to fire protection to female suffrage. The bills were debated and sent on to a second reading. When the debate focused on suffrage, Chilliwack women attended in large numbers, and the society hosting the event was so encouraged by the turnout that it decided to hold ongoing suffrage discussions every Monday evening.

Many nineteenth-century literary, church, and political clubs staged debates about suffrage. In 1874, William Fraser Tolmie debated suffrage at the Mechanics Institute in Victoria, and Nanaimo, Delta, Nelson, and Vancouver associations presented similar events during the 1880s and 1890s. In January 1893, the Nelson social and literary club debated suffrage, "with some of Nelson's greatest guns in the way of debate leading the attack and defence." Almost fifty people turned up to hear the spirited exchange between four men, which resulted in a slight majority (twenty-one to nineteen) voting against enfranchisement. Most such debates featured male participants, were formally structured with set questions, and were followed by public discussion. When the Vancouver Ward 5 Liberals presented an all-male debate in 1914, the pro-suffragists argued that "women are human as well as men." Their opponents countered that women would not take the trouble to vote and "did not even know enough to chew gum properly." Part entertainment and part education, these debates show high levels of local engagement with the enfranchisement issue.

As suffrage leagues developed, they hosted their own debates, taking the question out of the hands of male-dominated political parties and debating societies. The Kelowna PEL organized by Dora Kerr held an open debate every month. Sometimes, they were staged, with participants taking the roles of anti- and pro-suffragists – and sometimes they were dramatic exchanges between people of conflicting views. In Vancouver in 1913, Helena Gutteridge hosted a debate between two men, but the man who played the part of the anti-suffragist, James Conley, was "really in favor of the movement and afterwards spoke with much fervor for the cause." In the same year, the BC Woman's Suffrage League could not find an actual anti who was willing to debate Bernice Panagopolous, so the "ardent" visiting British suffragist Mrs. Parkyn took on the task. However, "in her great enthusiasm for the cause, [she] so far forgot that she was an 'anti' when presenting some of her strongest points that on the impulse of the moment she answered some of her own arguments." When the Victoria PEL hosted a debate in 1914, the two men chosen for the anti side apologized profusely to the audience, as they were "ardent suffragists." But a debate held at the Kitsilano Methodist Church between two suffragists (including Mary Ellen Smith) and two antis seems to have been real, as was the one organized by Reverend Henry Edwards at Vancouver's St. James's Anglican Church, where the sole man who opposed enfranchisement was "extinguished" by the arguments of Helena Gutteridge.

As mentioned at the beginning of this chapter, Mary Ellen Smith was at the centre of the decade's most dramatic debate, when she faced Father William O'Boyle at the Vancouver Labor Temple. In a sermon of June 1913, O'Boyle had come out strongly against suffragists, prompting them to suggest that he reconsider his views. That July, Catholic suffragist Ida Douglas-Fearn joined Susie Lane Clark in challenging O'Boyle to a public debate. "He shall not talk from a pulpit, over our heads," wrote Douglas-Fearn, "and we will claim no exemption on the basis of our sex. We will meet simply as human beings to discuss woman suffrage." To obtain O'Boyle's participation, Clark deployed flattery, suggesting that "a man of such prominence and scientific knowledge would be able to put up a strong argument and one that would be well worth hearing." But who would debate him? We do not know who chose his opponent, but it was the politically seasoned Mary Ellen Smith who took the stage in November 1913.

During the debate hosted by the BC Political Equality League, Smith's husband and Liberal politician Ralph Smith served as chair and sat onstage beside his wife. Newspaper accounts remarked on the overflowing audience, with people sitting on the floor and standing in the aisles and hallway. O'Boyle had not revised his opinions. He believed that political life would degrade women, who should concentrate on raising Christian families. Suffrage would be the "first step" in the "dissolution of that unit [the family] which is at the root and base of all the stability of society."

Smith rose to the occasion by simultaneously flattering O'Boyle and undermining his authority. She complimented him on his "brilliant" address but insisted that he had not managed to change her mind. At only thirty-eight, he was "young yet," she reminded the audience, and though he was to be "commended for coming out fearlessly on the opposite side of a popular question," he was either "mistaken or uninformed" *or* in favour of the "present exploiting and suffering of woman." "Which is it?" she wondered. Smith carefully took apart O'Boyle's points by arguing that enfranchised women would make better laws to protect their families and their children.

The evening itself seems to have ended in something of a draw. Susie Lane Clark reported that the audience was divided between those who favoured suffrage and those who did not. Assessing O'Boyle as ignorant and misinformed, she told the readers of her newspaper column that "we'll send him a complimentary copy" of the laws pertaining to women. Gutteridge was equally dismissive, asking, "Does the Reverend Father walk around Vancouver with his eyes closed? Perhaps [he] will devise some means of keeping the bodies and souls of women together without food, and their bodies warm without clothes or shelter that they may remain feminine and charming."

In addition to public debates, suffrage conventions brought together supporters and garnered media coverage. Members of the women's movement were familiar with national and international conventions, though few BC suffragists could afford to attend. But once the Political Equality League was formed, suffragists set about holding local conventions of their own. The founding conference of the league was held in Vancouver in May 1911. Mayor L.D. Taylor, under whose direction city council had recently enfranchised married women, was a featured speaker, along with Senator George F. Cotterill from Washington state, which had just enfranchised women. In a long speech peppered with applause and laughter, Taylor credited his mother for turning him into a

Born in Michigan, Louis Denison Taylor (1857–1946) was raised by his single mother. Upon immigrating to Vancouver in 1896, he prospected for gold before working as circulation manager for the Vancouver Daily Province. *In 1905, he purchased the* Vancouver Daily World *from Sara McLagan. A Liberal, union supporter, real estate booster, and populist critic of monopoly capitalism, Taylor was mayor of Vancouver eight times. In 1916, he married the* World's *business manager (Alice Berry). A suffragist, he gave Susie Lane Clark a regular suffrage news column in the* World.

suffragist and pledged that he would direct his newspaper, the *Vancouver Daily World,* to make a point of furthering the cause. Alice Townley finished off the day with a "witty" speech in which she stated that "although women of BC did not propose to use militant methods, it might be said that English women had been driven to it by forty years of rebuffs and indifference." At least, she told her audience, Mayor Taylor "had received the delegation which approached him on the subject with much friendliness and no visible symptoms of fear." Similar conventions were held over the next few years in Vancouver, Victoria, and Chilliwack as the league grew in popularity.

Canadian suffragists were reluctant to stage their own processions, such as those of Britain and the United States, but by 1913 they were confidently participating in civic parades. Vancouver suffragists entered a float in the 1913 Labour Day parade, claiming that it was the first in the province. Their contribution, a joint effort by the city's leagues, consisted of one float and three cars, with banners proclaiming, "BC Women Want the Vote." BC Woman's

Suffrage League member Bernice Panagopolous enjoyed the crowd's enthusiasm, remarking that it was "almost an ovation, with the men lifting their hats in courteous greeting, the women waving handkerchiefs and little groups breaking into cheers." Bertha Merrill Burns was less impressed, stating that the participants looked demure and a bit "frightened." On the whole, however, participants claimed that the response from the onlookers was positive and full of "good will."

That same month, the BC PEL designed a dramatic float for Carnival Week in Victoria. Rich with symbols of progress and justice, it would not have looked out of place at a parade in London or Washington. It was preceded by mounted women, three of whom held silver trumpets and were dressed in green habits and purple hats decorated with white plumes. Six white-robed young women stood on the float itself, labelled with the names of locales where women had the franchise: Australia, New Zealand, Finland, Norway, Sweden, and Canton, China. The *Champion* explained the symbolism of the design: "On a pedestal stood Liberty, holding in her hands a wreath of laurel similar to those worn by the woman citizens. This she was waiting to place on the brow of British Columbia, who knelt at her feet, praying for freedom." The float was pulled by horses and attended by young men (mainly the sons of PEL members) who wore purple, white, and green – the colours of the militant suffragettes.

Other forms of open-air meetings and displays attracted public and media attention. Between 1911 and 1914, the PEL rented booths at the August exhibitions in Vancouver and Victoria. One of the first public PEL actions in Vancouver was to rent a booth at the Made-in-Canada fair, where it sold crafts, pamphlets, and books by two of its members. At the Victoria Fair and Exhibition, suffragists in purple, white, and green sashes held open-air meetings and sold copies of the *Champion*. The PEL reacted with typical sardonic humour when someone vandalized its tent and removed the first two letters from the "Woman's Suffrage" banner so that it

Canadian suffragists rarely entered parades, but the Victoria
Political Equality League did so in 1913. Its float is preceded by
league members on horseback; the young woman with the silver
bugle might be Frances Willard Grant, youngest daughter of
Maria Grant. The men who walk beside the float wear purple,
green, and white sashes (the suffragette colours). On the float
itself, suffragists are dressed in white and crowned with laurel to
represent liberty, equality, and citizenship.

read "Man's Suffrage." In response, the group took out three more
letters so that the sign read "Man's Rage," apparently to "the delight
of the crowd." At the New Westminster Fair in the fall of 1912, the
local PEL sold candy named after PEL branches, including "Sunbeams from Summerland" and "Special Mixture P.E.L."

English suffragettes were known for their willingness to address listeners at Speakers' Corner in Hyde Park; women in Vancouver also tried their hand at outdoor public meetings. In the
summer of 1913, either the Evening Work Committee or the
Mount Pleasant Suffrage League organized Saturday night open-
air meetings throughout East Vancouver. In June 1913, a suffragist

who stood on a soap box was heckled and forced off the stand by a crowd of men banging metal cans. But the popular meetings continued through the summer. The numerous women who had the "nerve" to stand up and speak reported that they "were very pleased with the reaction the audience accorded them." Miss F. McGahey also had a positive reception that fall when she stood at the corner of Hastings and Seymour in downtown Vancouver, selling copies of the suffragette newspaper *Votes for Women.* She reported that most people had been courteous, except for a few women who treated her with a "silent, sweeping condemnation" or as if she were an "unsexed hooligan or some such monstrosity."

The New Westminster PEL combined a summer picnic to White Rock with an open-air beach meeting capped with a public address titled "Many Reasons Why Women Should Vote." A Cedar Cottage PEL picnic was a day-long affair that involved a trip by steamer from Vancouver to Gibsons Landing. The women wore white suffrage dresses, adorned with crepe bows of purple, white, and green. Although much of the celebrating involved picnicking and swimming, they also loudly proclaimed their suffrage sensibilities. They pinned bows on the boat's captain and crew, composed a song called "The Purple, White and Green," and developed a "suffrage yell" that they shouted to spectators as the boat docked upon their return. Their new "suffrage hymn" was clearly a hit because it was sung to close their subsequent meetings.

Suffragists loved to entertain and be entertained, and their events featured movies, music, poetry, and dramatic performances. Talks and debates combined entertainment with serious political speeches. In February 1915, a "suffragette" convention in Chilliwack advertised itself as "Funnier than the Old Maid's Convention" and a "sure cure for the grouch." It showed movies before and after the speeches. The period after 1910 witnessed an explosion of suffrage culture as original movies and plays circulated throughout the British Empire and the United States. In 1912, the PEL sponsored a provincial tour of the popular American movie

Votes for Women, a drama written by American suffragists that featured real-life American leaders Dr. Anna Shaw and Jane Addams. Most popular was the satirical one-act play *How the Vote Was Won.* Commissioned in 1909 by the British Actress Franchise League and performed hundreds of times across the world, it poked fun at anti-suffrage arguments that women should be supported and represented by men. The plot revolved around a suffragette-led woman's strike. When women subsequently leave their work and demand support from their male relatives, the men become overwhelmed and march on Parliament to demand women's enfranchisement. In fall 1911, the Victoria PEL presented a version of the play, as did the Cedar Cottage PEL in 1915. During the intermission, young women clad in white dresses and colourful suffrage sashes sold "home-made candy in tiny purple, white, and green baskets." The same play was staged as an opener for Dorothy Davis's suffrage tour to the interior, at the Vancouver University Women's Club in 1914, and by the PEL at its 1915 provincial convention in New Westminster.

Many suffragists were highly literate teachers, journalists, or writers, and were inspired to perform original music, stories, and poems. In Victoria, the league held a bazaar, performing an "original burlesque" called *A Suffrage Rummage Sale,* in which actors auctioned "prejudices, superstitions, fallen idols, curios, second-hand costumes, antique furniture and antiquated notions." A number of well-known Canadian suffragists such as Nellie McClung, Francis Marion Beynon, and Agnes Machar were celebrated novelists, and their work was part of a culture of women's writing that explored romance, marriage, and work in the lives of modern women. Vancouver author Alice Ashworth Townley was a prolific writer known for her prescriptive fiction for young women.

In her 1909 novel *Opinions of Mary,* Townley inserts herself into the plot as the sophisticated mentor to the kind-hearted but naive young Mary, who often makes unflattering remarks about educated women. A "new woman is just another name for the same

Alice Ashworth Townley (1860–1941). Born in Quebec, Alice
Ashworth moved to Vancouver in 1903. A quintessential club-
woman, she joined the Women's Press Club, the IODE, the PEL, the
Women's Institute, the Women's Canadian Club, and the LCW. She
co-founded the BC Equal Franchise Association in 1912, published
newspaper articles, and wrote instructive novels for children. She
was the first female Vancouver Park Board commissioner (1929–
35). This photograph was taken for the city in that role.

old maid," Mary states. When compelled to participate in a debate
on suffrage, she cries, "*I never wanted a vote! I know nothing about
women's rights – and care less.*" Forced to educate herself, she
soon learns the error of her ways. As she tells the author, "I think
it is preposterous that women have not had votes long ago. How
dare men refuse such a reasonable request?" Townley uses Mary's
transformation to demonstrate the irrationality of anti-suffrage
thought and to introduce readers to a range of contemporary

arguments for the vote. Mary ultimately defends the actions of the suffragettes as reasonable and points out that the "figure of Justice is a woman, that our greatest and wisest ruler was Victoria the Good – and what of Joan of Arc, who led an army?" The storyline reflects the suffrage belief that education and debate would change the minds of men and women who opposed female enfranchisement.

PRINT CULTURE

Suffrage ideals were circulated through print culture, which included news coverage and columns in the mainstream, labour, socialist, reform, and religious press. Many prominent suffragists were writers or journalists who used their pens to address their opponents. Suffrage-focused periodicals were rare. The *Champion* is the only Canadian example whose copies survive, though it was preceded by an Icelandic Canadian feminist periodical called *Freyja,* published between 1898 and 1910 in Winnipeg by suffragists Margret and Sigfus Benedictsson. Print culture was the primary medium through which to transmit local, national, and international suffrage news and to educate the public, but it also built shared values and a sense of community among people who might never meet.

The mainstream provincial press was a competitive industry, with dailies and weeklies in rural and urban areas. In a time before television or radio, people relied on newspapers for information about national and international events. Farmers, miners, small-town business owners, and political elites across the province read detailed stories and editorials about the national and global suffrage movement. Most newspapers were gradually asserting journalistic independence, but editors took partisan positions, just as they do today. For example, between 1871 and 1917, the *Colonist* did not adopt a consistent stance on suffrage, repeatedly changing its view depending on the political position of the editors and whether they supported the Liberal or the Conservative Parties.

An editorial enthusiastically endorsed the 1885 suffrage bill moved by Montague Tyrwhitt-Drake, but when Ralph Smith's bill almost passed in 1899, the editor proclaimed that the paper "is opposed to woman suffrage. It does not believe women want it." Three years later, the paper reversed its view, claiming that there was no "one single valid or satisfying reason why women should not vote, and we believe that if they did vote, their influence could be entirely for good and not for evil in our political life."

Mainstream editorials were not the only way in which the public learned about suffrage. Newspapers were motley assortments of editorials, letters, women's interest stories, and jokes, all of which created a lively discursive space where suffragists, politicians, and readers jockeyed for attention and attempted to convert the public to their cause. Mainstream newspapers published "all sides" to the enfranchisement question and printed anti-suffrage commentary to prove that women neither wanted nor needed the vote. At the same time, they routinely covered provincial, national, and international debates on the topic. Suffragists kept a close eye on the coverage and occasionally intervened. The constant to and fro was an extended public conversation about political equality, not one in which all participants had an equal voice, but one where suffragists could harness public interest.

Newspapers were dominated by male owners, editors, and journalists, but by the early twentieth century they needed to attract a female readership and draw on its purchasing power. To achieve this, they published women's pages, which focused mainly on domestic life but also discussed women's organizations and were edited by a small but growing number of female journalists. Vancouver's women's pages were known for their serious subjects, and many featured suffragists such as Lily Laverock, Ethel Cody Stoddard, and Isabel MacLean. Most papers also published the occasional women's edition, in which leading local women took editorial control to discuss domestic life, municipal and provincial suffrage, education, work, philanthropy, and recreation. The

Colonist offered such editions in 1895 and 1909, the *Victoria Daily Times* in 1895, and the *Vancouver Sun* in 1913.

None of the women's editions were fully pro-suffrage, but they made a sympathetic defence of the New Woman. Modern women could not ignore the wider world; they were responsible for ensuring that the political realm would protect the home and family. Columnists acknowledged their desire for meaningful paid work. M.E. Angus argued that all women had a duty to "place themselves side by side with their working sisters, ascertain the hardship and difficulties with which they are confronted, and seek to remove them." Constance Langford Davie pointed to the profound changes of the nineteenth century that made it incumbent on parents to provide their daughters with "a means of earning a livelihood." The *Daily Times* ran anonymous first-person columns written by a civil servant and a shop girl about wages and working conditions.

Both Agnes Deans Cameron and Maria Grant contributed pro-suffrage articles to the 1895 women's editions of the *Colonist* and the *Daily Times.* Cameron wrote that women deserved political equality, not because of their homemaking skills or their motherly qualities, but because of "simple justice." After all, they had to obey the law, their property was taxed, and they worked to "provide for their families and those dependent on them." "Anyone with reason," Cameron insisted in the *Colonist,* "has a right to help in determining what laws shall govern him. Women have reason, and, therefore, should vote." In the *Daily Times,* Maria Grant wrote a humorous column explaining why women should vote and men should not. Men would have to absent themselves from work while they cast their ballots, and their tendency to engage in political arguments with their wives jeopardized marital harmony. Even worse, Grant joked, "man in political matters is an emotional creature ... Men go into a state of ecstatic frenzy, cheering, throwing hats in the air, and disporting themselves like a set of irresponsible maniacs!"

Only a few newspapers and periodicals commissioned columns that were penned by suffragists. Among them was the *Vancouver Daily World*. A liberal and pro–Liberal Party paper, it was one of the few Canadian dailies that extensively covered local suffrage events, and it consistently endorsed votes for women, stating in 1891 that the "enfranchisement of women is as certain as that the world goes round." Under the ownership of Vancouver politician L.D. Taylor, the paper offered a column to Susie Lane Clark, providing historians with a unique window into activism in British Columbia. Clark valued non-partisanship and presented her readers with an unprecedented range of perspectives on women's political equality. "The only thing we ask the women to stand pat on is votes for women on the same terms that it has or may be granted to men," she wrote in 1913. Clark recognized the value of reaching out to anti-suffragists, encouraging them to submit reasons why women should not be permitted to vote (no one responded).

Though Clark was non-partisan, her socialist and labour sympathies shaped the perspective of her column, and she featured contributors who wrote about socialism, motherhood, and militancy. Bertha Merrill Burns had a regular "Sauce Box" column in the *Daily World* and the BC Federation of Labour newspaper, the *B.C. Federationist,* in which she crafted witty commentary on current events, often mocking gender norms and anti-suffragists. "In many homes 'Papa' is more humored than the baby," she quipped in 1913. "He is so much more disagreeable when crossed, and, unfortunately, he is too big to be spanked." Clark published Nora Tutty's appeal to the socialist women of Vancouver, laying out why both socialism and suffrage were central to women's political equality. Clark tracked all the suffrage activities in the city, and her columns are evidence of a busy and lively community.

Outside the mainstream press, suffrage news was covered in a flourishing national and transnational print culture of religious, reform, and farm periodicals. In 1914, the *Western Methodist Recorder* gave Florence Hall a regular column on suffrage, and the labour and socialist press also featured suffrage writers. The column by Bertha Merrill Burns in the socialist *Western Clarion* took up topics including suffrage and women in the labour force, and Helena Gutteridge edited a column in the *Federationist* that argued that working women needed both unions and suffrage. But coverage was inconsistent in the hands of male editors and newspaper owners, and suffragists eventually decided that only a dedicated suffrage press could guarantee reliable content and editorial control.

SUFFRAGE PERIODICALS

However, launching a suffrage publication was difficult. Production costs were high, geographical distances were great, and the potential readership was small. As a result, Canadian suffragists had few independent print cultures, unlike their counterparts in the United States and Britain. Only two dedicated suffrage publications have been identified in Canada, both in British Columbia. The *Pioneer Woman* was launched by Helena Gutteridge and was the organ of the Vancouver Evening Work Committee, which foregrounded the concerns of working women. Though it soon folded, its vision persisted in the *Federationist* column.

More lasting was the *Champion,* published in Victoria between 1912 and 1914 under the auspices of the BC Political Equality League and edited by Maria Grant and Dorothy Davis. Its editorials were strongly marked by Grant's philosophy that female enfranchisement was "in harmony with the law of Life," which she saw as a universal and inherent desire for liberty, equality, and freedom. The *Champion* provided editorial control, a way to share information, and an opportunity to challenge anti-suffrage ideology. Its writers contributed extended takedowns on the "absurdity" of forcing women to prove that they would vote responsibly and tried their hand at satire and persuasion. As much as the magazine intended to build a sense of solidarity, its editors also hoped to sway those who rejected suffrage. They worked hard to boost circulation, convinced local businesses to advertise in its pages, sold issues at public events, and in 1913 persuaded the CPR to sell copies on westward-bound trains. The volume of advertising in the *Champion,* for beauty products, fashion, appliances, and real estate services, speaks to the editors' success at fundraising and to the fact that many retailers saw female consumers as good for business. Suffragists were not afraid of using the media to circulate their ideas. Whether they were securing ads, selling ribbons and badges at local fairs, or flying a "Votes for Women" banner, they harnessed the media and modern consumer culture to raise money and increase visibility.

By 1912, BC suffragists were self-consciously aware of their relationship to the global movement, so the *Champion's* editors tried to bring an internationalist flavour to the magazine. Using articles reprinted from other publications, including the suffragette paper *Votes for Women,* they featured writing by leading American and British suffragists. Reading about global suffrage forced some women to reconsider their assumptions about British superiority. For example, though the "Women of Other Lands" column in the *Champion* could be condescending, asserting that enfranchisement was spreading to places that were ruled by superstition, it also highlighted suffrage work in South America, Turkey, China, Japan, the Middle East, and eastern Europe. In doing so, it introduced BC women to the names of people and organizations whom they would never otherwise have heard about. Suffragists slowly realized that no women were completely free from sexism and disenfranchisement. The *Champion* reported that Hindu, Buddhist, Confucian, Muslim, Jewish, and Christian women were working together "to make a common plea for the liberation of their sex ... from those artificial discriminations which every political and religious system has directed against them." The involvement of women and men from around the world seemed to prove that political opposition could not "hinder [this] evolution" and captured the feeling that the women's movement was part of a larger global awakening. But North American suffragists were unwilling to link enfranchisement with ending colonial rule, lifting restrictions on Asian immigration, or criticizing the dispossession of Indigenous peoples.

Not everything in the *Champion* was serious. Its word play and amusing columns were intended to make readers laugh, revealing a joyful sense of humour and a sheer delight in writing. It delved into political satire with "Our Men's Cosy Corner," a column that spoofed both anti-suffrage thought and the writing style of mainstream women's columns. Penned by "Uncle Pry," it advised men on their "personal affairs" and provided "helpful little sermonettes" about the manly virtues of courage and reticence. Uncle Pry offered fashion tips (avoid wearing purple, white, and green shirts) and pretended to wilt in the face of men's "boisterous language." He counselled on marriage as well: when a letter writer wondered whether a suffragette might make a "good wife," Pry addressed his reply to "A.S.S." (often used as an acronym for Anti-Suffrage Societies), telling him that suffragette wives were opinionated and unfashionable. Moreover, they forced their husbands to keep house while they amused themselves with "audiences of hysterical women." Another column mocked anti-suffragists by celebrating the "Knights of the Square Box," an "association to deprive men of the vote, on the ground that it unfits them for business life and distracts them from the far more vital matter of Real Estate Transactions."

Suffragists relied on a range of tactics to bring political change and win over the public. They launched countless petitions, wrote letters to the editor, and met with both their allies and their opponents. They used their skills and increasing confidence to build a culture of debate, disagreement, and dissent. The suffrage communities they created were intended to be open to a diverse group of women, regardless of political affiliation, religion, or class. But the movement was not racially diverse, and its arguments for equality rested on deep feelings of British superiority and entitlement.

Mothers of the nation must necessarily be interested in the country's rights, laws, and progress; they must take an interest in the matters of those laws, which they have to obey with others. Why should they not vote for law makers as well as men? ... No taxation without representation was the cry that gave Vancouver Island its first legislative council. Let this apply to women if they are not to have the franchise. Do not allow them to remain in the same situation as the Chinaman, who is taxed and has no voice in the matter.

– LETTER TO THE EDITOR,
COLONIST, 21 MARCH 1897, 7.

FIVE

THE POLITICS
OF RACE

Jane Constance Gilbert Cook (Ga'axsta'las) (1870–1951)
was born in Port Blakely, Puget Sound, grew up in her maternal
village of Taxis, and lived in Yalis after her marriage to Stephen
Cook in 1888. She was president of the Anglican Women's
Auxiliary, worked as a translator and interpreter, and sat on the
executive committee of the Allied Tribes of British Columbia. She
is pictured here with the Allied Tribes in 1922, standing to
the left of Peter Kelly (centre, front).

IN 1913, A DEPUTATION of almost seventy women met with Premier Richard McBride to present a ten-thousand-name suffrage petition to the government. Their leader, Maria Grant, listed the grave problems that women and children faced, and attempted to convince McBride that enfranchisement would help the country move forward:

> In this wonderful land we stand looking to the future with a record at present almost blank, with a sheet at present almost free from National stain. Remove from the Women of the Race the stigma of inferiority attached to disenfranchisement, and we shall all work together to make our National history the cleanest in the history of the world.

This speech, and the quote that opens this chapter, helps to place the suffrage movement within the racial politics of the province. Did Grant's "women of the race" include women from all religions and ethnic and racial backgrounds? Or were they solely of British descent? How could suffragists claim that Canada had a clean slate, when Indigenous people were dispossessed, immigration laws discriminated against people from China, South Asia, and Japan, and immigrant men were blamed for "unfairly" holding more rights than white women of British background?

The question of who was entitled to vote was shaped by many factors, including race and national origin. When British Columbia entered Confederation in 1871, it was a small male-dominated settler society with a visible Indigenous population. Building a "white man's province" was a top priority for its politicians. But who was white? The definition of "race" was messy, though it generally placed people of white British or northern European descent at the highest level of civilization. British superiority was reinforced by a belief that Christianity would civilize the "other" – a broad category that included Indigenous people and all non-British and non-Christian immigrants.

Beliefs about British superiority were reinforced by differential access to political citizenship. Asian immigrants were thought to be so racially different that political citizenship was an impossibility for them. At various times, eastern and southern Europeans were seen as having racial characteristics that made them a threat to the province and the nation. The federal Indian Act made First Nations wards of the state and forced their assimilation through residential schools and the criminalization of cultural traditions. Indigenous dispossession, accompanied by white settler immigration, established British Columbia as a broadly based British society by the end of the nineteenth century, and most settlers believed that provincial prosperity resulted from a uniquely superior British work ethic.

Suffrage campaigns built on these assumptions. A common argument for enfranchisement rested on the unfairness of allowing eastern European immigrant men to vote while simultaneously denying the right to women of British background. Maternal feminists often declared that the "mothers of the race" would help protect the province from an influx of undesirable immigrants. These beliefs existed in awkward tandem with suffragists' growing knowledge of global suffrage politics. But most of them favoured restrictive immigration laws, saw colonialism as beneficial, and failed to make significant connections with reformers or activists from marginalized groups, even when they shared similar concerns about improving the status of women and children.

FAIRNESS, IMMIGRATION, AND POLITICAL
CITIZENSHIP

By the 1870s and 1880s, suffragists throughout North America were emphasizing the unfairness of excluding educated white women from political citizenship while simultaneously granting it to men whom they saw as less deserving. In British Columbia, arguments related to fairness were two-fold. The first expressed resentment about the voting rights of foreign-born men. The second positioned women's potential vote as a bulwark against Asian immigration to Canada. Both views expressed ethnic and racial entitlement.

Anti-immigrant sentiment increased after 1896, as the federal government brought immigrants from eastern, central, and southern Europe to farm prairie land and to work in the expanding industrial and resource extraction economy. Immigration reached a height in 1913, when over 400,000 immigrants entered Canada. British Columbia never relied heavily on what most people referred to as "non-preferred" immigrants, but it did receive them in increasing numbers after about 1900. However, the arrival of large numbers of Europeans in Alberta, Saskatchewan, and Manitoba, and their visibility in parts of British Columbia, provoked fears that the Western provinces were accepting too many non-British immigrants. They typically held dangerous jobs in mines, railways, and smelters or worked in logging or construction and were commonly feared as labour radicals. If they brought their families (as they did to the Prairies), they were viewed with suspicion because they were Catholic and had many children; if they came as transient unmarried labourers, as they did to cities and some interior mining communities, they were viewed with suspicion because they lived outside a family unit. Instead of understanding that racism contributed to low pay and poor living conditions, many Canadians blamed immigrants for poverty, crime, and alcoholism, and for stealing jobs. But, despite these deep suspicions, European men could be naturalized once they satisfied the residency requirements, after which they were entitled to vote in provincial and federal elections.

The political rights held by immigrant men roused a strong sense of resentment among BC suffragists. The WCTU lamented the political influence of the male immigrant, who

> can neither read or write, but who by residing on Canadian soil one year and taking the oath of allegiance, though he may know nothing of our laws, nothing of the men who aspire to office, perhaps he cannot speak one word of English, and yet he can say, who shall be our legislators, while we women are placed side by side with idiots, lunatics and children.

The question of European immigration was central to Dorothy Davis's trip to the interior in 1912. She asserted that Canadian men should not "deny their countrywomen that recognition of citizenship ... which they accord to any European immigrant, when he has been in the country the stipulated time and has taken the oath of allegiance, however far removed his traditions and ideals of life, social and political, from Canadian standards, who has happened to be born a male." This rhetoric of injustice and unfairness persisted throughout the suffrage campaign in British Columbia.

But in contrast to their almost wholly negative view of Asian immigration, suffragists could imagine extending the vote to European men and women under certain conditions. Assuming that non-British Europeans were culturally backward, the editors of the *Champion* claimed that "ignorant foreign immigrants who come here are fully imbued, both men and women, with all the Old World ideas as to the inferiority and subjection of women." But once they were Canadianized, such men and women could become competent voters and "valuable citizens." The advent of the First World War, however, deepened the suspicion of European men who had immigrated from enemy countries. Some suffrage supporters, such as Liberal politician J.S. Cowper, suggested that delivering the vote to "Anglo Saxon women" would balance those of "alien men." But others called on the government to remove such men's voting rights, and the federal government did so with the Wartime Elections Act of 1917.

Suffragists were not just angry about the voting rights of European men. They were horrified by how their disenfranchisement placed them into the same category as the voiceless others in Canada. Most suffragists saw themselves as the embodiment of the highest ideals of citizenship: they were of British background, English speaking, educated and literate, rational, and able-bodied. Maria Grant felt it profoundly unjust that "the mother, the wives, the sisters of our most intelligent citizens, children of our own Empire are considered unworthy or incapable to exercise this privilege and are placed side by side with felons, Chinamen and idiots. Is it fair?" Mary Ann Cunningham argued that women "do not consider themselves children in mental growth; neither do they feel inclined to be ranked politically with savages, lunatics, and criminals." This sense of injustice combined with a strong feeling of cultural and intellectual superiority meant that suffragists wanted to lift themselves above the category of the other rather than dismantle it.

The maternal feminist argument that women deserved the vote because they were responsible for raising the next generation was often expressed with the phrase "mothers of the race" or "mothers of the nation." Most nineteenth-century nation-states placed enormous value on women's reproductive role in raising healthy future citizens, and women's movements in Canada, the United States, Britain, China, Turkey, South America, and elsewhere often used the language of mothering. Socialist Bertha Merrill Burns referred to "mother wit," by which she meant the

ONE ARGUMENT FOR WOMAN SUFFRAGE

A VOTER.   A NON-VOTER.

This 1911 *Vancouver Daily World* cartoon uses the common trope
of an educated, literate, intelligent, and respectable white woman
(who was denied the vote) portrayed in opposition to a dissolute,
inebriated, unintelligent, and corrupt man (who could vote).

dignity of domestic labour and the right of mothers to a political
voice. The term was often used as a shorthand to criticize the glor-
ification of motherhood in a system that simultaneously under-
valued mothering – all of which "concerns the mothers of the
race, whether they be black or brown, white or yellow."

But "mothers of the race" and "mothers of the nation" are what
scholar Mariana Valverde calls "slippery" concepts. Sometimes,
the words were intended to encompass humanity as a whole, but
they could also refer exclusively to white settler women of British
background. This latter definition informed the claim of settler

women that the civilizing force of their votes would help governments restrict immigration. While visiting Creston, for example, Dorothy Davis stated that the "rapid influx" of the "foreign element" had led to "an urgent need for an increase in the British born electorate if this country is to become true to the traditions and ideas which have made our Empire what it is today."

Armed with the vote, suffragists believed that women would offset the European immigrant vote and help staunch the flow of immigration from China, Japan, and South Asia. The province was home to Canada's largest proportion of Asian immigrants, with the 1901 census identifying 10.9 percent of the total population as Asian. The vast majority were Chinese men, mainly from Guangdong province, who typically laboured in railway construction and coal mining. Less numerous were Japanese men, who worked primarily in fishing, farming, and logging. Later, South Asian men from the Punjab would migrate to the province, working mainly in the lumber industry. Both government and private industry benefitted from low-paid immigrant labour, but neither wanted Asian men to stay permanently. Indeed, various racist policies were designed to discourage settlement – including disenfranchisement, head taxes on Chinese immigrants, immigration restrictions, and legislation that barred employment in public works and the professions. In September 1907, anti-Asian sentiment exploded into violence when the Asiatic Exclusion League organized a "White Canada" rally in Vancouver. For two nights, rioters attacked Japanese and Chinese neighbourhoods and properties. As a result of these policies, Asian communities in British Columbia were mostly male. Only a few Chinese merchants could afford to sponsor their wives or bring in young women to work as domestic servants. After 1908, Ottawa restricted male Japanese immigration while allowing Japanese women to enter Canada to marry. The resulting "picture bride" system brought several thousand women to the province until new restrictions were imposed in 1928.

Support for anti-Asian policies linked suffragists with various women's organizations, politicians, and labour unions, all of which drew on mainstream racist beliefs that Asian men were unclean and unhealthy drug users who lured innocent white women into sexual relationships and who could never assimilate into white society. The fact that they worked for low pay was seen as harmful because it diminished the wages of white male breadwinners. Socialist MLA James Hawthornthwaite supported a 1906 female suffrage bill in part because he considered it outrageous that white women did not possess the franchise, whereas "Indians and Hindoos might have it." A column written by Susie Lane Clark for the *B.C. Federationist* used openly racist language in protesting the arrival of the *Komagata Maru* – a ship carrying South Asian migrants that attempted to land in Vancouver in 1914, setting off a province-wide firestorm of anti-immigrant protest. As Clark explained, women who lacked the vote could exert only an "indirect" influence regarding the "occupation of these shores by hordes of dark-skinned immigrants from the Far East."

Both organized labour and suffragists prioritized the needs of white working women and advocated for restrictive immigration and bans on Asian employment. The Women's Employment League was founded by Helena Gutteridge in 1914 during a time of global economic recession and rising unemployment. An alliance between suffragists, city council, and organized labour, it aided unemployed Vancouver women through programs including a co-operative toy-making factory and the provision of meal tickets. It also supported the Trades and Labour Council's 1915 campaign to protest "against Asiatics being employed in hotels and restaurants of their city." At the behest of the LCW and the Trades and Labour Council, Gutteridge asked the YWCA to replace its Chinese cook with a white woman.

Though most suffragists supported restrictions on Asian immigration, they were divided on the question of South Asian women. After 1903, the province had a small population of about two thousand Sikh men, almost all of whom came from the Punjab to work in the logging industry. As British subjects, they should have been treated like other British subjects, but they too were labelled as a threat to the dream of a white province. By 1907, they had been disenfranchised. In 1908, legislation was introduced that required all immigrants to make a continuous journey from their country without stopping en route, a policy that targeted South Asian men because ships travelling from India to Canada stopped at Hong Kong. By 1914, only nine South Asian women had succeeded in immigrating to Canada. This gender imbalance raised concerns around mixed-race relationships, even as many feared that allowing women to immigrate would inevitably increase permanent South Asian settlement.

The leaders of BC South Asian communities hoped to win over politicians and suffragists by arguing that, as male British subjects, they should have the right to vote and to bring their wives to Canada. The Khalsa Diwan Society, established in Vancouver in 1906 to provide aid for new immigrants, protested immigration restrictions and disenfranchisement. Its president, Bhag Singh, and other members submitted petitions and lobbied provincial and federal governments but to no avail. In 1912, Husain Rahim, a member of the Socialist Party of Canada, attempted to vote in Vancouver. He managed to get his name on the voters' list and to cast a ballot but was subsequently arrested. South Asian community leaders had slightly better success with arguments that were based on their status as men and husbands. For example, Dr. Sundar Singh called upon Canadians to live up to the obligations of Christianity and the British Empire by demonstrating the "universal brotherhood of mankind." He added that it was God's "design for a man to have a wife." Without marriage, South Asian men would "have to clean their own homes, cook their own food, and attend to their own clothes." Furthermore, they would be "exposed to temptations of gambling, liquor, and immorality."

Born in the Punjab, Dr. Sundar Singh (1882–death date un-known) received his medical training in Britain. He emigrated to Canada in 1909 and moved to Vancouver, where he became a community advocate and strong supporter of South Asian immigration to Canada. After moving to Toronto, he helped establish the Canada-India Committee, which lobbied for fair immigration laws and nurtured support from allies, including Dr. Lelia Davis, a suffragist and Theosophist who worked at the Ontario Medical College for Women.

The argument that Canada should amend its immigration laws so that South Asian men could be joined by their wives touched sympathetic chords in some reform and suffrage circles. Although most British Columbians felt that South Asian women should not come to Canada, the "Hindu Woman's Question" remained a matter of debate, and there was some approval for limited female immigration. Suffragists were not united on the issue. Supporters emphasized the imperial ties that bound Sikh soldiers to the British army, suggested that lonely South Asian men might form sexual liaisons with white women, and cited the right of men to marry and have children. The National Council of Women and the IODE pressed Ottawa to lift the restrictions, with the former passing a 1912 resolution in favour of the measure, on the basis that denying British subjects the right to a family life was unfair.

But the Local Councils of Women in major BC cities were divided. The Vancouver LCW stated that permitting the immigration of South Asian women was "irresponsible" and not "wise or beneficial." It tried unsuccessfully to block the 1912 resolution of the national council. Vancouver suffragist and journalist Ethel Cody Stoddard penned a newspaper column that blamed the Eastern provinces for "dumping" the immigration problem on British Columbia and suggested that South Asian men treated women poorly. Suffragists in Victoria disagreed. In 1912, the local LCW debated whether to lobby the federal government to allow the immigration of "Hindu wives." Those who favoured the idea won the day, but only after amending their statement to read that restricting South Asian immigration was unfair, given that "less desirable" Chinese immigration persisted. Eventually relenting, Ottawa announced in 1917 that wives of South Asian men would be allowed to immigrate, but the policy did not become operational until 1919 – and the paperwork was so complex that the first group of South Asian women arrived only in 1921.

MODERN PROGRESS AND THE WEST

By the late nineteenth century, suffragists espoused the belief that the modern world was characterized by progress and was evolving toward justice and equality. Their cause was a march of enlightened reason away from the "barbarism" or "dark ages" of earlier societies, where women were held in bondage or slavery. This idea fit with the beliefs of evangelical Christians, Theosophists, and socialists, who argued that a nation's treatment of women revealed how civilized it was. The faith in progress relied on popular interpretations of Darwin's theory of evolution and adaptation, as well as Marxist understandings of history, all of which asserted that societies evolved and moved forward from simple or primitive to complex and civilized.

According to suffragists, societies that kept individual women in legal and sexual bondage were corrupt and lazy, whereas modern, progressive nations championed women's right to democratic participation. "The educated women of our century are totally dissimilar to the slaves of the barbarous ages," wrote Mary Ann

Cunningham in 1894. They "are taking their places side by side with the most advanced thinkers and workers of the world." Terms such as the "stone ages" evoked a past when humans were ruled by superstition rather than by law or reason. In contrast, modern women would be freed from the "ghosts and ghouls of the dark ages." Suffragists commonly referred to undoing prison chains or throwing off the shackles that bound women to dependence. Some were developing theories of what feminists would eventually call patriarchy: that male domination throughout world history "has always meant the serfdom of woman, no matter what class she belonged to."

The belief that modern British civilization was the most advanced in the world was complicated by evidence that women in pre-modern Britain had held paying jobs or enjoyed positions of political influence. The growth of suffrage internationalism also challenged assumptions that the British Empire was the sole standard-bearer of modern values, especially as certain supposedly uncivilized nations had enfranchised their female citizens. The *Champion*'s "Women of Other Lands" column showed a growing awareness of women's global progress. Its writers drew on tropes of victimized Middle Eastern women in "harems" gradually awakening to their oppression. But they also noted that men and women in Egypt used the Koran to argue that women's equality was an Islamic value, and they discussed how activists in China saw female enfranchisement as part of political reform. Sometimes, they used this information to shame their opponents. Addressing the Men's Society at St. James's Anglican Church in Vancouver, for example, Reverend Henry Edwards declared that "today women have not half the power held by the negro women of darkest Africa." One of his listeners pointed out that women in non-British countries enjoyed high status: "In the far east, even among the Mohammedans, each wife, even the least favored of four, has better rights than women in BC." In Kelowna, socialist

R.B. Kerr told an audience that "even in China" women could vote for members of the provincial assembly. If this were true of China, surely British Columbia should be ashamed by its lack of progress.

This rhetoric of progress played well in British Columbia, where politicians celebrated growth and opportunity. The completion of the transnational Canadian Pacific Railway in 1885 and industrial and demographic growth were evidence of what historian Patricia Roy calls the "boundless optimism" of the period. An article in the September 1912 issue of the *Champion* celebrated ongoing industrial development and added, "We hope that through our ports may pour the golden harvest of the North-West." Suffragists enthusiastically embraced the belief that white women were key partners in taming the rugged Western frontier and in building a permanent and prosperous society, and from this belief they developed a powerful myth of the West as more egalitarian than elsewhere in North America. This framework was foundational to settler colonialism in Western Canada, where the language of pioneering independence presented British settlement as an affirmation of hard work and egalitarianism rather than the dispossession of Indigenous land.

BC suffragists connected with the rhetoric of the West as a modern frontier that encouraged women's "pioneering" independence. Idaho and Wyoming had offered white women early voting and homestead and property rights, hoping that they would migrate, marry, and help populate the West. But Canadian provinces did not take the same steps. As historian Sarah Carter shows, Canadian authorities believed that agriculture and landownership rightly rested in the hands of men. Prairie settler women were the first in Canada to be enfranchised, but the majority of the provinces quickly followed suit between 1916 and 1918. The West hardly lived up to its self-image as a beacon of gender equality. And suffragists saw no contradiction between the reality of racial disparity and their faith that the West had the "broadest vision" of gender equality and would acquire "justice for all, especially for the suffering and oppressed."

Nevertheless, BC suffragists felt that there was something distinctively egalitarian about their province and came to believe that it was peopled by a particular kind of Western woman, who was characterized by ambition, independence, and a strong work ethic. The *Prince Rupert Journal* celebrated the new women of the "Pacific Slope" as unique in comparison to their "slower, eastern sisters." Full of the "western spirit," they were strong and educated but also feminine and accomplished housewives, like "one of those confections with a frothy meringue on top and a good deal of satisfying custard beneath." In 1911, Vancouver suffragist Blanche Murison praised the educated women of Vancouver by linking them with the "tireless efforts of these indomitable women workers of the west, with their broad-gauged judgement." Such women were part of the "progress that made the story of their Last Great West such wonderful reading."

Central to the belief that new women were being forged on the Pacific Coast was the idea that new men – who were modern and egalitarian – were being created there as well. When Seattle suffragist Adela Parker spoke in Vancouver, she contended that "the men of the West have a particular regard for women and their work. This not only includes the man who has been born here, but the man who has been here long enough to become imbued with the great spirit of the West." Suffragists flattered male supporters as visionary men who were "broad-minded enough to grant women political equality." Organizations showcased male supporters such as Seattle city councillor Max Wardell, whom they described in glowing terms as a "splendid type of the 'new man' who today is espousing woman's cause by securing for her equal justice." The Vancouver PEL invited Mayor L.D. Taylor and Seattle Democratic senator George F. Cotterill to speak at its first convention, where Taylor enthusiastically assured the audience that he had long been a "woman suffragist" and that women would soon achieve full political rights.

Although some men clearly enjoyed being described as modern and egalitarian, this language was also designed to flatter and shame politicians to move faster on suffrage legislation. After suffrage wins in Washington state (1910), California (1911), and Oregon (1912), Susie Lane Clark remarked that most of the Pacific Coast currently "boasts of political equality for its women" and wondered, "Are the men of British Columbia going to be less just[?]" Suffragists were not afraid to shame men as weak and cowardly for failing to live up to progressive standards of manhood. When the Pioneer Political Equality League failed to get Vancouver mayor Truman Smith Baxter to support suffrage, it wondered whether "the suffragists' trusting faith in the generosity of 'our big Western men' is somewhat misplaced and that perhaps the vote will not come by crying for it." Dorothy Davis and the PEL repeatedly challenged Premier McBride to demonstrate that he was the "strongest" leader in Canada. "The Men of this Far West have always been Pioneers in the struggle for a wider, freer, greater physical existence," Davis claimed. "Have they the courage to show themselves Pioneers on a loftier plane, and break the trail for their Women into a land of moral and social and political freedom?" By the time McBride resigned, the answer for suffragists was clear: as a man who rejected their claims to citizenship, McBride was out of place in the "progressive west" and the rapidly advancing world.

ACTIVISM IN AFRICAN CANADIAN COMMUNITIES

During the nineteenth century, both African American women who moved to British Columbia and women of Indigenous maternal descent were active in its early women's movements. But by the end of the century, white settlement had changed the demographic profile of the province. The mainstream suffrage movement was dominated by white women of British background, and it paid little attention to women who did not belong to this group.

Suffrage would never be the main vehicle through which racialized women fought for political rights.

Black settlers began to arrive in British Columbia during the
late 1850s, as race-based laws endangered African Americans on
the Pacific Coast. The first large group came from San Francisco
and settled in Victoria, on Saltspring Island, and later in the
Lower Mainland. The BC African Canadian community was much
smaller than those in Eastern Canada, where well-known women
such as the journalist Mary Ann Shadd Cary called for abolition,
racial equality, and women's rights.

In Canada, African Canadian men could vote and run for office,
although racism often prevented them from doing either. Many
black settlers were committed to Christian reform and temperance, and had ties to the American anti-slavery movement. Shared
religious views allowed for connections between black and white
settler women, and several churches in nineteenth-century Victoria refused to segregate their parishioners on the basis of race.
One of the earliest charitable organizations in the province was
the Committee of Coloured Ladies, established in Victoria in 1862
by leading black women in the colony. Cross-referencing census
information with signatures on the 1885 and 1897 suffrage petitions confirms that at least twenty-one black men and women
(and another likely seventeen) supported suffrage. Some of them,
such as Mary Hamilton and Mabel Carter, were also active in
Victoria women's groups. For example, the Mrs. S. Pointer who
attended the founding meeting of the provincial WCTU in 1883
was probably Sarah Pointer. She and her husband, Nathan, were
African American Methodists and small-business owners who
had emigrated to Victoria in the 1850s. The extended Alexander
family was also visible due to its membership in women's and
religious organizations and because several family members
signed suffrage petitions in the 1880s and 1890s. Saanich residents Nancy and Charles Alexander, who came to Victoria in 1858,
had much in common with many reform and religious families

Corinthia Pierre Alexander (1868–1939) was born in Victoria to
Thomas Whiting Pierre and Ann Elizabeth Deal Pierre, Baptists
who came to Victoria in the early 1860s. Trained as a dressmaker,
Corinthia married Thomas Alexander, son of Charles and Nancy.
She signed the 1897 suffrage petition along with her mother, her
sister-in-law Georgina Pierre, and possibly her mother-in-law,
who is listed as Mrs. Alexander. Her sister Louise Pierre signed
the 1885 suffrage petition.

elsewhere in the province. A school trustee, farmer, and carpenter,
Charles helped form a temperance society and was a founding
member of the Shady Creek Church. Nancy belonged to the
Women's Institute and the WCTU. Both were important and re-

THE POLITICS OF RACE 135

spected members of their community, with deep connections to white and black communities in the region. The names of their daughter-in-law Corinthia Pierre Alexander and her family also appear consistently on suffrage petitions of the period.

The racism experienced by African Canadians in the West intensified after 1905, when over 1,500 black Americans fled to the Prairies in response to ongoing violence and lynching in Oklahoma. In 1911, Prime Minister Wilfrid Laurier passed an Order-in-Council to ban members of "the Negro race" from entering Canada, because they were "deemed unsuitable to the climate." Though the ban was repealed, it reflected growing hostility toward black migration. Because racism had a significant impact on black women's work and family lives, community organizations and churches rather than the white-dominated suffrage movement were their main vehicle for fighting racism and inequality. Women and men established the Negro Christian Alliance, the United Negro Improvement Association, and the African Methodist Episcopalian Church, all of which allowed black citizens to claim rights through the language of "racial uplift" – the "moral, social and general advancement of the race."

Such bodies offered important leadership roles to black women. For example, the Negro Christian Alliance was founded in Vancouver in 1911 by Harriet Blanche Davis, an Iowa-born Canadian who was its president by 1913. A multi-pronged organization, it supported prohibition and female suffrage, and it campaigned against racism in the city. It challenged the portrayal of black people as violent and uncivilized, spearheading a 1915 protest against the staging of a play titled *The Clansman* and the movie *Birth of a Nation,* both of which glorified the Ku Klux Klan. The alliance held open meetings every Sunday in Mount Pleasant, and in February 1914 it hosted a public debate on whether female suffrage would be "a benefit to humanity." After Mrs. A.W. Walker and two men spoke in favour of enfranchisement, and Mrs. Declaybrooke and two men came out in opposition, a vote at the end of the meeting concluded that Mrs. Walker and her team had won the day.

But despite some shared values, there is no record that black women's organizations collaborated with the suffrage movement in Vancouver, and the names of leading black women do not appear in newspaper coverage of suffrage events. Given the deepening racism directed toward African American immigrants, this is not surprising. The politics of Dr. Ella Synge, a leading New Westminster suffragist, illustrate the depth of this racism. Before moving to British Columbia, she lived in Edmonton, where she led a 1911 protest against the government's "foolish" stance on black migration. Drawing on stereotypes that characterized black men as sexually dangerous, Synge suggested that they might visit "outrages" on white women. Previous tentative collaborations did not last into the twentieth century, and women's organizations remained racially segregated in the years leading up to the suffrage referendum.

INDIGENOUS WOMEN'S ACTIVISM

Just as black women carved out a small space in the early women's movement, the daughters of fur trade officials and Indigenous women participated in Victoria's nineteenth-century reform community. Men such as Governor James Douglas – himself of black and Scots heritage – saw respectability as key to building the city of Victoria. In the 1880s, many daughters of fur trade marriages were active in women's movements. Sarah Work Finlayson (daughter of trader John Work and Josette Legacé) was involved with the Protestant Orphans Home and the WCTU, and many members of the extended Finlayson family signed the 1885 suffrage petition, demonstrating their involvement with temperance and their support for enfranchisement. In some families, interest in Indigenous stories, languages, and kin connections persisted despite the pressures of assimilation. Lucy McNeill Moffatt, the daughter of trader William Henry McNeill and his

Born in 1854 in Fort Victoria, Martha Douglas was the youngest
daughter of Governor James Douglas, who was born in Guyana,
and his wife Amelia (Connolly), who was born in Fort Churchill.
Educated in England, she returned to British Columbia and
married engineer Dennis Reginald Harris in 1878. A member of
many women's groups, including the Lace Club of Victoria and
the Women's Institute Weavers Guild, Harris was a founding
member of the Victoria Political Equality League, hosting events
and fundraisers at her home.

Haida wife, Mathilda, signed the 1885 suffrage petition and seems
to have maintained trading ties to her Indigenous relatives.

Most mainstream suffragists, however, showed little concern
for the impact of colonization on Indigenous families and communities. Some Ontario and American suffragists were aware of

As It Should Be

Miss B. C. (to the women of British Columbia)—There is now nothing within my gift which you may not attain.

Representations of the nation often took highly gendered forms – perhaps as the innocent and feminine Miss Canada or the hardy Johnny Canuck. In her analysis of newspaper cartoons, historian Carmen Nielson shows how stylized images of Indigenous women brought readers into the "colonial gaze." This 1917 cartoon from the *Vancouver Sun* represents British Columbia as an Indigenous woman who (although not entitled to vote herself) welcomes a newly enfranchised settler woman to full political citizenship.

Haudenosaunee women's political power, but BC suffrage leaders were not interested in learning about Indigenous women's long histories of community leadership. Only a few women who were descended from Indigenous mothers remained active in the suffrage movement into the twentieth century. The most visible example was Martha Douglas Harris, youngest daughter of Governor James Douglas and his Metis wife, Amelia Connolly. Harris maintained an interest in her mother's ancestry and published a book of Indigenous stories that her mother had related to her, but her father trained her to be a respectable upper-middle-class woman of British background. After receiving a liberal arts education at an English finishing school, Harris inherited property in her own name and married British-born civil engineer Douglas Harris in 1878. She was active in the LCW and is frequently mentioned in Victoria newspapers as an enthusiastic suffrage supporter and founding member of the Political Equality League. However, women like Martha Harris were assimilated into mainstream society and were not defined as "Indian" under the terms of the Indian Act (she was listed as "Scotch" in the 1881 census).

First Nations women did not participate in the mainstream suffrage movement. But looking for direct connections between the suffrage movement and Indigenous women does not capture the complex history of Indigenous women's lives, activism, and community leadership. Many joined Anglican and Methodist Women's Auxiliaries on the northwest coast, and though they shared concerns with settler women about maternal health, children's education, and temperance, those concerns were shaped by the impact of colonialism on their communities. The Methodist Women's Auxiliary in the Tsimshian territory of Port Simpson (near present-day Prince Rupert), for example, included both white settler and Indigenous women, and the Anglican Women's Auxiliary in the Kwakwaka'wakw territory of Alert Bay (on Cormorant Island, off the northeast coast of Vancouver Island) served

Indigenous mothers and women. Many Indigenous women were interested in temperance and concerned about the impact of men's alcohol use on women. Some also spoke about the harmful impact of early marriage, especially on young women who married older men, as well as the lack of choice in marriage partners.

First Nations women did not need the suffrage movement to take on leadership roles, and they drew on the traditions of their communities, where they were leaders, elders, and traders in their own right. The life of Ga'axsta'las (Jane Constance Cook) shows the importance of broadening the lens in order to understand gender equality activism in British Columbia. Anthropologist Leslie Robertson has collaboratively documented the legacy of Kwakwaka'wakw leader Cook (1870–1951), whose life bridged the nineteenth and twentieth centuries. After converting to Christianity, Cook helped establish the Anglican Women's Auxiliary in Yalis (renamed Alert Bay) and worked as an interpreter in court, at political meetings, and during church services. As colonization disrupted community-based practices such as the potlatch, she criticized the treatment of young girls and women in her community, especially early marriage and the practice of a woman's family choosing her husband, seeing these as a challenge to women's liberty. Cook was a prominent voice because she was active in the Allied Tribes of British Columbia, a provincial Indigenous rights organization that fought for Aboriginal title. But it is likely that members of the women's auxiliary were discussing these issues as well, and at least some of her statements were made on their behalf. It is important to understand Cook's activism as rooted in both Indigenous rights and concern for women's status. She held provincial and federal governments accountable for dispossession, demanded land and fishing rights, and pushed for better education and health care funding – demands that settler reformers and suffragists showed little interest in supporting. These long-standing forms of Indigenous activism continued into the twentieth century and were central to 1940s efforts to win the provincial vote.

Although women in the mainstream suffrage movement and those from racialized communities shared concerns about the status of women and children, interaction between them was rare. Suffragists failed to draw Asian, immigrant, or Indigenous women into larger reform movements, favoured exclusionary immigration laws, and supported racial restrictions on the vote. Few suffragists understood racial and gender inequality as interconnected, and they were unwilling to see the impact of racial disparity or their own role in maintaining it. These failures, however, did not prevent all marginalized women from supporting suffrage and rights to full citizenship. But not until later in the twentieth century would mainstream feminists begin to address the racism embedded in Canadian society and the women's movement itself.

The women workers must see to it that they are organized both politically and industrially. Each are necessary to bring about economic freedom of women in industry.

– HELENA GUTTERIDGE,
B.C. FEDERATIONIST, 17 OCTOBER 1913, 5.

SIX

LABOURING
WOMEN

The newly founded Social Democratic Party of BC held a
celebratory picnic in Capilano Canyon, North Vancouver, in 1907.
Ernest Burns is in the third row at the right, just above the
woman holding the violin. Above him sits his wife, Bertha. To
her right sits Frank Parr; his suffragist wife, Louisa Parr, is
probably one of the women in the back row.

IN OCTOBER 1913, socialist feminist Bertha Merrill Burns stood on stage at a Social Democratic Party meeting in downtown Vancouver, where she criticized socialists who claimed that there was no "sex war" and who aimed only to win the class struggle. Burns was not afraid to censure the sexism of her political world. Many male socialists and union members viewed men as rightful breadwinners who deserved a "family wage" – an income high enough to support a dependent wife who remained at home to raise the children. To Burns, however, the economic, cultural, and legal subordination of women was evidence of a "sex struggle" that had to be fought if women were to achieve equality and liberation. "The chains that bind are the chains of thought," she argued, "and so soon as one thinks in freedom, so soon may one unite with others to achieve the widest liberty." For Burns, and for many of the socialists, labour organizers, and working-class women who are profiled in this chapter, economic and women's liberation were equally essential to the attainment of political freedom and full autonomy.

The best-known suffrage leaders in Canada were of middle-class or elite British background. But the BC movement had many working-class and socialist leaders and members. Socialist critiques of women's economic subordination, capitalist exploitation, and political disenfranchisement in Canada dated from the late nineteenth century. Committed suffragists who were socialists or trade unionists (such as Burns, Dora Kerr, Helena Gutteridge, Laura Jamieson, Mary Norton, and Susie Lane Clark) were part of a thriving left, labour, and socialist political culture in the province. As increasing numbers of women took on paid employment, suffragists prioritized their concerns and sought ways to build more inclusive organizational structures. They worked within organized labour and socialist parties to bolster support for workplace reforms and for suffrage. When Vancouver Island coal miners went on an extended strike, a few labour suffragists offered support to them and their families. But it was Vancouver that became the only city in Canada to establish an independently organized suffrage movement created and led by a working-class woman, which was designed to reach working women and to nurture alliances between labour and suffrage leaders.

THE LIVES OF WORKING WOMEN

The paid workforce in British Columbia – as in the rest of the country – was dominated by men. And the BC economy was dominated by primary resource industries such as logging, fishing, and mining, all of which relied heavily on male labour. Although a minority, women workers were an increasing presence across the country. By 1911, 15 percent of British Columbia's adult women worked for wages, making up about 8 percent of the paid workforce. Expected to work for pay only prior to marriage and motherhood, women were much less likely than men to work in union shops, were paid less, were not permitted to enter certain jobs and professions, and were blamed for driving down men's wages. Most worked in domestic service, although in Vancouver, the professions (mainly pink-collar stenography, teaching, and nursing) were their second-most common employment. They were also hired in fish canning (which retained Indigenous, Japanese, and white women) and factories, mainly in the garment industry. A few Chinese women were employed in the sweated trades, typically in tailoring, where wages were low, hours long, and conditions poor. White women found places in the expanding field of office and sales work. As Star Rosenthal and Melanie Buddle note, during the first decades of the twentieth century, British Columbia had the highest percentage of women who worked after marriage, who were self-employed, or who worked in the professions. And their labour in the household and on the farm remained unpaid.

By the turn of the century, many suffragists had been employed in white-collar jobs such as stenography, teaching, nursing, and journalism. Some were from working-class families or had married respectable and skilled working-class men. For example, Mary Ellen Smith was a trained teacher and the daughter of a coal miner; Vancouver's Susie Lane Clark taught school and married a printer; and Cecilia Spofford retired from teaching upon her marriage to William, a carpenter. Helen Gregory MacGill was a journalist, and Bertha Merrill Burns had worked as both a teacher and a journalist. It would be impossible to list the number of unmarried or "self-supporting" women who joined Political Equality Leagues across the province after 1910. Teacher Evelyn LeSueur later became one of Vancouver's first female police officers, and two of the province's best-known suffragists, Helena Gutteridge (a tailor) and Agnes Deans Cameron (a teacher), remained unmarried and self-supporting while active in the movement. Helen Badgley performed at numerous suffrage events and worked as a music teacher and elocutionist in Vancouver. A few practising female doctors – a distinct minority at this time – also joined the PEL, including Etta Donovan (Victoria), Belle Wilson (Vancouver), and Ella Synge (New Westminster). Even relatively well-off suffragists tended to be formally educated, had once worked for pay, and possessed skills that were useful in political activism.

Perhaps the presence of so many working women prompted women's organizations to call for equal pay long before the province introduced such legislation in 1953. The number of teachers

This photograph of suffragist, labour organizer, and politician
Helena Gutteridge (1879–1960) was taken in 1911.

in the movement probably influenced this demand. One of the
few professions that was open to women, teaching was female-
dominated. But even here, women were concentrated in the lower
grades and were expected to retire upon marriage. Agnes Deans
Cameron was a proponent of equal pay for female teachers, spoke
against funnelling girls into domestic science education, and
opposed age discrimination against teachers. Suffragists pushed
labour organizations to support equal pay platforms as well; as a
delegate at the national Trades and Labour Congress in 1915,

Helena Gutteridge delivered a speech on behalf of female workers and moved a resolution for equal pay.

Suffragists valued paid labour because they understood that marriage did not guarantee lifelong economic security for women. Separation, divorce, or widowhood were often accompanied by financial vulnerability. Despite her middle-class background, fifty-four-year-old Maria Grant found herself in precarious economic straits when her husband died in 1908. She was forced to sell her home and find employment to support herself and her children. At one point, she ran a boarding house for working women, where she lived with her youngest daughter, and she held a position as secretary of the Children's Aid Society. When Grant died in 1939, her estate consisted solely of personal effects and was valued at a mere $100. After Laura Jamieson was widowed, she took in boarders and managed a co-operative house. Ida Douglas-Fearn, who grew up well-off in England, married (and divorced) a labourer and worked as a midwife in Fort Langley before moving in with her adult children in New Westminster. Helen Gregory MacGill's first husband relied on her acumen as a journalist and businesswoman to help finance his medical career. After his death, however, she married a lawyer whose poor business decisions and unwillingness to inform her about their finances drove them to economic uncertainty more than once.

Given that many women would be working for pay at some time in their lives, suffragists argued that they should be taught a profession or skill. Dora Kerr stressed the necessity of job training – "the experience of life which women need as much as men and in which they are so often deficient can only be gained by girls taking their part in the industrial work of this world." Accepting paid employment was often a point of pride, not just a modern necessity. For example, when the BC PEL held a fundraising event with the theme "Why self-supporting women need the ballot," it asked members to contribute both a dollar and a story about how they had earned the money. Suffragists accepted that working women should speak for themselves. Winning the vote would give them a "voice" in regulating their labour conditions rather than relying on men – or women of other classes – to ask for reform on their behalf.

SOCIALIST SUFFRAGISTS

Dangerous work and low pay concerned suffragists, social reformers, trade unionists, and socialists. All agreed that workers were exploited under unregulated capitalism but differed in their analysis of how to address the problem. Labourists and union supporters felt that, as the main producers of wealth, workers were entitled to a greater share of the profit and that organized labour was the best way to improve their wages and working conditions. Socialists agreed that capitalism was exploitative, but they sought to abolish the wage system and establish collective ownership of the means of production. Their aspirations were embodied in a dizzying array of political parties, including the Socialist Party of British Columbia and the Social Democratic Party of BC. Both wished to eradicate capitalism, but the former was often labelled "impossibilist" because after it merged with the Canadian Socialist League to form the Socialist Party of Canada (1904), it increasingly rejected both an alliance with labour and the idea that capitalism could be reformed through political measures. Frustration with this approach led to the emergence of the Social Democratic Party of BC (SDP) in 1907, which was open to reforms that would improve the lives of workers. Both organized labour and socialist parties attempted to win provincial and federal office, and in the 1903 provincial election, socialist and labour parties combined received 15.8 percent of the vote. During this election, the Socialist Party of British Columbia sent its first MLAs to the legislature, James Hurst Hawthornthwaite of Nanaimo and the Welsh-born former coal miner Parker Williams of nearby Newcastle. These two MLAs sat alongside former Slocan miner and labour representative William Davidson. In the 1912 election, Parker Williams was joined by SDP MLA Jack Place.

Many women were attracted by the socialist promise of a more egalitarian world in which both men and women could live free from poverty and economic despair. The Canadian Socialist League endorsed suffrage and even ran a female candidate for office in Toronto in 1902. Its newspaper, the *Citizen and Country* (later titled the *Western Socialist* and the *Western Clarion*), featured a regular column by Bertha Merrill Burns. A journalist who wrote extensively on socialism, suffrage, and economics, Burns worked closely with socialist publisher Richard Parmater (Parm) Pettipiece. Her columns – and those of other socialist feminists – argued that socialism and feminism together would liberate women from poverty, low wages, and workplace exploitation, and would place proper value on motherhood and domestic labour.

Women enthusiastically attended party meetings during the lead-up to the 1903 provincial election, and the Socialist Party of BC catered to them by offering ladies' and mothers' nights. At a Victoria ladies' night, for example, Ada Clayton, Bertha Merrill Burns, and several others spoke, sang, and gave readings on women's work, birth control, and the high cost of living, to "loud applause" and acclaim. Irene Smith, a socialist organizer from Washington state, was a popular speaker who highlighted the role of women in socialism. She attracted such large and enthusiastic crowds on Vancouver Island that the party hired her to remain in the province through the autumn of 1903 to rally support leading up to the election.

Despite this interest, many socialists believed that female enfranchisement was of secondary importance to the larger goal of abolishing capitalism. The party was heavily male-dominated, believed that suffrage and legislation on equal pay and a minimum wage were too reformist, and claimed that capitalism forced women to work for a living. Men occupied the party's key leadership positions, leaving socialist women with little say in policy. When the party dropped suffrage from its platform at its 1902 convention, Bertha Merrill Burns was furious: "Not a woman delegate was present, not a woman's name appeared in the proceedings report and, apparently, not a woman's hand or tongue or brain in any way influenced the convention." She stayed in the party until 1907 but remained a vocal critic. Accusing some men of believing that they owned women and of treating them like children, Burns objected to the party's approach to its female members. Though it permitted women to join, some members argued that they should not vote on party policy, because they were not provincially or federally enfranchised. This attitude incensed Burns: "She is supposed to be incapable of forming convictions of her own on any subject under the sun, or of exercising the right of criticism for herself on any subject." The *Western Clarion* cancelled Burns's regular column in 1903, possibly because her criticisms did not go over well with party leaders.

All of this made it difficult for suffragists to determine how much they could rely on socialist support. The party often expressed hostility regarding the movement. A 1905 *Clarion* editorial stated that suffrage was imported from England and mocked Vancouver suffragists for imploring male politicians to offer them the vote. It labelled English suffragettes – many of whom were elite women – as "pillars and props of the capitalist system." And an unflattering 1907 column described them as bearing a "striking resemblance to a farm yard during the season when eggs are cheap." When the Vancouver Political Equality League asked for support, it was told that the party was not "violently opposed" to enfranchisement but that "we simply don't care a cuss ... We know only two kinds of people. Not men and women but masters and slaves." Nonetheless, the party's opposition was rooted in sexism, given its efforts to have its male candidates elected to office.

Even so, individual party members and elected politicians were often supportive. Dora and R.B. Kerr, who sat on the provincial executive of the Socialist Party of Canada, argued that women should not wait until the defeat of capitalism for enfranchisement. Two socialist MLAS – James Hawthornthwaite and John Thomas (Jack) Place – introduced five pro-suffrage private members' bills between 1906 and 1916. The Irish-born Hawthornthwaite worked as a real estate agent for a coal-mining company in Nanaimo before becoming a labour politician and a founding member of the Socialist Party of Canada. Although he believed that winning the franchise would not be enough to free women from economic dependence on the "master" class, he perceived it as an issue of justice and a sign of progress. He also felt that female voters were a potential "civilizing force" that would counter South Asian male immigration. He urged the legislature to reject partisanship in order to enfranchise working women, who were the "most oppressed of all." His Socialist colleague Parker Williams claimed that women's "greater purity and simplicity" might improve the tone of provincial politics.

The refusal of the SPC to officially endorse suffrage and other reforms such as old-age pensions, labour regulations, and access to education compelled Bertha and Ernest Burns to establish the Social Democratic Party of BC (SDP) in April 1907. The *Western Clarion* mocked its platform, especially its support for suffrage, in 1910: "Keep your eyes on the blackboard, boys! Our next number is a hell-cracker. Woman Suffrage! What an inspiring theme! ... How we have all dreamed of the day when woman would descend from her pedestal and take part in the more prosaic things of life!" Suffragists who joined the SDP found more room for participation. Bertha Merrill Burns was elected its recording secretary and was soon delivering public talks on socialism in Vancouver, as was Dorothy Parr, the suffragist daughter of founding members Louisa and Frank Parr. In October 1912, the SDP hosted a meeting on the

topic "Votes for Women" with Burns and two visiting British suffragettes, who argued that opposition to suffrage was rooted in a
conservative desire to protect the interests of business and property. The SDP women's branch included Burns and two working-
class suffragists from Victoria – Helen Christopher and Ada
Clayton – in executive positions. Burns was convinced that socialism was a viable alternative to capitalism, but she refused to
accept that women's liberation would easily arrive once socialism
triumphed. She chided those who believed that "when the working class shall have acquired possession of the means of production, and so attained economic freedom, ... nothing else is
necessary."

SUFFRAGE AND ORGANIZED LABOUR

Labour had a similarly complicated relationship with the suffrage
movement. After the federal Trade Union Act legalized unions in
1872, labour bodies were founded throughout the country. Many
Canadian cities had a Trades and Labour Council that represented
individual craft unions, with Vancouver and Victoria forming
their councils in 1889. The Trades and Labour Congress of Canada,
established in 1883, was a national umbrella organization for
labour, and the BC Federation of Labour, its provincial equivalent,
was created in 1910.

Although most unionized employees were men, labour increasingly supported suffrage and partnered with women's groups on
reforms that benefitted working women and families. Both saw
enfranchisement as a crucial way to improve the working conditions of women and were generally unified around demands for a
minimum wage, shorter working hours, health regulations, and
safety inspections. For their part, employers usually asserted that
women's low pay was justified because they would retire upon
marriage and be supported by men. But suffragists saw social
problems as stemming from what many described as starvation

pay and proposed a minimum wage and equal remuneration for equal work. In Vancouver, Helena Gutteridge worked tirelessly to bring together unions, socialists, and women's groups to lobby the provincial government. The LCW supported her visits to Lower Mainland factory workers and her recommendations to the 1913 Royal Commission on Labour Conditions in British Columbia.

But protective legislation that applied specifically to female employees was often double-edged. Working women certainly pushed for better pay, shorter hours, and Sunday store closures. However, the support for such measures was often grounded in fears that paid work would jeopardize women's futures as wives and mothers. Helena Gutteridge maintained that long working hours harmed women and led to "rapid aging [with] injurious effects on the next generation." This concern for women's maternal health reflected mainstream gender values, but it also allowed critics of capitalism to stress the toll that hard physical labour exerted on working-class bodies. Labour leaders sometimes supported a minimum wage for women because they believed it would prevent women's low-waged labour from undercutting men's wages. Achieving a family wage and preserving high wages for white settler men remained of utmost importance. Even Gutteridge drew on this rhetoric to win union support, telling the BC Federation of Labour in 1914 that a minimum wage for women benefitted men because it would prevent employers from using women as a supply of cheap labour.

Union support for reforms that targeted working women gradually translated into support for suffrage. In 1910, the Vancouver Trades and Labour Council and a number of locals endorsed it, followed one year later by the BC Federation of Labour. The federation hoped that female working-class voters would "support and expand working class pressure" on the state. But its relationship with suffragists grew fraught toward the end of the First World War for a number of reasons. The federation feared that women would deprive returning veterans of jobs and was critical of women's turn to the reformist Liberal Party when it adopted a pro-suffrage platform. In two 1916 editorials, most likely written by Parm Pettipiece, the *B.C. Federationist* denigrated suffragists as "noisy advocates" who had a "pet hobby." It blamed women for "invading" the labour force and stealing men's jobs, and for being "a bulwark of defense to everything that is conservative in political and industrial life." The paper did not report on the 1916 suffrage referendum or the enfranchisement bill of 1917. The fragility of alliances with socialist parties and unions explains why socialist and labour suffragists continued to work within independent women's organizations.

WORKING-CLASS SUFFRAGE LEAGUES IN VANCOUVER
The birth of focused suffrage associations in 1910 opened up the possibility of reaching larger groups of women. At the same time, the growth of Vancouver, now by far the biggest city in the province, shifted suffrage leadership from the older generation of middle-class reformers in Victoria to a younger generation of Vancouverites. Though it is difficult to assess their exact class background, many of Vancouver's highest-profile suffragists had worked for a living before marriage, had been taught a skill or a profession, or were married to skilled tradesmen, such as carpenters, printers, or machinists. They were part of a culture of skilled working-class families, generally of British background and often connected to trade unions, who perhaps lived in a single-family home in a respectable neighbourhood. Keenly aware that marriage would not protect them, they strongly believed that women must be economically independent.

Three individuals were the driving force behind the working-class suffrage movement: British-born Helena Gutteridge, American-born Susie Lane Clark, and Ontario-born Bertha Merrill Burns. A tailor and labour organizer, Gutteridge was one of the

Susie Lane Clark *(left)* and Helena Gutteridge at a CCF event in 1938.

few suffrage leaders who worked for a living. She was equally dedicated to enfranchisement and unionization, and her ability to bring together groups of women across ideological divides was key to suffrage success in Vancouver. Gutteridge worked closely with Susie Lane Clark, who had been active in the California suffrage movement, and Bertha Merrill Burns, a journalist. All three shared socialist sympathies and a commitment to combatting women's subordination. Burns was a lifelong Marxist, and Gutteridge and Clark later joined the social democratic Co-operative Commonwealth Federation (CCF). Gutteridge believed that organized labour was the best vehicle for the emancipation of working women, so she collaborated closely with union leaders. Clark felt a populist anger at the treatment of workers, whom she believed rarely received a fair deal, and decried the negative impact of monopoly capital on women and children. All imagined a different world in which women enjoyed political, economic, and social equality and where the exploitation of capitalism was eliminated.

Working-class and socialist women were active in suffrage movements across the country, though Vancouver was the only Canadian city with an independently organized suffrage league that was designed for and led by working-class women. The chance to build such an association was first seized by Gutteridge when Vancouver split from the PEL, becoming the Pioneer Political Equality League (PPEL) in 1913. Gutteridge immediately founded an Evening Work Committee, secured the Labor Temple in downtown Vancouver for its meetings, and published a short-lived newspaper. The committee met once a week, reportedly with an average attendance of a hundred women.

The Evening Work Committee was so successful that it declared autonomy from the PPEL in July 1913 and renamed itself the BC Woman's Suffrage League (WSL); its purpose was to appeal to working-class women and to seek union support for enfranchisement. A number of working-class and socialist women took on executive positions in the WSL, including Gutteridge, Bernice Panagopolous, and Mary Brennan. Among its members were Susie Lane Clark and socialist supporters Esther Crosfield and Nora Tutty. Neighbourhood leagues in Grandview and Mount Pleasant quickly emerged and affiliated with the WSL, suggesting that it was seen as the head branch of a larger network. The Mount Pleasant League was particularly active and was organized at the home of socialist Louisa Parr. Though open to all women, it focused on reaching out to those who lived in its largely working-class neighbourhood. Its leadership positions were held by socialist and working-class women, with Clark as its first president and Bertha Merrill Burns on its executive. Its members included Louisa Parr and her daughter Dorothy.

Organizers for both the WSL and the Mount Pleasant leagues attempted to lift barriers to working women's participation. Gutteridge acknowledged that women who earned a living had far less time to devote to the movement than did "women of leisure." The "parlour" meetings of mainstream suffrage groups were often held in private homes during the day, which meant that most working women could not attend. Nor would many have felt comfortable in breaching the class barriers of Vancouver society. Aware of this, the suffrage leagues met in public venues during the evening or on weekends. The Mount Pleasant League met on Monday nights at Lee Hall, and the WSL meetings were on Wednesday nights at the Labor Temple. Children were welcome, an acknowledgment that their mothers were probably unable to afford child care. The leagues also held open-air meetings on neighbourhood streets, handed out pamphlets on street corners, and entered a float in the 1913 Labour Day parade.

The leagues had their own organizational structure and working-class identity but were integrated into the larger suffrage scene. Their members regularly gave talks to the PPEL on women's unemployment, and they in turn hosted PPEL members at their own meetings. One WSL member, American-born Bernice Panagopolous, who was married to a Greek cook and who lived in Mount Pleasant, spoke throughout the city on suffrage and labour. Most suffrage socialists belonged to multiple associations, including socialist parties, unions, suffrage leagues, and women's groups. Helena Gutteridge willingly shared the stage with representatives from almost any organization, as long as they favoured enfranchisement and worked to improve the legal and economic status of women. Suffragists often worked together across class divides, especially after Gutteridge formed the United Suffrage Societies to bring the various Vancouver leagues into a unified lobbying body. This ability to collaborate was crucial to the success of the 1916 referendum campaign.

Despite these alliances, however, most middle- and upper-class women did not endorse systemic changes to capitalism. Throughout this era, the most common form of female employment was domestic service – a job characterized by low pay, long hours, and poor working conditions. Yet middle- and upper-class women seemed less concerned with the exploitation of servants than with the personal inconvenience of a servant shortage. The *Champion* supported domestic science education partly to reduce the stigma associated with such work but also to aid in the creation of "a class of helpers sadly needed" in the province. Because Chinese men worked in service, there was concern that not enough young white women were employed in the field. When servants themselves tried to organize – as they did in Vancouver's Home and Domestic Employees Union in 1913 – middle- and upper-class women came in for criticism. As union president Lillian Coote remarked, they happily took steps to address their own problems, but they ignored the obvious solutions to the exploitation of servants – shorter hours and higher wages – because these "touch[ed] their own pockets." And when working women or their husbands were on strike, they could not necessarily count on support from suffragists. For example, when female laundry workers went on a three-month strike in the fall of 1918, the wife of a laundry company owner, who was also a PPEL member, physically assaulted one of the strikers.

Burns, Gutteridge, and Clark used their connections with powerful Vancouver labour leaders to promote suffrage. The WSL allied itself with the labour movement and had won endorsements from sixteen local unions by late 1913 (including longshoremen, bricklayers, plasterers, painters, masons, and sheetmetal workers). The unions passed a resolution calling on Victoria to enfranchise women on the same terms as men. Burns and Gutteridge drew on their association with Parm Pettipiece, editor of the *Federationist*, and convinced him to publish a regular column to highlight

WSL activities. This column became the WSL print organ, calling for suffrage and discussing "issues that relate to women's place in the labour market." Clark and Gutteridge edited it at various times, and numerous suffragists regularly contributed to it. The column persisted until the First World War, when rising tensions over women's labour resulted in its cancellation.

The leagues also enjoyed extensive coverage in the *Vancouver Daily World* after its owner gave Susie Lane Clark a regular column, the "Suffrage Movement News." Launched in 1913, the column ran every week for more than a year, documenting the lively activities of local suffrage leagues and devoting extensive coverage to working-class activism. An early contribution came from Nora Tutty, who encouraged socialists to join the suffrage movement in order to "secure this tool for the work which we want done in the world." Worried that too many people on the left saw women's equality as secondary to the "great mission of Socialism," Tutty argued that enfranchisement would increase women's power and hasten the coming of socialism. "Delay no longer!" she exhorted her readers. "To quote the familiar slogan of Karl Marx: You have a world to win; You have nothing to lose but your chains."

The leagues argued that working women's interests were not well served in an unregulated economy or a patriarchal political order. The WSL believed that a working woman was doubly oppressed by both her class and her gender: "She is the bottom dog, her interests are not considered, point of view not represented." Gutteridge saw economic independence and the franchise as equally necessary and strongly believed that only collective action – in women's groups *and* in unions – would secure both. Like others of her time, she saw enfranchisement as a progressive force that would radically change power relations between women and men, and between workers and capital. "The woman and the worker stand side by side," she wrote in December 1913: the "women's movement and the labour movement are the expressions of a great revolutionary wave that is passing over the whole world."

League members pointed out that capitalism was structured and controlled by men and that it valued profit over decent living conditions and well-being; as Nora Tutty suggested, it sacrificed women and children on the "altar of mammon." Clark argued that male capitalists – whom she called the "money interests" – opposed women's political equality precisely because they benefitted from the "slave wages" they paid for women's labour. Similarly, Ida Douglas-Fearn believed that business owners resisted suffrage because they feared that restrictive labour laws would reduce their profits. A September meeting of the WSL erupted into an intense discussion about the root causes of the high cost of living, including the role of monopoly capital.

The leagues also concentrated on the daily problems that plagued the lives of working women and their families, and they detailed how poor pay and the high cost of living made it difficult for female workers to support themselves or their children without resorting to charitable aid. Starvation wages hindered the ability of women to survive independently of men and contributed to their entry into sex work. League members condemned the fact that poverty forced some women to surrender their children to institutional care. They also took up intensely local issues, such as fare increases on public transit, which made it difficult for women to commute to work affordably.

League members stressed the link between the profit-seeking goal of capital and poor child and maternal health. Bertha Merrill Burns had long made this a part of her socialist critique. "A woman buys sugar and finds it half sand; she buys milk made of half chalk and water," she wrote in 1902. "How then is a woman to provide pure food for her family? She can never do it so long as the present profit system prevails in our mercantile world." Similarly, Louisa Parr stated that under capitalism, "everything is made for profit and not for use" and that "it was time the women, who were the national housewives, were seeing to the production of better foodstuffs." Clark believed that women could be convinced of the need for suffrage by highlighting how the profit imperative in food production contributed to illness: "If mothers were awake to the fact that today everything is made for profit, and for that reason the manufacturer puts up every article as cheaply as possible, never considering the health of the nation, they would desire the vote so they could ensure better pure food laws."

Many women saw the appeal of this argument. Infant and maternal mortality rates were highest for Indigenous, poor, and working-class families, but no woman could avoid risk. In British Columbia, the rate of infant mortality was higher than the national average: 17 percent of children born in 1901 and 12 percent in 1921 died before their first birthday. These figures do not capture the number of miscarriages experienced by women who were vulnerable to disease, nutritional deficiency, and poor prenatal care. High infant mortality was connected to communicable diseases, such as diphtheria, measles, whooping cough, and tuberculosis, which were worsened by overcrowded housing and bacteria-ridden water and milk. Many suffragists had seen their own young children or those of a friend die from disease or had suffered from dangerous pregnancies. Margaret Jenkins lost six of her children to diphtheria, and Maria Grant, Laura Jamieson, Nancy Alexander, and Revelstoke suffragist Helen Sturdy had at least one child die in infancy. A member of the Victoria PEL study club spoke about the death of her infant daughter due to unregulated formula. She believed that women's political participation was necessary because "man was so liable to place commercial and private interest before the consideration of human life." Concerns about maternal and children's health were a response to suffering and to heartbreaking losses, and an attempt to value the bodies and well-being of children and women.

The WSL expected that enfranchised working women would collectively improve their own conditions of labour rather than allowing men of any class to define their needs. Because they were disenfranchised in relation to men, the "need for political power for the working woman [is] greater than that of any other class." Winning the vote would give them a voice and force governments to legislate solutions. But labour and socialist women also understood that mothers could not necessarily take on paid employment, so they supported social welfare measures such as mothers' pensions, which would serve the dual purpose of "relieving pressure in the labour market" and recognizing the "obligations of the husband and the state to the mother."

Suffragists were willing to collaborate with unions and socialists but did not hesitate to confront them if they derailed discussions of women's equality. Attendees at a league meeting might hear addresses from visiting socialists and labour leaders on issues including co-operative food pricing and the need for public utilities. But suffrage leaders pushed back if socialists tried to downplay the importance of women's enfranchisement. When a group of socialists disrupted a WSL meeting in 1913, Clark and Gutteridge made it clear that attempts to divert the focus from suffrage would not be entertained. Socialist Bernard Roseman's opinion that suffrage was a worthless "palliative," and that "raucous" suffragists should focus on collaborating with men to end capitalism, reflected a class politics that frustrated many suffragists. Clark published the letter he wrote to the *Daily World* but caustically suggested that such advice should be accompanied by a donation and reasserted her belief that enfranchised working women would offset the corrupt vote of male-dominated capital.

WOMEN AND COAL-MINING COMMUNITIES
Most working-class participation in the suffrage movement came from Vancouver women, but there was also some interest in

enfranchisement in the coal-mining towns on Vancouver Island. Coal mining first developed on the island during the 1870s, reaching a production height in 1911. Between 1910 and 1920, island mines employed about four thousand miners, and slightly smaller numbers worked in the hardrock mines of the Kootenays. Organizations such as the Miners' Mutual Protective Association (1877) and the Miners' and Mine Labourers' Protective Association (1890) emerged in Nanaimo, Ladysmith, and Wellington to improve the dangerous working conditions and raise the low wages of white miners. These bodies and later the Western Federation of Miners and the United Mine Workers of America supported numerous strikes from the 1870s through to an extended strike of 1912–14.

Workers in the coal-mining districts of Vancouver Island voted for politicians who promised to improve wages and broaden suffrage for men and women. In the 1890s, Vancouver Island miners endorsed the Nanaimo Workingman's Platform, which supported women's suffrage and a range of labour reforms. Suffragist Mary Ann Cunningham identified herself as an "independent" in opposition to the government and in support of this platform. Three candidates who were nominated by the Nanaimo-based Miners' and Mine Labourers' Protective Association ran on the platform and were elected to the legislature in 1890: miner Thomas Keith, former miner Tom Forster, and farmer Colin Mackenzie. All three advocated a range of reforms, including the single tax, and all voted in favour of women's suffrage bills. Liberal Ralph Smith of Nanaimo drew his political backing from the same region, which elected him to provincial and federal office. His approval of suffrage was rooted in his labour politics and coal-mining background, his Methodist faith, and his partnership with his wife, Mary Ellen. Support was especially high in and around Nanaimo, where 70.0 percent of the vote in the 1903 provincial election and 82.2 percent in 1907 went to labour and Socialist candidates combined. Socialist Party of British Columbia candidates Parker Williams and James Hawthornthwaite both lived in the Nanaimo area, and they consistently favoured suffrage while sitting in the legislature.

There is also evidence that the wives of Vancouver Island miners favoured female enfranchisement, a topic that may well have been part of the conversation because of the demographic makeup of the mining communities. Unlike most Kootenay miners, who were unmarried and transient European immigrants, Vancouver Island miners were mainly of British background. A significant minority of them – about 40 percent – were married and living with their families. Although women were not permitted to work in the mines, the men's low wages and dangerous working conditions directly affected them. In the midst of a March 1891 strike, a group of wives protested the death of a Wellington worker. During ongoing protests, about forty of them marched in support of suffrage, the first such public demonstration in the province.

During the 1912–14 coal strike led by the United Mineworkers of America, Vancouver Island mining towns were subject to state violence, mass arrests, and the imposition of martial law, with over a thousand soldiers stationed in Nanaimo. Women from the United Mineworkers Women's Auxiliary harassed and attacked company managers and strikebreakers, though their gender protected them from arrest. A few suffragists publicly sympathized with the plight of mining families, spoke in favour of the strikers, and criticized state violence. Gutteridge supported the miners at a protest rally in Vancouver, and Esther Crosfield joined a group of socialist supporters protesting at a Conservative Party meeting, where she handed out suffrage leaflets to those in attendance. Bertha Merrill Burns attempted to convince readers of the *Vancouver Daily World* that the deployment of the militia was a terrible expense that all "taxpaying women" should criticize.

Sympathetic labour activists connected the exploitation of miners with the political exploitation of women. A *B.C. Federationist* column linked the incarceration of miners in Nanaimo with that of suffragettes in England: "The miners of Nanaimo and their parliamentary representative also, are getting an object lesson on the state of the jails in British Columbia. The revelations made by suffragettes who were sent to prison in England have caused the reform of many abuses." Laura Jacobs of Nanaimo wrote a passionate column for the *Federationist*, sympathizing with the miners and their wives. Comparing miners to chattel slaves, she suggested that women were in an even worse position because at least the men could vote. Jacobs argued that the strike had "awakened" island women, whom she believed would "fight for emancipation at the ballot box. The mothers of the new century will be strong and free, their children glad and happy. The mothers of Vancouver Island are already organizing towards a purer, safer, nobler heritage on God's beautiful earth." After the strike ended, the *Vancouver Sun* and the *Federationist* quoted coal-mining wives who claimed that it had inspired them to support suffrage because enfranchised women would force mine owners to apply safety standards. Sympathy for mining communities notwithstanding, however, there is little evidence that the mainstream suffrage movement made any formal connections to mining women. Nanaimo did have a middle-class WCTU, but the region had no independent suffrage league to unite women across class divides.

Suffrage rhetoric commonly emphasized the importance of women's role as wives and mothers. But the BC movement had become deeply concerned about the exploitation of working women by the turn of the century, and it was influenced by socialist and labour critiques of capitalist profit and wage labour. Working-class, socialist, and labour suffragists argued that working women must win the vote to achieve liberation as workers, women, and citizens. Although socialist and working women were active in the movement across the province, Vancouver suffragists created the deepest formal connections with labour, and it was there that women founded an independent and visible working-class suffrage movement.

The news that reaches us from various corners of the world as to the extraordinary progress of the Woman's Cause should be an incentive to every suffragist in B.C. to spur her or him on to determined effort. The women of this Province are surely at least as capable of conducting a Political campaign as the women of other lands, and one can hardly believe that the men have so little of the pioneer spirit, or so little sense of the dignity of their women-folk, as to be content that they should eventually be cast ashore in lifeboats, so to speak, rather than ride triumphantly into harbour on the crest of the wave of this great Movement.

– EDITORIAL,
CHAMPION, NOVEMBER 1913, 3–4.

SEVEN

A GLOBAL
MOVEMENT

Kang Tongbi (1881–1969) was born in Guangdong, China,
to reformer Kang Youwei. She travelled globally with her father,
often acting as his interpreter, and undertook her own North
American speaking tour in 1903, organizing the Chinese Empire
Ladies Reform Association in Victoria. She studied at Barnard
College between 1907 and 1909. Returning to China after the 1911
revolution, she wrote articles for a women's newspaper, led an anti-
footbinding campaign, and authored a biography of her father.

WHEN WELL-KNOWN British suffragette Barbara Wylie toured Canada in 1912–13, she expected to find a sleepy suffrage movement waiting for militant British women to inspire it into action. Upon her arrival, however, she was met by enthusiastic and articulate audiences that were well versed in British militancy and its relationship to political conditions in Canada. Speaking in Victoria, Vancouver, and New Westminster, Wylie delivered a clear justification of the suffragette strategy. "We are at war with the men," she stated, and "we are destroying property and we will continue to destroy it until we obtain our rights." Many wondered whether Canadian women should follow suit. Wylie herself was uncertain, but she insisted that "if window breaking is necessary to obtain the vote, why, the Canadian women must smash windows." BC women never did smash windows, though they were inspired by suffrage triumphs around the world as they debated how to force their own governments to enfranchise women.

During the first two decades of the twentieth century, suffrage seemed to be within sight as New Zealand, Australia, Norway, and neighbouring American states granted it. This message of global progress was spread by a growing number of women who toured internationally and spoke to suffrage leagues in the province. Many suffragists were inspired by the British movement and sympathized with the direct actions of the Women's Social and Political Union. And they were attuned to victorious American campaigns in California, Oregon, and Washington. They also turned their eye to the burgeoning women's movement in China, which successfully fought for increased political rights.

Suffragists identified as members of a larger global community, albeit one that was limited by class, race, ethnicity, and national origin. But where did they learn about global suffrage? Although some wealthier women travelled to conventions outside the province, most learned about international suffrage at public talks or through newspapers. By the 1910s, suffrage societies were hosting visits by international speakers that instilled a sense of being part of a modern, global, and unstoppable movement. Audiences in cities and towns across the province could learn about custody and divorce law in British Columbia, footbinding in China, and suffragette militancy in Britain. Media coverage allowed suffragists to assess global tactics, understand their place in world events, and imagine themselves as part of a larger community, even if they never left home.

TRAVELLING SPEAKERS
As BC suffrage organizations grew, they hosted famous speakers from around the world. Among them were Americans Dr. Anna Howard Shaw, Charlotte Perkins Gilman, Jeannette Rankin, and Susan B. Anthony. Celebrated suffragettes Emmeline Pankhurst, Emmeline Pethick-Lawrence, and Barbara Wylie also spoke, as did Canadian reformers such as Nellie McClung. Suffragists also enthusiastically attended talks by lesser-known activists. And though most speakers confined their visits to the Lower Mainland or Victoria, the interior welcomed a number of them: between 1913 and 1918, the Revelstoke Political Equality League, for example, hosted talks by McClung, Pankhurst, Cecilia Spofford, and Miss Pease, who was visiting from Bristol, England. The tide of speakers reached its height in 1913, just before the First World War made international travel difficult.

The first suffrage speaker in the province was Susan B. Anthony, who came to Victoria during the fall of 1871 as part of a speaking tour of the Pacific Northwest managed by Oregon suffragist Abigail Scott Duniway. She delivered four public lectures in

Alhambra Hall. The press covered her talks, but Anthony and Duniway were dismayed by the unexpectedly small turnout of about a hundred people, only a small proportion of whom were women – press reports indicate that about twenty attended each lecture. Perhaps neither woman fully understood the demographics of the region – its white settler population was small, with only a tiny middle class. But Duniway commented on the interest shown by Victoria's black community; familiar with Anthony's anti-slavery and women's rights work, its members arrived "in force to every lecture."

Despite her disappointment, Anthony delivered rousing speeches, which generated detailed press write-ups and spurred debate. A seasoned speaker, she knew how to orate with finesse and humour, even when her points were serious. She suggested that women's political citizenship could end war and that women should have the legal right to separation and divorce. During her third lecture, she deliberately took a provocative stance, repeating stories about Victoria women being flogged by their husbands. This strategy increased the size of the audience for her final lecture. Anthony's deeply ironic style was in full force when she pretended that women in Victoria enjoyed being physically abused. Every time she made this claim, the crowd roared back "No!" along with applause and laughter. When Anthony reported that "there was no town in America in which wives got so many floggings as in Victoria," the audience was "convulsed in amusement."

Her listeners may have been enthusiastic, but the press was ambivalent. The *Colonist* headline, "Victoria: A City of Woman Whippers!" suggests that the paper did not take Anthony's accusations of domestic violence particularly seriously. The paper printed letters in opposition, several of which resorted to gendered insults. One woman suggested that a woman's true job was "submitting herself to her husband," and another dismissed Anthony as a "shrewish mischiefmaker ... content to make her more fortunate sisters miserable by creating dissension in their households." "An Insulted Husband" called her a "sexual mistake," and "A Male Biped" maintained that women were "physically unfit to perform the avocation of men." And "Minnie" stated that most men were too "gentlemanly" to challenge Anthony and that "met with the opposition of an intelligent woman ... her arguments would be upset."

Minnie would probably have been delighted to learn of the opposition that dogged Anthony's footsteps, a determined nemesis in the figure of Oregon anti-suffragist Jennet (Jo) Blakesley Frost. Resolutely opposed to suffrage, she followed Anthony throughout the tour and heckled her continuously during the lectures. Frost cast aspersions on Anthony's unmarried status and called her an "old maid who had neglected to fill the office in society for which God ... had wisely created her." For her part, Anthony dismissed Frost as the "weakest and silliest acting and talking woman I ever saw." After engaging in public showdowns at agricultural fairs in Washington state, Frost came to Victoria in January 1872, where she delivered three lectures that were marketed in opposition to Anthony. She attacked Anthony's ideas as "calculated to destroy society, civilization and religion, and to degrade womanhood." When she described suffrage as a "calamity" that would devastate the nation, she was met with cheers, applause, and "shouts of 'hear hear.'" The *Colonist* sided with Frost and stated that suffrage was "causing many women in the States to neglect their household duties and babies and become politicians." Apparently, however, Frost left Victoria in disgrace, having failed to pay a local merchant for a purchase of clothing.

The talks by Anthony and Frost were the only major public lectures on suffrage delivered in British Columbia during the 1870s, but newspapers reported on the movements in Britain and the United States. And the formation of women's organizations during the 1880s placed BC suffragists within international circuits of speakers from Australia, the United States, and Britain. Eventually, conventions with international delegates visited the

Born in Ireland, Patience "Lilla" Swanton (1863–1934) married Robert Scott Day, an architect and civil engineer, in 1888 and emigrated to British Columbia in 1891 after living in South Africa. She was on the executive of the Victoria LCW and was involved in the National and International Councils of Women, the Alexandra Club, the IODE, and the relief committee of the Canadian Patriotic Fund during the First World War.

province. When the National Council of Women had its annual convention in Vancouver in 1907, the delegates held public meetings and visited nearby cities. In 1909, when the International Council of Women hosted its annual conference in Toronto, suffragist Lilla Day was the sole provincial delegate and one of only nine Canadians in attendance. An LCW member, Day belonged to the Victoria elite and was wealthy enough to make the trip to Toronto. Dr. Anna Howard Shaw gave a keynote address that was printed in the *Colonist,* accompanied by a poetic ode to women's voting: "Let those who oppose take warning/And keep this motto in sight/No question is ever settled/Until it is settled right."

After the conference, a group of delegates embarked on a twenty-five-day train trip across the country, stopping in present-day Thunder Bay, Winnipeg, Regina, Calgary, and Edmonton before heading to the coast. In Vancouver, Marie McNaughton secured funding from city council and organized a mass meeting at the downtown Opera House, where 1,700 women and men heard the delegates speak on global suffrage achievements. The rhetoric of Canadian advancement was wrapped in admiration for the British Empire, the stage was draped in a Union Jack, and the meeting ended with the singing of "God Save the Queen" and "The Maple Leaf Forever."

The delegates then took the ferry to Victoria, where the lieutenant governor held a reception whose guests included socialists Dora and R.B. Kerr, Dr. Etta Donovan, Margaret Jenkins, Cecilia Spofford, and May Fraser Tolmie, daughter of early suffrage ally William Tolmie. The *Colonist* posted a journalist to interview the delegates about the suffrage movement as they toured the city by streetcar. The paper was enchanted with Chrystal Macmillan, a well-known Scottish lawyer whom it described as "tall and muscular," "keen in intellect," and able to command attention. Though the paper took pains to note that she was not a suffragette, Macmillan declared that militants deserved respect for their "courage in facing ridicule, abuse, and misrepresentation," and foretold suffrage success in Great Britain.

The regular press coverage of British debates about suffragette militancy made a huge difference in the public's exposure to the global movement. Visiting British suffragists helped organize local leagues and inspire women. In 1911, members of the Vancouver PEL came to hear Mrs. Brignall, of the National Union of Women's Suffrage Societies, speak about the differences between constitutional reform and direct action. The militant Women's Social and Political Union (WSPU) was well represented by visits from Barbara Wylie, Emmeline and Frederick Pethick-Lawrence, and Emmeline Pankhurst. When WSPU member Dorothy Pethick gave a talk in Vancouver, the tickets sold out so quickly that many members of local leagues could not obtain one. British speakers addressed constitutional reform, militancy, global activism, and almost every other topic of interest to Canadian suffragists.

British suffragists were not alone in providing encouragement. The ease of movement across the American border enabled BC suffragists to call on Americans for support and solidarity. Famous speakers Anna Shaw, Jeannette Rankin, and Charlotte Perkins Gilman provided symbolic inspiration and generated mass enthusiasm. But meetings with American suffragists from states in which women had recently won the vote were a more regular source of inspiration. After Washington state enfranchised women in 1910, its suffragists travelled north to give public addresses and to support local organizations. Adela Parker, a Seattle lawyer and publisher of the *Western Woman Voter,* was a popular visitor who delivered talks to provincial leagues and accompanied them on delegations to lobby the premier. In summer 1913, she gave a series of public lectures in Vancouver, Coquitlam, and New Westminster on the successful campaigns in Oregon, Washington, and California, arguing that everywhere suffrage had been introduced, the social order had been improved. She described suffrage as a "western movement" that was both "sane" and effective in its methods. Suffrage organizations were also delighted to showcase male political allies from Washington, which had recently enfranchised women at the state level. The advent of the First World War slowed the frequency of public events, but years of listening to international speakers helped local suffragists hone their own skills of argumentation, which were pulled into service during the referendum campaign of 1916.

"DEEDS, NOT WORDS": BRITISH MILITANCY

The growth of suffragette militancy in the United Kingdom helped determine how BC suffragists imagined their own activism. The WSPU was founded in 1903 by Emmeline Pankhurst and a group of socialist women in Manchester, England. Adopting the motto "Deeds, not words," the WSPU condemned the sexism of all political parties and was designed to disrupt politics through direct action until the vote was won. The mass parades, physical and verbal confrontations with politicians, property damage, and arson generated a violent police and state response (arrest, assault, and forced feeding in prison) that shook conventional assumptions about how far women would go to secure political equality. The press was fascinated and repulsed by militant women marching

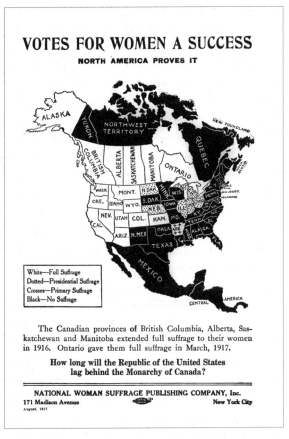

VOTES FOR WOMEN A SUCCESS

NORTH AMERICA PROVES IT

White—Full Suffrage
Dotted—Presidential Suffrage
Crosses—Primary Suffrage
Black—No Suffrage

The Canadian provinces of British Columbia, Alberta, Saskatchewan and Manitoba extended full suffrage to their women in 1916. Ontario gave them full suffrage in March, 1917.

How long will the Republic of the United States lag behind the Monarchy of Canada?

NATIONAL WOMAN SUFFRAGE PUBLISHING COMPANY, Inc.
171 Madison Avenue   New York City
August, 1917

The acquisition of suffrage was often portrayed as a global race between nations. According to this 1917 poster from the National Woman Suffrage Association, an American group, the fact that some provinces in Canada (a constitutional monarchy) had passed suffrage legislation while many states in the American republic had not is presented as politically embarrassing.

in the streets, spitting on politicians, and breaking windows. Were they inhuman Amazons? Overtaken by hysteria? Although the portrayals of suffragettes were often negative, Canadian suffragists would use that fascination to their own advantage.

Many were sympathetic to the suffragettes, but the BC leagues developed the strongest sense of solidarity with them. Before they emigrated to British Columbia, a number of British-born suffragists had witnessed or participated in direct action, or they had friends and family members who were affiliated with the WSPU. Leading Victoria suffragist Margaret Pethick was the sister-in-law of the famous Emmeline Pethick-Lawrence, and both she and her husband, George, were in close contact with the WSPU. Most BC leagues adopted the official WSPU colours of purple (dignity), white (purity), and green (hope), whereas those in other provinces opted for the American combination of gold and purple. The use of the simple and striking WSPU colour scheme could transform almost any object into a recognizable symbol of militancy. Leagues made tri-coloured banners, sashes, badges, and ribbons, sold them

Emmeline Pethick (1867–1954) was born in Bristol, England. Influenced by socialism and Methodism, she did volunteer work for a Methodist mission in London. She married Frederick Lawrence (1871–1961) in 1901, and the two merged their surnames, becoming the Pethick-Lawrences. Emmeline was the WSPU treasurer, and Frederick acted as its legal adviser. They founded the WSPU newspaper Votes for Women in 1907. The Pethick-Lawrences were jailed in 1912 during the WSPU window-smashing campaign, after which they came to Victoria to stay with Emmeline's brother Harold and his wife, Margaret. They were expelled from the WSPU in part because they had expressed reservations about its tactical use of violence. Emmeline was involved in the international women's peace movement during the buildup to the First World War and ran for office as a Labour Party candidate in 1918.

to raise money, and distributed them at exhibitions and public meetings. Even the petitions presented to Premier McBride were wrapped in purple, white, and green ribbons.

Suffrage leagues hosted talks given by militant British women. During a visit to Victoria, Emmeline Pethick-Lawrence detailed the failures of the British government and stated in an interview that suffragettes would rather die than "surrender." In the fall of 1911, the infamous Emmeline Pankhurst came to Victoria on a North American speaking tour. She believed that Canada was "ripe" for the leadership of militant British women. In actuality, the BC movement was curious but circumspect about how militancy applied in Canada. Her lecture, titled "The Militant Methods of the Suffragettes in England," was chaired by Maria Grant and delivered to prominent local citizens, including Mayor Alfred Morley and Agnes Deans Cameron. After acknowledging that not everyone would approve of direct action, Pankhurst declared that media reports of violence were sensationalized, that suffragettes had attempted peaceful methods, and that she "did not think that the legislators of Canada would ever be so hard upon women as had been the Liberal government in Great Britain." Her talk inspired Victoria suffragists to set up a WSPU-affiliated branch at the home of Dorothy Davis, with Margaret Pethick as its first president. It did not last long, but its existence demonstrates a strong sense of solidarity with, and admiration for, Pankhurst and the suffragettes.

Suffragists were further informed about WSPU activities during a 1912–13 Canadian tour undertaken by Glasgow organizer Barbara Wylie. The WSPU may have chosen her for the tour because her brother was a Saskatchewan MLA or because she had been part of the delegation that confronted Prime Minister Robert Borden during his 1912 visit to London. After joining the WSPU in 1909, Wylie had been imprisoned and had participated in a hunger strike. But she seemed to know little about Canada, and her focus on the federal vote ignored the constitutional relationship between the provinces and Ottawa. In Vancouver, she insisted that she would lead a delegation to the capital to force Prime Minister Borden to grant the federal vote. Her tour was anticipated by the local press shortly after she set sail from Britain. One paper warned that a "hysterical suffragette" was headed for Canada and joked that when "the suggestion was made that she might be refused a landing, her reply was 'we still have aeroplanes.'"

Wylie visited Toronto, Ottawa, Montreal, Winnipeg, New Westminster, Vancouver, and Victoria. She was unapologetically militant, informing the *Vancouver Daily World* that "moral suasion" was not a useful tactic in the "war" with men. She firmly believed that the British government would grant suffrage only if forced to do so and that only full citizenship would end the "sex war" between men and women. She lauded aggressive measures and attacks on property, telling a New Westminster audience that "it was only by making themselves unpleasant that they could hope to get what they wanted." She urged suffragists to "make the homes and businesses of men uncomfortable."

Wylie's talks attracted media attention because they promoted attacks on property, but militancy was not her only topic. She also drew on liberal humanist ideals to argue that "when citizenship is conferred on women the attitude of the sexes will be changed. Men will treat women as their equals, not as their toys or chattels." Wylie spoke about unequal pay and the relationship between poverty and high infant mortality. And she pointedly noted that working-class men held a degree of political authority as voters and union members, whereas women had little collective power, regardless of whether they were workers or mothers.

When Wylie spoke on two consecutive nights at the Vancouver Labor Temple, local papers described the meetings as overflowing, with people jammed into "every conceivable nook" and women "sitting on the floor around the speaker." Audience members cheered in agreement with her points or shouted their opposition.

Leading male suffrage supporters such as Anglican minister Henry Edwards and Dr. Ernest Hall were present to offer encouragement and to take up collections for the WSPU. The New Westminster Political Equality League invited Wylie to speak, and the turnout was "attentive and appreciative." She was well received by the *New Westminster News,* which stated that she was so charming, eloquent, and humorous that "almost every reasonable person now admits that there is certainly much to be said in favour of the militant methods." Her speech in Victoria was chaired by Socialist MLA Parker Williams, and though the editors of the *Champion* carefully stated that most Canadian women did not approve of militancy, they believed that Wylie's speech "aroused a good deal of sympathy" and made some converts.

Even as BC suffragists expressed their opposition to violent tactics, they insisted that suffragettes were fighting for a just cause. Florence Hall criticized militant tactics as misguided because they might alienate sympathetic allies and make political women look undignified. Furthermore, as a devout Christian, she felt that women should not emulate men's "brutality" or do anything that might bring harm to others. Even so, she believed that suffragettes courageously made sacrifices for the greater good of womankind and that their actions were "brave and dauntless and even heroic." Victoria's Elsie Baer did not endorse their tactics, but she believed that suffragettes "redeem[ed] the womanhood of England from the loathsomeness of apathy and indifference." In 1913, the Port Coquitlam PEL declared support for the "action of the militant suffragettes in England."

Most BC suffragists echoed Hall and Baer's ambivalence regarding political violence, framing it as the reluctant response of women who had been pushed too far by the failures of the parliamentary system. As one suffragist asked in 1912, "Can we condemn militancy in those who for fifty years have without avail petitioned Parliament to amend laws which permit such evils and such miscarriage of justice?" Although the language of being pushed into radicalism underplayed suffragette choices, it allowed sympathizers to express solidarity without breaking entirely from respectable womanly behaviour.

Even in otherwise cautious organizations, women contradicted propaganda that portrayed the suffragettes as hysterical and out of control, and instead emphasized the suffragists as heroic and brave freedom fighters. When Marie McNaughton spoke to a middle-class audience at the Canadian Club in Victoria, she mentioned that she knew many suffragettes and believed them to be courageous women who were "enduring a great deal for the sake of the freedom of womanhood." PEL president Maria Grant claimed that she did not support militancy but added, "I stand ... with uncovered head and without censure before the brave women who are fighting so fearlessly, fiercely for imprisoned womanhood and childhood." Suffragettes were often likened to Christian saints or martyrs such as Joan of Arc , heroically sacrificing their bodies for women's liberty. Ida Douglas-Fearn's poem in the *Vancouver Daily World* was dedicated to militant suffragettes, whom she addressed as "our saints, our martyrs/In whose great fellowship we crave some part."

Other suffragists explicitly justified the necessity of property violence in Britain. Dorothy Davis presented an apologia for direct action to an audience in Kelowna, arguing that attacks on property were "necessary" to call attention to police violence against suffragettes. Perhaps Rose McCready, a Kelowna suffragist, sat in the audience that day. Two years later, she delivered a lecture detailing her memories of the violence at WSPU protests in England. From her perspective, the militants were "ingenious and tactical" operators whose actions demonstrated the underlying violence of the police and the state. Bertha Merrill Burns pointed out that "persons deprived of a ballot logically use a brick. After all Mrs. Pankhurst is no more 'unwomanly' than Joan of Arc, to whose memory we build statues."

Most BC suffragists were frustrated with media stories that exaggerated the extent of militancy and focused "the limelight" on a small group of people. They encountered similar sensationalism during the summer of 1913, when they themselves were accused of torching a tree in Stanley Park and setting fire to Selkirk Hall, the Revelstoke theatre. Such rumours, which were stoked by reports of arson in Britain, confirmed their fears of unfair media coverage. At a September 1913 debate, Helena Gutteridge voiced her ongoing frustration: "The one fly in the ointment at these meetings," she said, "is that some are insisting on bringing up the subject of militancy ... But what has militancy to do with votes for women in B.C.? What?"

Suffragists debated the pros and cons of militant tactics until the advent of the First World War. In May 1914, for example, the PEL hosted a meeting to debate whether it should adopt more confrontational methods. Suffragists often insisted that violence was not necessary in the province – at least, not yet. Most politicians would not have missed this equivocal note: if respectable women in Britain could be pushed into violence, might government stubbornness produce the same result in Canada? As Maria Grant told Premier McBride in 1913, "if many of them are growing impatient and rebellious it can hardly be wondered at." When these meetings with McBride failed, Davis informed him that "never again ... would the women come to the government in the same way." It would be more pleasant for the government to enfranchise women without further struggle, she told McBride, apparently adding with a smile, "Not that we have any intention of adopting the tactics of militancy."

Suffrage leaders always kept in reserve the possibility that they might ultimately resort to more disruptive and militant tactics. The mainstream media's preoccupation with direct action suggests that anti-suffragists were indeed worried about this prospect. For example, the editor of the *Victoria Week,* William Blackmore, called for a boycott of the PEL because of Davis's vocal sympathy for militancy, and he mocked the Pankhurst family and made fun of British hunger strikers. Developments in Britain and expressions of admiration for suffragettes seemed to spark fears that if Canadian women were not granted the vote, they too might be pushed into similar action.

TRANS-PACIFIC CONNECTIONS

After 1910, BC suffragists also turned their attention to the growing women's movement in China. Although they typically opposed Chinese emigration to Canada, they admired the leadership of Chinese women and came to celebrate China as emblematic of political modernity. Suffragists were introduced to members of the Chinese women's movement when reformers and revolutionaries visited Vancouver and Victoria to build diasporic support for political change at home.

Why did so many Chinese activists come to British Columbia at this time? During the mid- to late nineteenth century, the ruling Qing Dynasty (1644–1911) struggled to maintain its hold on power. By 1898, reformers had failed to create a constitutional monarchy or make liberal reforms to the Chinese economic, political, and educational system. In the years leading up to the Chinese Revolution and the establishment of a republic (1911), exiled reformers such as Kang Youwei and Liang Qichao, as well as revolutionaries such as Sun Yat-Sen, fought for control of China's future. British Columbia was an important stop on their North American lecture circuit, as they attempted to win support from the diaspora.

Reformer Kang Youwei (1858–1927) visited Canada at least six times between 1899 and 1909. During his first trip, he founded the transnational Chinese Empire Reform Association (CERA) in Victoria, which supported political reform and a constitutional monarchy, and called for the end of discrimination against Chinese immigrants in North America. CERA eventually had more than 160 branches in North America, Asia, Australia, and Africa.

Treated as a celebrity, Youwei addressed large audiences in Vancouver, Victoria, and New Westminster, speaking about responsible government, decreased immigration restrictions, work mobility for Chinese labourers, the end of footbinding, and financial independence and higher education for women. His reform work was given a feminist spin by his second daughter, Kang Tongbi. She and her elder sister, Kang Tongwei (who published the women's newspaper *Nü Xue Bao*), spoke multiple languages and received extensive higher education. Tongbi accompanied her father on his travels, acting as his interpreter, and her own lecture tour of 1903 began with a two-week stay in Victoria and a series of public lectures about women in the Chinese reform movement.

Her first order of business was to connect with Chinese women who lived in the province. Due to racist immigration policies, their numbers were tiny, and they were mainly the wives or domestic servants of wealthy merchants. Fragmentary evidence suggests that a small group of wives in Vancouver, Victoria, and New Westminster, including Mrs. Chan Sing Kai (Kate), wife of Methodist minister Chan Sing Kai, engaged in philanthropic and reform politics. While in Victoria, Kang Tongbi organized the Chinese Empire Ladies Reform Association (CELRA), which quickly expanded, setting up chapters in Vancouver, New Westminster, Seattle, Portland, Chicago, and New York. Two surviving copies of posters for the Victoria and Vancouver CELRA branches feature the group's larger political aims and document its membership. The reformist Guangxu emperor appears at the top, under which are images of reformer Kang Tongbi and prominent local Chinese women. By October, the Vancouver CELRA "ladies" were participating in community events and had an executive structure in place. The poster tells us that CELRA championed the political and civic responsibilities of women in building a strong nation-state. Using language that BC suffragists would have recognized, it links CELRA members to heroic, brave, and accomplished women around the world, including Joan of Arc, Sophia Perovskaia, the revolutionary

The Chinese Empire Ladies Reform Association was founded
by Kang Tongbi in 1903. Two chapters were set up in British
Columbia – one in Victoria and another in Vancouver. Members
included the wives and daughters of leading Chinese merchants.
This poster shows the images and names of the women involved
in the Victoria chapter. The reformist Guangxu emperor appears
at the top, flanked by Kang Youwei (on the right) and fellow
reformer Liang Qichao, a journalist (on the left). Kang Tongbi
is pictured in the centre, below the emperor.

who assassinated Czar Alexander II, and Feng Liao, a diplomatic envoy.

Did the women of CELRA support women's suffrage? There is no definitive record that they did, but the possibility is not unlikely. For example, Kate Chan was active in the movement after her family relocated to Portland in 1901, where she attended suffrage events with her daughters. The family's Methodist faith and Kate's training as a physician make it likely that she nurtured sympathy for suffrage before moving to the United States. By 1905, Vancouver CERA members were sufficiently well versed in the women's rights movement to devote much of a December meeting to a discussion on suffrage, which unfolded "with considerable animation." Whether CELRA pushed CERA to debate this issue is not known, but the men would certainly have heard reformers speak approvingly of women's rights. The meeting ultimately concluded that despite their reform work, Chinese Canadian women were not "ready" for suffrage, because they had not yet developed "sufficient knowledge of the public questions."

British Columbian newspapers were fascinated by politics in China and covered many of the talks given by reformers on the Pacific Coast and elsewhere in North America. The San Francisco chapter of CERA sponsored lectures by Sieh King King, a San Francisco student and "new woman" from Shanghai, who supported reform and described footbinding as an "injustice to our sex." Journalist Mai Zhouyi (Mrs. Loo Lin, a "new woman" who edited the *Lingnan Women's Journal*) addressed Victoria audiences in 1903, as did Li Sum Sing, an editor at the *Chinese Mail*, in 1908. Mai Zhouyi was on a North American tour to proclaim women's equality. "My dear sisters," she told her audience in California, "we are human beings, not to be compared to animals or goods. We must work together so that we can stand in equality and liberty." The North American press was often ignorant of Chinese women's reform activities and tended to claim that every Chinese woman it covered was speaking publicly for the first time. The *Colonist* reported on Kang Tongbi in typically Orientalist terms, declaring incorrectly that her 1903 lectures were the "first occasion on which any Chinese woman has been known to speak in public."

Chinese "new women" typically invoked progress, equality, and modernity, rhetoric that was familiar to North American suffragists. They also believed that women had important roles to play in modern nation-building projects, as well as the right to economic independence and higher education. British-born and Canadian-raised writer Edith Eaton (Sui Sin Far), who moved to the United States in 1896, exemplifies the complexities of this reformist world. She criticized the individualist aspects of the American suffrage movement and praised the contributions of Chinese women to modernization, including dress reform, opposition to footbinding and arranged marriages, and access to higher education. As the Victoria CELRA poster asserted, "In the rise of the country or its fall, men and women share equal responsibility."

Because they identified Chinese immigration as a threat, members of the BC suffrage movement never reached out to the Chinese women who lived in the province. But by the 1910s, they had learned to see women in China as the embodiment of modernity. They were particularly interested in developments in Guangdong province between 1911 and 1912, where the government had briefly instituted enfranchisement unrestricted by gender, property, or education and had also introduced a quota of ten female representatives in the provincial assembly. Though the National Parliament soon reversed these measures (and returned them in some provinces only during the 1920s and nationally in the 1940s), this initial success evoked both admiration and envy in North America. "Even China is ahead of us," wrote the *Champion*, because the country had "openly recognized the equity and advisability of calling upon her women as well as her men to take their share in the direction of national affairs, and China will therefore rise, not sink, in the scale of nations." The 1907 lectures given by British Baptist missionary and suffragist Mrs. J. Creasey Smith in

Vancouver reached a similar conclusion. Smith and her physician husband had moved to Shenshi in 1898 to work at its mission hospital, and North American audiences were eager to hear her speak about Chinese feminism and political reform. Smith condemned Western prejudice and noted that Chinese women were well versed in projects of women's higher education and anti-footbinding. She tended to see the Chinese reform movement as proof that suffrage had reached the "Celestial Empire," but she did admit that true change in China had come from the hard work of women themselves. Although Smith, Kang Tongbi, and the members of CELRA were separated by nationality, race, language, and religion, they all shared an interest in political developments in the trans-Pacific world and the place of North America within it. The work of Chinese reformers in criticizing racial and gender inequality helped lay the groundwork for Chinese Canadian activism that would continue into the enfranchisement campaigns of the 1940s.

As suffragists researched women's inequality, exchanged information, and met or read about other women who were working for change, they became convinced that winning the vote was the inevitable outcome of humanity's progress toward equality. Despite their optimism, however, the Conservative government in Victoria remained stubbornly opposed to suffrage. The resignation of Premier McBride in 1915 and the looming provincial election initially brought hope for a political shift. But the government proved disappointing yet again, and suffragists entered 1916 with a new and unwanted problem: a referendum in which male voters would decide the fate of women's political citizenship.

Whereas, the British Columbian legislature has passed a bill submitting the question of woman suffrage to a referendum of male voters ... and whereas, such a proposal is an insult to women, and the women of British Columbia would make themselves contemptible if they took any notice of such a referendum; therefore, the Equal Franchise League of Kelowna hereby resolves that it will have nothing to do with the proposed referendum.

– KELOWNA EQUAL FRANCHISE LEAGUE,
VICTORIA DAILY TIMES, 21 JUNE 1916, 13.

EIGHT

ACHIEVING
THE VOTE

Vote for Woman's Freedom

THE WOMEN OF BRITISH COLUMBIA, WANT THEIR POLITICAL
FREEDOM BECAUSE

1. If woman has to obey the laws it is only just that she should have a voice in making them.
2. Woman's influence would be increased and laws for woman's protection would be more easily secured.
3. As Political Rights make man nobler, so they would make woman nobler also.
4. The Ballot is an educator. Woman needs the education of the ballot, the world needs the education of the woman's ballot.
5. Woman can better protect her home interests.
6. Woman has borne her share of the toil, suffering and loneliness in the pioneer work of this Province and she ought to have a voice in how it is governed.

WOMEN ARE FREED FROM POLITICAL SLAVERY IN NORWAY, SWEDEN, FINLAND, NEW ZEALAND, AUSTRALIA, TASMANIA, ISLE OF MAN, UTAH, WYOMING, COLORADO AND IDAHO, WITH THE RESULT THAT THE LAWS ARE BETTER AND CONDITIONS IMPROVED.

GIVE THE WOMEN THE BALLOT

In the buildup to the 1916 referendum, suffrage groups issued
propaganda that urged men to vote in favour of it. This placard
drew on almost every rhetorical argument from forty years of
suffrage activism. It was probably published and distributed
by the provincial Suffrage Referendum Association.

IN THE SPRING of 1916, Vancouver suffragists held a meeting at the local Labor Temple to protest the Conservative government's planned referendum on female enfranchisement, which would accompany the upcoming provincial election. Mary Ellen Smith, a Liberal, predicted the defeat of the government and also warned the male electorate that "if the men of British Columbia fail to give the women the vote this session, they will have written their epitaphs for themselves on their own tombstones: 'Unwept, unhonoured and unsung.'" Smith's prophecy proved to be partially accurate: the Conservatives lost the fall election, but the referendum passed with a healthy majority. In the aftermath of the election, Maria Grant described the victory as an out-of-body experience and said that she "took three days to come back to mother earth."

The referendum victory came after long years of hard work and political organizing. Indeed, after the Political Equality Leagues were founded throughout the province, suffrage had seemed to be gaining in popularity. But the advent of the First World War had halted this momentum as women concentrated on the war effort. With the resignation of McBride in 1915 and the government on the verge of collapse, suffragists hoped to convince the new Conservative premier William Bowser to introduce enfranchisement legislation. Disappointingly, however, Bowser declined, promising instead to present a suffrage bill only if the (male) electorate voted in favour of it. Though they were critical of the undemocratic nature of a referendum in which only men could vote, suffragists nonetheless campaigned to support it in the summer of 1916. The resulting victory and subsequent legislation were cause for celebration, but the success was partial in many ways. Suffragists had to push Ottawa to expand the federal franchise, and the government's 1917 response was limited to women who served in the military or were related to enlisted men. Wide-ranging racial exclusions remained in place. And even after African Canadian and Euro-Canadian women won the right to vote and run for office, breaking into electoral politics proved difficult, and they were consistently under-represented as candidates and office holders.

THE FIRST WORLD WAR

With well-organized suffrage leagues and support from clergy, unions, and politicians across the province, the long years of campaigning seemed to be bearing fruit by 1914. But the outbreak of the First World War dramatically slowed the movement's momentum. Some suffragists were highly critical of the war, with a few, such as Helena Gutteridge, opposing militarism and speaking out publicly against conscription. In the lead-up to hostilities, international suffrage groups had highlighted the importance of peaceful arbitration in resolving conflicts between nations, and the women's peace movement deplored the impact of war on women and children. In 1913, Susie Lane Clark noted that women were getting "wise to this war game" and added that "mothers should guard against the jingoism of politicians who endeavour to stir up false patriotism." She believed that the day would come when a mother no longer saw it as her "patriotic duty to put the sword into her son's hand." Florence Hall took pride in women's homefront work but was horrified by war's devastation: "We firmly believe that if the women of these warring countries had possessed the power of the ballot, this awful slaughter of precious life would never have clotted the twentieth-century civilization."

Fissures among feminists ran much deeper in Quebec, where riots against the profoundly unpopular policy of conscription were met with police violence.

But most Anglo-Canadian suffragists believed that women had a patriotic duty to back the war effort, and they curtailed the enfranchisement campaign while they focused on volunteer work. Talks by visiting suffragists tailed off, as transatlantic travel became increasingly dangerous and difficult. Emmeline Pankhurst diverted her energy from suffrage into building support for the war effort, and her 1916 visit to the West Coast barely touched on the vote. Political Equality Leagues across the province gathered every week to sew and knit clothes for soldiers or for people in German-occupied areas, but they did not entirely abandon their interest in the vote. In Creston, PEL members met to knit while they discussed suffrage and debated the "subject of the war." In August 1914, just as Canada was gearing up for war, Mary Ellen Smith went on a suffrage lecture tour in the Fraser Valley. According to Susie Lane Clark, her efforts demonstrated that the issue would not be "relegated to the background ... While assisting in this calamity as much as possible, women still must insist on having their political rights."

Although the war diminished the singular focus of suffrage activism, the high profile of women's voluntary work bolstered their demands for political citizenship. And even if women did not serve on the front lines, they too bore the cost of war, fearing for the safety of their loved ones and experiencing poverty while the main breadwinners were away. Without the vote, Clark argued, women had no control over important political decisions, "which so vitally affect them." Many suffragists would have agreed, as their sons, husbands, and brothers enlisted in the military and were often injured or killed in action.

PARTISAN POLITICS AND THE REFERENDUM
Political change was imminent by the time the referendum was

announced. The boom economy fuelled by land speculation and railway development had collapsed by 1913, and the province entered an economic depression characterized by high levels of debt and unemployment. The Conservative Party machine, built by McBride and Attorney General William Bowser through extensive patronage, was accused of corruption. Pushed by the Liberal Opposition and facing a general election, McBride resigned and was replaced by Bowser. Although the war had dampened their activism, suffragists optimistically secured a meeting with Bowser to lobby for his support of the private member's bill introduced by Socialist MLA Jack Place. But instead of endorsing the Place bill, Bowser promised to introduce one of his own, which would allow women to vote on the same terms as men. However, there was a catch – he would take this step *only* if the electorate approved of it in a province-wide referendum.

Most suffragists were furiously opposed to the referendum. Although prevalent in Western American states, referendums were not common in Canada except at the non-binding municipal level. The Pacific Coast states had all employed referendums to decide on suffrage (Washington in 1910, California in 1911, and Oregon in 1912). Idaho and Montana had done the same in 1896 and 1914. But there was no guarantee of success. In Oregon, for example, four referendums had failed between 1884 and 1910. Outcomes were closely contested: suffrage passed with only a 52 percent majority in Oregon and just 53 percent in Montana. Of greatest concern, however, was the fact that only registered voters could participate in a referendum. By opting for this approach, the BC government made it clear that male voters alone would decide the fate of women's political citizenship.

Moving swiftly, a delegation of thirty suffragists headed by Helen Gregory MacGill confronted the premier in April. They argued that women's rights should not be tied either to a general election or to a referendum and bemoaned the energy wasted on a referendum campaign instead of the war effort. But Bowser repeated the usual arguments, saying that women "had a long way to go before they had equal privileges with men." The hope that the Conservatives would introduce legislation was dashed when Jack Place's bill was defeated on second reading. Bowser then scheduled the referendum on women's suffrage and prohibition as part of the general provincial election that was slated for September 1916.

The situation was complicated by the Liberal Party's endorsement of suffrage and by its ascendency as the vehicle of reform under its social gospel leader, Harlan Brewster. With the election imminent, suffragists faced an important decision: should they maximize their chances by campaigning for both the referendum and the Liberals? Doing so would compromise their commitment to non-partisanship and risk introducing divisions among their supporters. If they poured their energy into electing the Liberals and lost both the election and the referendum, the triumphant Conservatives could potentially retaliate. Others worried that the Liberal promise of enfranchisement was grounded largely in political expediency. A number disliked the Women's Liberal Association because it funnelled the attention of suffragists into partisan politics and because it was dominated by elite individuals such as Evlyn Fenwick Farris, who had once been reluctant to support enfranchisement.

Suffragists debated these hard questions during the spring of 1916. Despite their general distaste for a referendum, they had some cause for hope. Suffrage was now supported by a wide range of clergy, labour leaders, politicians, media, and women's groups, including the formerly nervous National Council of Women. Furthermore, the national and international political landscape was shifting in favour of women's rights. Women had voted in municipal elections and served as school trustees throughout North America. Suffrage had been achieved in all the Pacific Northwest states, a number of European countries, Australia and

New Zealand, and in Guangdong, China. By the time Bowser committed to a provincial referendum, hopes had been bolstered by success in Manitoba, Saskatchewan, and Alberta, all of which granted suffrage between January and April of 1916.

In May, the BC PEL called an emergency meeting in Vancouver to decide how to proceed. A number of groups remained outraged: Mary McConkey, president of the PPEL, and Mrs. W.F. Gurd, president of the Equal Franchise Association, "stated that their organizations would not lift a finger to secure the passing of the referendum." The Kelowna PEL, led by Dora Kerr, also refused to participate. Unsurprisingly, the Women's Liberal Association dismissed the referendum as an attempt by a Conservative government to delude women and decided to concentrate on the election of Liberal candidates. After two days of intense disagreement, most suffrage groups opted to form a united front and established the Suffrage Referendum Association (SRA) to spearhead their campaign.

With fanfare, the SRA was officially launched on 1 June 1916 at the Labor Temple, and the Vancouver branch soon became the dominant force in the province. After being elected secretary, Anna McIntyre quickly wrote a constitution and set up standing committees on organization, voters' lists, meetings, literature, and publicity. Louise Bryan, an Ontario-born WCTU organizer and honorary president of the BC PEL, was elected chair. The SRA founded over twenty local committees throughout the province. The sheer size of Vancouver necessitated a set of six committees, broken down by ward and co-ordinated by the Vancouver City Central Woman's Suffrage Campaign Organization, which was led by Helena Gutteridge and Susie Lane Clark.

The SRA branches threw themselves into their work. Press reports confirm that Lower Mainland branches, especially those in Vancouver, Burnaby, and New Westminster, held meetings, concerts, and fundraising parties every week. The SRA had fortnightly meetings in Vancouver, and members travelled widely to give talks and drum up support. Vancouver lawyer and Conservative Leon Ladner accompanied Liberal Mary Ellen Smith "all over the Lower Mainland and other parts of British Columbia" in a "little T Ford which chugged and bumped over the rough roads." Ladner addressed a Young Conservative Club with the classic maternalist argument that women would bring "purifying power" to politics. He also evoked women's patriotism, telling the audience, "While our fathers and our brothers and our dear ones are shedding their blood to preserve civilization on the battlefields of Belgium, us men of British Columbia here at home, whether Liberal or Conservative, join hands by granting a vote to your women, heroes at home." SRA members spoke to church congregations, community groups, and political meetings, secured a tent at the Vancouver Exhibition, and bought placards on local streetcars to advertise the cause.

The SRA quickly initiated a province-wide propaganda campaign, printing posters and handouts that summed up the reasons for awarding women the vote. It sent thousands of flyers to soldiers at recruiting stations and at military encampments in England and across the country. It wrote to newspapers in the interior, asking that they print the text of the proposed bill, which was entitled the Woman Suffrage Act. The *Hedley Gazette* even published a friendly editorial, suggesting that "the ladies cannot make a poorer selection of [cabinet] material ... than their fathers, husbands, sons and brothers have done."

Suffragists used every available argument to persuade the electorate. The placard titled *Vote for Woman's Freedom,* which is pictured at the beginning of this chapter, boldly demanded "GIVE THE WOMEN THE BALLOT," followed by a list of justifications including women's right to political representation, maternal protection of the home, and "pioneer" toil. The Victoria SRA mailed

out circulars at the beginning of August that drew heavily on
maternalist arguments, suggesting that the branch believed
Victoria men might be most open to that form of persuasion:

> We do not claim that equal suffrage will be a panacea for all
> ills, but simply that it will bring about a fairer and more
> evenly balanced administration of affairs. It is just because
> men and women are different that women should have equal
> opportunity with the men to bring their own point of view
> to bear on the many political questions which affect them
> so vitally.

The SRA argued that wherever suffrage was granted, birth rates
increased, child mortality rates and government debt dropped,
and legislation that benefitted women and children was put in
place.

The SRA was truly a big-tent organization, bringing together
men and women, Liberals and Conservatives, Catholics, Jews, and
Protestants. Mrs. J.O. Perry, a WCTU member and a Catholic Liberal
supporter, headed the public meetings committee and often
spoke at them herself. The first chair of the Provincial Women's
Suffrage Referendum Association in Vancouver was lawyer and
former Conservative politician Sir Charles Hibbert Tupper, who
had become a strong critic of the corruption in his old party.
Encountering some resistance to his style of chairing the initial
meeting, Tupper quickly resigned. Regardless, the SRA was proud
of the support from prominent men and encouraged voters to
"show the whole civilized world how they stand by their women –
by rolling up a big majority on the suffrage question." Men took on
suffrage leadership roles in a new way as they headed up committees and addressed audiences. Ladner served on the Joint Finance
Board of the SRA along with Isaac Rubinowitz, a Vancouver Jewish

defence lawyer who was a Rhodes scholar, McGill law school graduate, and head of the local Red Cross. Rubinowitz also had labour credentials, defending Nanaimo miners who were arrested during the coal strike and speaking at events for the Independent Labor Party. The SRA headquarters worked from an office donated by prominent businessman and prohibition supporter Jonathan Rogers. Well-known Conservative MP H.H. Stevens, Socialist Lyle Telford, and numerous municipal politicians offered their services as volunteers and public speakers. Supportive clergy preached sermons in favour of suffrage. Accompanied by music, singing, and recitations from local performers, including Helen Badgley, Kitsilano Congregational pastor A.E. Cooke used the Bible to prove women's equality. His sermon was so "splendid" that he was asked to repeat it (which he did shortly afterward). A social gospeller who was critical of capitalist exploitation and land speculation, Cooke had authored a popular pamphlet charging McBride and the Conservatives with corruption.

Conservative candidates also seemed supportive, perhaps in recognition that the tide was turning and that they were in danger of losing the election. In New Westminster, the local SRA was chaired by the enthusiastic Mr. W.F. Hansford, secretary of the Conservative Association, who arranged debates between Conservative and Liberal candidates, usually with additional speeches by suffragists. At the August Conservative Club debate in New Westminster, Liberal David Whiteside took on Conservative candidate Thomas Gifford, who declared himself in favour despite having voted against the suffrage bill in the spring. Across the province, Conservative candidates now agreed that women deserved the vote and praised their contributions to society. At the Conservative campaign rally in Kelowna, the mayor shouted down hecklers as he introduced Premier Bowser and complimented women's presence in the audience. A Conservative paper, the *Cranbrook Herald* endorsed suffrage by asking, "Is the vote of a drunken miner or lumberjack better than the vote of a hard-working and respected woman?"

The campaign of the Victoria SRA branch was more muted than that on the Lower Mainland. Headquartered on Fort Street, the branch was chaired by lawyer Richard T. Elliot, with a small but active group of suffragists. It founded two subcommittees, one to seek out the opinions of socialists, unions, and political candidates, and another to obtain the co-operation of local organizations. The Victoria branch published circulars encouraging people to support suffrage because political women improved the standard of living, women had contributed to the war effort, and "our women are by birth, breeding and education, universally intelligent and sound enough in mind to use the vote sensibly." It placed regular ads in the Colonist, requesting more help from the community.

Although Victoria had a long tradition of suffrage activism, the media paid little attention to the referendum campaign. Nor was the Victoria SRA as popular as its Vancouver counterpart. Just two weeks before the election, the Liberal Party held a rally in Victoria, which was attended by so few women that the Liberal candidate commented on their absence and expressed disappointment at the presence of "so few ladies." In early September, the PEL was still encouraging Victoria women to step up their activism, saying that though their minds might be "at present occupied with other matters" – probably referring to the war effort – they should still take the referendum seriously. Why the Victoria campaign was somewhat lacklustre is unclear. Perhaps the city was more conservative than Vancouver; the returns for the referendum showed that its support for enfranchisement was lower than in the province as a whole. Also, suffrage leadership had largely shifted to Vancouver by this point.

Despite the involvement of Liberal supporters, the SRA remained officially non-partisan, and most branches hosted talks by Liberals, Conservatives, and Socialists in hopes of winning over all potential voters. Helena Gutteridge and Maria Grant addressed Liberal, Conservative, and Social Democratic Party rallies and spoke alongside all supportive political candidates. Mrs. D. MacLachlan of the Victoria SRA joined Social Democratic candidate George Winkler at an August 1916 Miners' Union meeting in Cumberland. Grant addressed a Conservative rally in Esquimalt, stating that the war had "brought a change in the feeling towards women and that it had effected a realization of their ability to take their part in the upbuilding of the nation." She also emphasized women's war work to a Conservative rally attended by Bowser, claiming that it revealed the ability of a woman to stand "beside her men folk in the time of stress." Of course, many suffragists chose to campaign for the Liberal Party and spoke glowingly of its record. Mary Ellen Smith travelled ceaselessly to Liberal meetings on Vancouver Island and the Lower Mainland. But Helena Gutteridge remained defiantly non-partisan, even when pressed to declare her affiliation. She insisted that referendum campaigners endorsed no political party and added that, in her opinion, "one party was as bad – or as good – as the other. Both were ready at all times to adopt reform legislation if it suited their purposes."

Despite all the evidence of support, suffragists walked a fine line during this period. No formal anti-suffrage campaign emerged, but opposition persisted among some politicians, media, and unions. Although some local Trades and Labour Councils pledged their support, the BC Federation of Labour attempted to persuade male workers that women were taking advantage of wartime conditions to steal their jobs. The *Colonist* remained opposed, arguing that the vote was a privilege, not a right, and that men should grant it to women only if it benefitted the "public interest." Neither the *B.C. Federationist* nor the *Colonist* devoted much space

to the referendum campaign. Speaking to a Methodist congregation in New Westminster, Gutteridge mentioned the "unbounded
confidence that the movement was to be strikingly successful,
which was heightened daily and hourly by the inclusion of prominent men of both political parties." But she warned women to
stay "vigilant" and hardworking, and not to "become too optimis-
tic in respect to the outcome." Similarly, the editors at the *Vancouver Daily World* cautioned suffragists not to be too "sanguine,"
because a quiet but real opposition to enfranchisement did exist
in the province.

As referendum day approached, the SRA recruited women for
training in election procedures and to act as scrutineers at polling booths. A total of 103 women (and a lone man) volunteered
in Vancouver, as did 30 in South Vancouver, 30 in Burnaby, 29 in
Revelstoke, and 29 in North Vancouver. Scrutineers came from
wide-ranging backgrounds: some were working class, some were
elite, and some were mother-daughter teams. In Vancouver's
working-class Ward 5, twenty-two female scrutineers, including
Susie Lane Clark, "marched in formation" to the polls, where men
who were waiting to vote greeted them with "three cheers." A
team of female scrutineers in New Westminster proudly posed for
a portrait in the local newspaper. The SRA also recruited female
scrutineers to work the polling booths set up for the soldiers who
were stationed at military camps around Vancouver. Eventually,
every ballot had been cast. All that remained was to await results.

The final count revealed that 70 percent of the electorate had
opted for suffrage: 43,619 voted in favour, whereas 18,604 voted
against. Although the margin of victory was not as great as many
had hoped, it was a clear majority and certainly more decisive
than that of many neighbouring American states. The results
also showed the regional basis of support. Overall, 67 percent
of Vancouver men voted in favour, whereas only 57 percent of

Victoria men did. On the whole, rural citizens chose suffrage in higher proportions than did urban voters. In Revelstoke, the pro-suffrage vote doubled the opposition, and in miner-dominated Cumberland, it was almost triple. Vancouver Wards 5 and 6, where Susie Lane Clark and Gutteridge had deep roots, voted over 70 percent in favour. But the result was not solely class-based; other Vancouver working-class districts voted over 60 percent against suffrage. The soldier vote, delayed because of problems counting the overseas ballot, was tighter than the provincial one, with 8,273 in favour and 6,002 opposed. Perhaps these differing outcomes were linked to the depth of campaigning in certain locations or neighbourhoods. Or perhaps the soldiers associated suffrage with the referendum question on prohibition, which they did not generally support. Regardless, the results showed beyond doubt that the majority of BC voters now approved of female enfranchisement.

Overjoyed, suffragists wanted the government to introduce legislation as soon as it took office in November 1916. When this had not occurred by mid-February, the Political Equality League and the Vancouver-based United Suffrage Societies co-ordinated a joint delegation to "speed" legislation forward. Sixteen suffragists asked Brewster to introduce legislation, advocate for the federal franchise, and propose an infant guardianship act. Ultimately deciding not to wait until all the overseas returns had been counted, the Liberal government soon passed a bill giving women the franchise and the right to run for office on the same terms as men, made formal on 5 April 1917.

The amendment to the Provincial Elections Act was met with delight, but the celebrations underlined suffrage critiques of partisan politics. Brewster invited prominent Liberal suffragists to the floor of the legislature while leaving their non-Liberal colleagues to watch from the galleries. Liberal supporters Mary McConkey and Helen Gregory MacGill offered flowers to the premier and

Attorney General J. Wallace Farris. Wallace's wife, Evlyn Farris, took centre stage, and some resented that she claimed credit for the success of a movement she had previously shunned. An angry Susie Lane Clark wrote a scathing letter to the *Vancouver Province,* stating that Farris had "never been an active suffrage worker" and that victory had not come "through a small coterie of women working for a political party." In Victoria, Maria Grant registered similar complaints, noting that neither Farris nor the Liberals should take credit for suffrage success – it sprang from hard work and numerous factors, including the non-partisan nature of the movement.

That the Liberals wanted to claim the suffrage triumph for themselves is clear in their treatment of Maria Grant, who had remained non-partisan throughout the campaign and who was not acknowledged in the public festivities. Her friends in Victoria rectified this slight by holding a reception in her honour. The members of the now defunct PEL wrote their own congratulatory proclamation, tied it in a purple, white, and green ribbon, and asked Elsie Baer to read it aloud. Baer praised Grant's "beneficent influence and power," her "faith in woman hood," and her "consistent and unremitting labour ... to obtain women's political representation." The *Colonist* remained virtually silent regarding the referendum victory and the ensuing celebrations, probably because it had endorsed the losing Conservative Party. After the election, it published a short editorial, neither congratulating nor encouraging newly enfranchised women but condescendingly schooling them on how politics functioned in a democracy.

ELECTION AFTERMATH
Winning the referendum did not end questions about women's political citizenship. Nor did it undo the race-based exclusions from the vote. By the end of the war, most provinces had enfranchised women, with New Brunswick and Prince Edward Island

soon following, though Quebec women would have to wait until 1940. Furthermore, being entitled to vote provincially did not automatically make one eligible for the federal franchise. In 1917, the Borden government introduced the Military Voters Act, which permitted women serving in the military (including nurses) to vote federally, and the Wartime Elections Act, which enfranchised the female relatives of overseas soldiers. These two pieces of legislation enfranchised approximately 500,000 Canadian women, even as Ottawa employed the Wartime Elections Act to disenfranchise many men who had been born in "enemy" nations but who had been naturalized after 1902. Although this measure was repealed when the war ended, the wives of naturalized enemy aliens faced additional hurdles in getting their names on the federal voters' list, including a requirement for a special certificate issued by a judge. These obstacles affected a significant number of women who had immigrated from Germany and eastern Europe.

Furious that the legislation excluded the majority of white settler women, BC suffragists pressed Borden to change it. Victoria suffragists denounced the Wartime Elections Act as "contrary in its spirit to the freedom for which we as a nation are today making great sacrifices." In Vancouver, fifteen members of the United Suffrage Societies confronted MP H.H. Stevens at his office and argued "back and forth" with him about the act, which he defended by stating that the inclusion of "alien" female voters could be dangerous. His listeners refused to accept this justification, suggesting that denying patriotic women the federal franchise was profoundly unfair. They were deeply disappointed in Stevens, feeling that he had "fallen down" on suffrage after volunteering for the Suffrage Referendum Association. Vancouver's recently established New Era League wrote to federal politicians and Prime Minister Borden, calling the act a "gross, flagrant injustice" that excluded loyal Canadian women. In May 1918, the Dominion of Canada finally extended the federal franchise to female British subjects, but it maintained the racial restrictions set by the provinces. And the legislation arrived too late for women to vote in the December 1917 federal election, an important wartime contest that returned the Unionist government of Robert Borden to power.

After April 1917, women were able to run for municipal (with property restrictions), provincial, and, soon after, federal office. The election of Mary Ellen Smith to the provincial legislature in 1918 – and her later appointment to a cabinet position – seemed to foretell a new era in which enfranchised women might work at the highest levels of political power. Smith ran as an Independent Liberal in a federal by-election and soon joined Liberal ranks as the first female MLA in British Columbia and only the second in Canada. Suffragists were overjoyed, and hundreds of women turned out to fete Smith at receptions in her honour. Her victory had enormous symbolic value. She was showered with praise and presented with two particularly meaningful gifts from her fellow suffragists. The first was a gold and diamond medallion inscribed with her name and those of her "willing workers" from Vancouver's suffrage leagues. Presented to Smith at her home before hundreds of well-wishers, it showcased the images of women's equality and liberty: a laurel-crowned figure of victory was engraved in the centre, and the entire medal was edged with laurel leaves. A second gift came from Victoria, where suffragists designed a large floral ship of state, reminiscent of the one carried by Maria Grant on her many trips to the legislature. Built of purple, white, and green flowers, it also sported three miniature flags (the provincial Coat of Arms, the Union Jack, and the Canadian Red Ensign). Smith brought it with her to a final luncheon hosted by Susie Lane Clark and the United Suffrage Societies, where it sat as the centrepiece at the table of honour. After a standing ovation, Clark remarked that Smith's election win was "second in importance only to the gaining of the franchise itself." Woman after woman stood to toast her fearlessness and courage. Pledging herself to improving society and sponsoring effective legislation, Smith challenged women to stay political in a feminist way, by "learning the game, but never lowering their standards."

Smith proved to be a popular MLA and was re-elected in 1920 and 1924. Her politics were well received by the reformist Liberals, and she worked closely with Attorney General Farris to sponsor legislation that was favoured by women's organizations, labour, suffragists, and reformers. In 1921, she became the first woman in the British Empire to be appointed as a cabinet minister, though she had no portfolio and thus lacked the influence she had hoped for. Smith soon resigned her cabinet post, saying, "I have been in the unfortunate position of having to assume the responsibility of actions of the government without being in a position to criticize or advise."

Despite the hopefulness of Smith's electoral victory, women remained under-represented both as candidates and elected officials. Only a few ran for office during the interwar period, comprising about 4 percent of all candidates. They achieved some success at the local level. In 1918, the Kootenay town of Kaslo, which had an active Political Equality League, became the first in the province to elect women to municipal council – of the six who ran, two were elected. In 1928, Alice Ashworth Townley became the first female commissioner of the Vancouver Park Board, and in 1937, Helena Gutteridge was the first woman elected to Vancouver City Council. Not until 1944, when Stella Gummow was elected reeve of Peachland, would a woman head a municipal government. In Ontario, Agnes Macphail was elected MP in 1921, but the country waited fourteen years for the next – and British Columbia sent a woman to the House of Commons only when Co-operative Commonwealth Federation (CCF) candidate Grace MacInnis was elected in 1965.

Running for office under the discipline and structure of a party was often unappealing to suffragists, many of whom maintained a strong attachment to independent and non-partisan politics. Esther Crosfield and Cecilia Spofford ran as Independents, and Maria Grant founded the non-partisan Women's Independent Political Association in Victoria to sponsor women for local elections throughout the 1920s. The National Council of Women continued its stance of non-partisanship, telling delegates at its annual meeting in 1917 that women should vote in unity on issues that related to women and children, rather than supporting the traditional parties. That year, the council put forward a "Women's Platform," which called for state-funded social welfare programs, along with nationalization of coal and certain food industries. But women who ran provincially with party backing achieved the greatest success. Even so, only seven were elected to the BC legislature between 1918 and 1949; three ran for the Liberals, three for the CCF, and one for the Conservatives. All but one represented Vancouver.

By the early 1930s, a number of former suffragists had found a more welcoming home in a new party – the CCF. Its broad-based approach to socialism appealed to suffragists, many of whom had struggled to find a comfortable space in male-dominated socialist parties. Gutteridge was elected to city council under the CCF banner, where she tried unsuccessfully to convince her colleagues to end property qualifications on municipal voting and to establish social housing. Her long-time collaborators also joined the CCF and ran for office: Clark was elected to the Vancouver Park Board in 1937 and again in 1938, and Laura Jamieson won a seat in the provincial legislature three times (1939–41, 1941–45, and 1952–53). As members of this generation took on greater responsibilities in the party, they worked with younger socialist MLAs such as Grace MacInnis, Dorothy Steeves, and Mildred Osterhout, all of

In the 1941 provincial election, twelve women ran for office and
five were elected. Three successful candidates, all representing
the CCF, are pictured here. From left, Laura Jamieson (Vancouver
Centre), Dorothy Gretchen Steeves (North Vancouver), and Grace
MacInnis (Vancouver Burrard).

whom had benefitted from the intersection of suffrage with
labour and socialist politics.

During the post-suffrage era, only a few female candidates
won office, and many former suffragists expressed disappointment
about women's lack of representation. This under-representation
was true for white women of British background, but the political
barriers encountered by racialized and Indigenous people were
even higher and longer lasting. The suffrage movement did not

fight for the enfranchisement of these groups. In the end, it was racialized and Indigenous people themselves, and the community organizations they built over time, who finally forced the provincial government to remove racial restrictions on the vote after the Second World War.

Isn't this what we have been clamoring for the last 100 years? Clamoring for the removal of a false racial barrier? Now this may be the turning point in our long history. We are stepping on the threshold and there is no turning back.

– WILLIAM FREEMAN,
KLEMTU BC, *NATIVE VOICE*, MARCH 1949, 2.

Chinese have lived and worked in B.C. for 90 years. We are proud of our record as citizens and taxpayers. The vote is coming to us, and now at last I think we're going to get it.

– GORDON CUMYOW, ON THE MUNICIPAL VOTE,
VANCOUVER PROVINCE, 7 SEPTEMBER 1948, 2.

NINE

EXTENDING SUFFRAGE

Born at Nass Harbour, Frank Calder (1915–2006)
was sent to the Coqualeetza residential school and
received a theology degree from the University of British
Columbia in 1946. He was working in a cannery when he won a
CCF seat in the provincial legislature in 1949, the first
Indigenous person to do so. He served on the Nisga'a
Tribal Council (1955–73) and was awarded the
Order of Canada in 1987.

IN APRIL 1949, over thirty years after the 1916 suffrage referendum, Indigenous residents in the Gitksan village of Kispiox (north of present-day Hazelton) gathered to register their names to vote for the first time in an upcoming provincial election. The long day of registration included guest lectures by prominent activists and was followed by a celebratory banquet prepared by the Native Sisterhood. A reporter from the *Native Voice* spoke to Isaac Skulsh, the "oldest man" in his village, who said, "I never thought I would live to see this day." His son Walter, a member of the Native Brotherhood of British Columbia, explained, "My father is walking in a dream today." Both Walter Skulsh and long-time suffragist Maria Grant described winning the franchise in evocative terms: for Skulsh, it was like a dream; for Grant, it was a euphoric out-of-body experience.

Although suffrage victories were emotionally, symbolically, and politically meaningful, they were not the end of the story. In 1917, the women's movement understood that the suffrage legislation had not eradicated gender inequality. Former suffragists immediately developed new associations to educate women about the importance of the vote and to press the provincial government to implement legal and workplace reforms, especially mothers' pensions and a minimum wage. Women also used their newly acquired power to demand participation in the organizational structures that administered and monitored reforms related to women and children.

The victory celebrations of 1917 ignored the continued disenfranchisement of Indigenous and Asian people. Along with

Saskatchewan, British Columbia was the only province that with-held the vote on the basis of race, and its racial exclusions were the most extensive in Canada. The Dominion Elections Act of 1920 stipulated that anyone who was barred from voting provincially would not be permitted to vote federally, meaning that posses-sion of the federal franchise depended on both race and regional location. After many years of campaigning, the BC government finally enfranchised First Nations, Japanese, Chinese, and South Asian Canadians, removing race-based barriers by 1949. But like women's suffragists before them, the activists of the 1940s knew that achieving the provincial vote would not solve all problems of social, political, and economic inequality.

POST-SUFFRAGE ORGANIZING

Delighted though they were by the 1916 referendum result, suf-fragists knew that having the vote would not automatically lead to women's equality. Suffragists focused their energy on new in-itiatives, such as the New Era League and the Voters Education League, both of which emerged in Vancouver and concentrated on non-partisan lobbying and political education. Established in 1916, the New Era League was the longer-lasting organization. Presided over by Susie Lane Clark, it enjoyed support from a range of women, called for mothers' pensions, and defended relief camp strikers during the Great Depression. Some older groups remained active, including the Pioneer Political Equality League and the United Suffrage Societies. The Revelstoke Women's Forum was established in the fall of 1916 in response to the referendum. Headed by suffragist and former teacher Helen Sturdy, it educated women on the practical details of how to get on the voters' list, the status of reforms undertaken by the new government, and larger questions about the "duties arising out of the parliamentary fran-chise." Such associations were intensely interested in voter educa-tion: everything from how to volunteer as a scrutineer at a polling booth, to run for a municipal board, or to help with an election campaign. In 1919, the Local Councils of Women banded together to found a provincial council to consolidate and push for more reforms. Many former suffragists retained their commitment to non-partisanship, working with LCWs, the CCF, churches and synagogues, and members of the Communist Party of Canada – especially the Women's Labour Leagues – on Vancouver's Mothers' Council, established in 1935, to support unemployed relief camp strikers.

This newly developed confidence was evident in the birth of organizations such as the National Council of Jewish Women, which founded a Vancouver local in 1924. By this time, the city's small Jewish population had founded synagogues and a Ladies Aid Society. Like other women's groups, the local council embraced the language of democracy and citizenship rights, and it established a Neighbourhood House (1926) to assist immigrants and a well-baby clinic (1927). Professional women organized into Business and Professional Women's Clubs, setting up branches in Victoria in 1921 and Vancouver in 1923. Encouraging women to vote and run for office, the clubs also played an important role in advocating for pay equity. But they were conservative in other ways, focusing mostly on white-collar, professional, and middle-class members and excluding Asian women from their ranks until 1929. Local Councils of Women, the National Council of Women, and members of the University Women's Club became increasingly involved in the international peace movement, hoping to avoid a repeat of the First World War. Progressives such as Laura Jamieson and Helena Gutteridge worked with the Women's International League for Peace and Freedom, espousing its critique of the connections between capitalism and war. The Vancouver branch, started by Jamieson in 1921, slowly reached out to non-settler women in the name of peace and racial reconciliation – inviting, for example, Indigenous rights activist and journalist Ruth Smith to address one of its meetings in 1948. The branch was adamant in its support for disarmament, as well as collective bargaining and labour rights, and it attracted former suffragists such as Gutteridge, Mary Norton, and Evelyn LeSueur well into the 1940s. Even less radical women, such as Evlyn Farris, joined the League of Nations Society and supported international relations and peaceful resolutions to conflicts between nation-states.

INTERWAR REFORMS

Some of the greatest legacies of the suffrage movement came to fruition in reforms affecting wages and child welfare, which were consolidated after the First World War. Military recruitment revealed widespread poverty and illness among Canadians, and high soldier casualties were compounded by the devastating influenza epidemic that killed 4,000 British Columbians, 30,000 to 50,000 Canadians, and 20 to 100 million people around the world. The period was ripe for reforms that promoted the health and welfare of the family and increased the birth rate of the most "healthy" and productive citizens. During the war, the government had intervened in the economy and had established a link between income taxation and citizenship status. After the war ended, it became increasingly clear that state intervention would be needed to provide greater social and economic stability.

The 1916 BC election of the reformist Liberal Party after thirteen years of Conservative rule coincided with this trend, and the party enlisted prominent suffragists to help implement and institutionalize reforms. Shortly after taking power, the Liberals introduced legislation that made British Columbia the first province to create equal guardianship rights for mothers. A slew of other reforms followed. In 1922, women were allowed to sit on juries, and the property qualifications were slowly removed from the School Act. Helen Gregory MacGill and Attorney General Farris worked out a new property rights bill in 1920 that limited men's ability to will away their property and that forced an estate to furnish "adequate provision" for all family members. Suffragists welcomed the enforcement of public health measures, including immunization and milk sterilization, along with the formation of a Child Welfare Association (1918).

Outside of equal guardianship rights, two reforms had dominated the twentieth-century suffrage agenda: a minimum wage and the mothers' pension. Both were priorities for newly enfranchised women in the post-war moment. Legislating a minimum wage was one of the first major initiatives of the Liberal government. Helena Gutteridge created the cross-class Minimum Wage League in 1917 with the Vancouver Trades and Labour Council and the University Women's Club, drawing on support from the New Era League, the BC Federation of Labour, the Women's Forum, LCWs, and the Victoria Trades and Labour Council. At the league's first public meeting, Gutteridge and her socialist colleagues James McVety and Victor Midgely convinced twenty-five working women to join. League membership was limited to wage-earning women, but the twice monthly meetings at the Labor Temple were open to everyone. Mary Ellen Smith had campaigned on the promise of a minimum wage, and the league worked with her to press for quick legislation, sending a delegation to the government and holding multiple public meetings, social events, and a fundraising campaign involving a masquerade ball.

On one level, the wage campaign was a success for working women. The Liberals passed the Minimum Wage Act in March 1918 and created a board that summer, appointing Helen Gregory MacGill and two others to consult with the public and make recommendations for setting wage rates. But Gutteridge and MacGill were disappointed by the final results. Most suffragists had hoped for a living wage that would be set high enough for a working woman to support herself independently. But the government set the rates lower than the cost of living and forced employers and employees to negotiate the rate of the minimum wage, an oppositional process that favoured powerful employers and prompted Gutteridge to claim that the Department of Labour was acting more like a department of "capital and labour." The act excluded vulnerable groups, such as servants and farm workers, and it allowed employers to pay a lower wage to women under the age of eighteen and to a certain percentage of workers in training. Some people did benefit – average wages for female employees increased, and those of laundry workers almost doubled. Even so, the minimum wage was never close to the cost of living. By 1921, protective labour legislation had prohibited night work for women and children, shortened working hours, and established a minimum age of fifteen for the industrial employment of girls. Welcome though these changes were, they fell short of what many suffragists had hoped for.

A similar trajectory marked the 1920 Mothers' Pensions Act. During the 1920s, many provinces established this form of pension (sometimes called an allowance), which was intended to support mothers who could not do so themselves. Tapping into maternal feminist beliefs about the value of motherhood, Helena Gutteridge saw pensions as a way for the state to acknowledge women's caring labour as productive and deserving of a wage: "If a woman's place is in the home, then they who are so fond of telling us this, should get to work and see that provision is made for widows and deserted wives that they may stay at home and care for their children."

After Susie Lane Clark led delegations in 1918 and 1919 to meet Liberal premier John Oliver, he established a commission to examine the possibility of mothers' pensions and appointed several commissioners (including Cecilia Spofford) to hold public hearings. They found strong approval for a generous pension plan. Working-class and poor mothers welcomed a pension that would allow them to opt out of poorly paid jobs and resist low-quality charitable child care or the institutionalization of their children.

Many reformers and labour organizers hoped that the pension would keep women out of the workforce and prevent employment competition with men.

The pension proved so popular that the government received twice as many applications as it had anticipated during its first year of operation. But the pension did not meet suffragist expectations. It was set below the lowest female minimum wage rate in the province, and most recipients had to supplement it with paid labour or another means of support. Contradictions about the relationship of women to paid employment and mothering remained unresolved. Politicians were wary of "encouraging" women to leave their husbands. And though many felt that wage work was not ideal for the mothers of young children, they feared that social welfare programs would create dependency on the state and reduce the work ethic. As a result, most social welfare programs were built on the principle of "less eligibility," meaning that the payments were set lower than the wage that a general labourer could be expected to earn. And the obvious popularity of the benefit sparked concerns about spiralling costs.

Most recipients of the pensions – and the architects who designed the policy – saw them as an entitlement rather than a form of charity, on the same level as veterans' pensions or workers' compensation. In British Columbia, reformers and suffragists had successfully campaigned to include a broader range of women in the pension legislation than elsewhere in the country. Most significantly, unmarried mothers and those with only one child were eligible. Yet, the legislation still permitted the exclusion of mothers who were deemed unfit. Unmarried and divorced mothers were included only on the basis of a discretionary clause and could be rejected by investigators, as could those who were seen as capable of finding work or another means of support. And eligibility was determined by investigators who visited women's homes and assessed their suitability as mothers.

Neither women's organizations nor the government imagined that racialized mothers were entitled to the pension. As with other forms of social welfare, only British subjects could apply, which meant that most First Nations mothers were ineligible. The Allied Tribes of British Columbia protested this exclusion and lobbied the government for mothers' pensions that were "comparable to those provided for white women in the Province." Naturalized British subjects were also eligible, though the Naturalization Act of 1914 had raised their required period of residency from three years to five. And the pension also required an eighteen-month residency in the province. At this time, approximately a thousand naturalized Chinese people lived in British Columbia, and it was technically possible for the mothers among them to apply, but there is no evidence that any of them applied for or received a pension. And the vast majority of Japanese and Chinese residents were not British subjects.

Suffragists also wanted a role in administering and enforcing the new reform legislation. Women's organizations lobbied Victoria to appoint prominent women to government agencies, a step that would also expand paid work for white settler women, as factory inspectors, movie censors, police officers, and members of Minimum Wage and Mothers' Pensions Advisory Boards. Premier Brewster rewarded several high-profile suffragists with appointments to the civil service, along with their husbands. Helen Gregory MacGill sat on the BC Minimum Wage Board, and Cecilia Spofford was appointed to the commission on mothers' pensions and to the Mothers' Pensions Advisory Board (along with Susie Lane Clark). These positions – both the prominent ones held by well-known women and the everyday ones such as that of pension investigator – were filled by white settler women across the province as pink-collar work expanded in the growing welfare state.

The range of reforms introduced during the interwar period reflected the recognition that women were subject to long working hours, poor work conditions, and lack of access to medical care. But the articulation of these concerns often emphasized women's reproductive capacity – their ability to birth and raise healthy children. Scientific theories of evolution had already aroused fears of population decline, which intensified after the First World War. If species could become extinct – as scientists had now proved – could the same thing happen to the human race? This anxiety grew increasingly powerful in the wake of the war's devastation, the deadly influenza epidemic, and a drop in white settler birth rates.

By the 1910s, major cities in most provinces had established juvenile, domestic, and family courts to address problems related to youth and the family, and these increased in size and personnel during the 1920s and 1930s. They were seen as progressive at the time – instead of penalizing offenders through incarceration, they typically sought to reform them via the expert supervision of court officials and medical and social welfare professionals. Women sought work in this emerging welfare state, filling the ranks of court investigators, probation officers, and social workers. Some prominent figures received judicial appointments: Helen Gregory MacGill became a Vancouver Juvenile Court judge in 1917, as did Laura Jamieson in Burnaby in 1927. Women believed that they were using their newfound power to solve social problems in a more caring way, but in fact the state was deepening its control over the lives of poor and working-class youth and their families. With the aid of legislation – especially the 1908 Juvenile Delinquency Act and a 1924 amendment that criminalized "sexual immorality" – these judicial systems targeted interracial sex, promiscuity, skipping school, and theft.

Such increased state power intersected with long-standing desires to protect the health of citizens, which laid the groundwork for restrictive legislation around sexuality and reproduction in ways that upheld hierarchies of ability, race, and class. Many former suffragists and women's groups supported eugenics legislation in the 1930s, arguing that numerous physical and mental illnesses – including tuberculosis, sexually transmitted diseases, epilepsy, and depression – were caused by hereditary "feeble-mindedness" to which poor, eastern European, and Asian immigrant populations were thought to be particularly prone. The Sexual Sterilization Act was implemented in 1933, and before it was repealed in 1973, almost two hundred people who lived in government institutions had been involuntarily sterilized. By 1925, the National Council of Women was favouring the sterilization of what were termed "mental defectives," a measure that was approved by the mainstream press, members of all political parties, doctors, and former suffragists such as Emmeline Pankhurst, Helen Gregory MacGill, and Mary Ellen Smith. These values also played out in legislation that claimed to protect innocent white women from Asian men: for example, Smith ushered in legislation in 1919 that banned Chinese businesses from employing white women and that was extended as the Women and Girls' Protection Act of 1924. Such legislation underscored the deep limitations of many post-suffrage approaches to ameliorating women's poverty and inequality.

By the 1930s, non-Indigenous and non-Asian women held a high degree of formal legal equality in British Columbia. But such advances did not eliminate the systemic inequalities of class and race, which were resistant to change. To be fair, most suffragists did not believe that enfranchisement would fully resolve economic inequity, though they hoped it would ameliorate the worst problems. Some suffragists – particularly those who became more prominent after 1916 – were vocal about the limitations of reform. Laura Jamieson, for example, felt that women were "sitting back" after enfranchisement and was disappointed in the slow rate of progress toward more structural change. Some suffragists had hoped that women would vote as a non-partisan bloc or might even found a women's political party. A "party aloof from either faction," argued Maria Grant in 1917, "was the thin end of a wedge that would crack the skull of party government." But this hope never materialized. Although many suffrage ideals would be incorporated into the expanding welfare state after the Second World War, cultural expectations of gender, along with hetero-normative family structures, would remain strong until the second wave of feminist activity arose during the 1960s and 1970s.

TOWARD UNIVERSAL SUFFRAGE

Like the struggle for gender equality, the battle for universal suffrage did not end in 1917. African Canadian and white settler women of British and European descent could vote and hold office by 1917, whereas Asian and First Nations individuals were not entitled to vote at the municipal, provincial, or federal level. Nor could they enter the professions of law, medicine, pharmacy, or accounting. These restrictions became key issues in the human-rights-based enfranchisement campaigns of the 1930s and 1940s. For Asian Canadians, post-war activism was also tied to ending discriminatory immigration laws. And for Japanese Canadians, the post-war period involved protest against permanent disloca-tion and forced "repatriation" to Japan after the trauma of intern-ment. For many Indigenous activists, acquiring the vote was important for achieving broader goals regarding land title and improved funding for health and education. But attaining provin-cial voting rights was complicated by the federal Indian Act, which linked enfranchisement to the loss of status.

The Second World War changed the political landscape and prompted a rethinking of the relationship between race and cit-izenship. The push to reconsider voting rights came from both international and domestic sources. In the wake of the Holocaust, Canada signed the 1948 United Nations Declaration of Human Rights, which prohibited discrimination on the basis of race and was drafted in part by Canadian lawyer John Humphrey. Canada's race-based immigration laws and provincial voting restrictions were becoming an international embarrassment. In 1946, a *Montreal Standard* editorial claimed that "B.C. is being held up to ridicule all across Canada! It denies full rights of citizenship to those of minorities which have colored skins." Domestically, the Canadian Citizenship Act (1946) replaced the category of British subject with that of Canadian citizen. Under this legislation, women no longer automatically took on the nationality of their husband when they married. But First Nations and Inuit would wait another decade to be considered full citizens, as only those born on or after 1 January 1947 were included in that category.

Wartime military service provided powerful language for disenfranchised men. Chinese Canadian and Indigenous communities argued that the state had taxed their incomes and conscripted their bodies for the war effort while refusing to award them the vote. The experiences of Chinese Canadian, South Asian, and First Nations veterans opened further possibilities for criticism: if they had fought for democracy, surely Canada was obligated to grant them all the rights of citizenship? First Nations were particularly attentive to the irony of the term "Canadian citizenship," pointing out that they were the original inhabitants of the land yet remained wards of the state under the Indian Act. This emphasis on military service, however, had the consequence of deepening male leadership of enfranchisement campaigns.

These campaigns reached their height after the Second World War but drew on earlier community protests against racism and discrimination. The few Asian women who lived in British Columbia built women's associations, but in communities with a heavy gender imbalance, the work of resisting disenfranchisement fell largely to men. Early attempts came from Tomekichi Homma in 1900 and Won Alexander Cumyow in 1902, both of whom challenged their exclusion from the voters' list and launched (unsuccessful) lawsuits against the provincial government. Cumyow's son Gordon engaged in a similar fight in 1918, when he took on the Law Society for refusing his application to clerk. As he noted, "by right of Birth, I am considered a British subject, one who should enjoy the full rights of citizenship." But the provincial courts consistently upheld the right of the province to disenfranchise on the basis of both race and gender, and to bar Asian men from practising the professions.

In Chinese Canadian communities, organizations such as the Chinese Freemasons, the Chinese Benevolent Association, and the Chinese Empire Reform Association had a long tradition of protest against head taxes and immigration restrictions, opposition to segregated schooling, and support for suffrage, all to "enjoy the same privileges" as Canadians. Because China was an important Canadian ally in the Second World War, Chinese Canadian contributions to the war effort helped build public support for enfranchisement. Women's voluntary war work – similar in many ways to that taken on by white settler women – also allowed them to claim the status of deserving citizens. The Daughters of China (1941) raised money for China through community fundraising, dances, and fashion shows, and Chinese Canadian women in Vancouver's Chinatown formed an Ambulance Corps platoon in 1941. In turn, men cited the rights associated with military service and modern citizenship to argue for enfranchisement. Soldier Jack Chew wrote to the *Vancouver Province* in 1945, asking whether the legislature would soon grant the vote and civil rights to Chinese Canadian communities: "I am fighting for democracy and yet on the other hand I do not know what I am fighting for." Chinese Canadian workers in Vancouver launched a series of strikes in 1943 to protest Canada's decision to disallow income tax deductions for dependants living in China. By forcing historically anti-Asian unions to support their cause, workers helped to advance the human rights discourse.

Community groups such as the Chinese Benevolent Association and the Chinese Canadian Association pushed the provincial and federal governments to extend the franchise, sending

Wong Foon Sien (1899–1971) was born in Guangdong, China, and moved with his merchant parents to Cumberland in 1908. Relocating to Vancouver, he attended law school at the University of British Columbia but could not be called to the bar, because Chinese Canadians were legally excluded from practising law. He became a court interpreter, contributed to numerous newspapers, and was involved in the Chinese Benevolent Association (established 1906). He advocated for the right to vote and to enter the professions, and for an end to racial discrimination in immigration policy.

petitions, briefs, and delegations to Premier John Hart and cabinet ministers throughout the 1940s. A 1944 petition from the Chinese Canadian Association emphasized the willingness of Chinese Canadians to "lay down their lives in defence of this country" and argued that "being deprived of the right to vote is an unfair and arbitrary derogation of our rights as citizens of Canada." The petition was signed by several men, including Foon Sien and Gordon Cumyow, and one woman, Esther Fung. Both Sien and Cumyow were well-known leaders of Chinese organizations, and Cumyow's family had been active in agitating for full citizenship rights since the turn of the century. Esther Fung's leadership grew from her social work background and her involvement with community associations. Born in Vancouver, she graduated from the University of British Columbia and was employed in San Francisco as a social worker before returning to take up the position of Chinese club secretary at the YWCA in 1942. Fung was also active in interracial outreach, working with African Canadian Vernice Carruthers, a local vocalist, to speak at "race friendship services" in city churches. But even winning the federal and provincial franchise in 1947 did not automatically confer municipal voting rights. Community groups sent delegations to lobby the Union of BC Municipalities in 1948 to force it to end race-based exclusions in the civic franchise.

Like Chinese Canadians, South Asians drew on their war service and status as taxpayers to argue for the vote and the end of restrictions on immigration. With a storied tradition of service in the British military, South Asian men relied heavily on their status as both soldiers and British subjects. Through the 1930s and early 1940s, community leaders hired and worked alongside well-known lawyers and political figures from India as they petitioned provincial and federal governments. In 1943, a twelve-man delegation that met with Premier John Hart included prominent members from the Khalsa Diwan Society, along with First World War veteran Bahoo Singh and two young enlisted men. Singh sported his military service medals, and the young soldiers were dressed in full uniform, both pointed reminders of the South Asian record of loyalty and respectability. Naginder Singh Gill of the Khalsa Diwan Society implored Hart for enfranchisement, stating that "we have tried to be good citizens of this province ... We, the Canadian Sikhs, are willing and anxious to play our part and to fight for Canada, too. We want our children to grow up as good Canadians and responsible citizens, playing their part as respected members of the Canadian community." They were joined by Opposition leader Harold Winch and Harold Pritchett, president of the International Woodworkers of America. But the government remained unmoved. Minister of Labour George Sharratt Pearson, a Nanaimo MLA, claimed in 1944 that South Asian men should never be enfranchised, because they were "unreliable, dishonest, and deceitful."

Once overseas conscription was introduced in 1944, both Chinese and South Asian men adopted a "No Vote – No War" policy. However, Ottawa responded by simply exempting South

Asian men from military service. Community leaders continued to leverage international pressure against the Liberal-Conservative coalition government, drawing support from Indian political figures and trade commissioners, British colonial officials, the UN Charter of Rights, and the CCF, all within the context of India's looming independence. This unrelenting activism finally resulted in provincial enfranchisement in 1947, though restrictive immigration policy on the basis of national origin was not addressed until the 1960s.

For Japanese Canadians, the extension of the franchise was connected to ongoing protest against the province's plan to retain restrictions on their freedom of movement. They too used court challenges and lobbying to protest exclusionary immigration and voting legislation. The Canadian Japanese Association was established in the late nineteenth century to aid Japanese immigrants, but it also called for enfranchisement and challenged racial exclusions in court as early as 1900. Over two hundred Japanese Canadian men had served in the First World War, and when veterans opened their own branch of the Canadian Legion in Vancouver, president Masumi Mitsui used it as a point from which to press for the vote. In 1931, Japanese Canadian veterans were provincially enfranchised. By the 1930s, the community had a few mainstream allies, including the United Church, the CCF, and Helen Gregory MacGill. In 1936, the Japanese Canadian Citizens League sent a four-person delegation to meet with Prime Minister William Lyon Mackenzie King to ask for the federal franchise. One of the delegates was a Vancouver activist and teacher named Hideko Hyodo, who argued that Japanese Canadians deserved the vote not only on the basis of their human rights and fundamental equality, but also because of their hard work and loyalty to Canada.

But Canada and Japan were enemies during the Second World War. After Japan attacked Pearl Harbor in 1941, politicians, unions, newspapers, and citizens' groups accused Japanese Canadians of disloyalty and began to demand their forced removal from the

Vancouver teacher Hideko Hyodo (later Shimizu) and three
other representatives of the Japanese Canadian Citizens League
spoke in favour of enfranchisement at the federal Special Committee on Elections and Franchise Acts in 1936. Hyodo was one
of the first Japanese Canadian women in British Columbia to
receive a teaching certificate. During the Second World War, she
set up schools for children in the internment camps. She appears
(from left to right) with Samuel Hayakawa, Minoru Kobayashi,
and Edward Banno.

Pacific Coast. In 1942, after a series of orders restricting movement and removing a range of civil rights, Ottawa ordered the removal of 22,000 Japanese Canadians living within a "protected" area near the coast and incarcerated many individuals and families in internment or labour camps in the interior. Their property was confiscated and sold. At the end of the war, the federal and provincial governments debated whether they should be permitted to return to the coast, be dispersed throughout the country, or be deported to Japan. Even the federal and provincial CCF supported the dispersal policy, claiming that it would "protect Canadian living standards." Many local and national Japanese Canadian organizations protested both dispersal and "repatriation," continuing to fight for the end of all restrictions on movement and for full citizenship rights. With the declaration of war on Japan and their treatment as "enemy aliens," Japanese Canadians from BC were barred from military service between 1941 and 1945. This meant that, unlike other racialized groups who volunteered or were conscripted during the war, Japanese Canadians found it difficult to cite wartime service as fundamental to their demand to vote. But after 1947, community groups successfully harnessed the new language of human rights and equality in the new Citizenship Act. George Tanaka, national secretary of the Japanese-Canadian Citizens' Association, noted that the denial of the franchise felt particularly harsh after 1947, when other Asian Canadians had won the provincial vote. Due to the leadership of Tanaka and Seiji Homma (president of the provincial branch of the citizens' association) and support from the provincial CCF, multiple church groups, and the Canadian Civil Liberties Union, the government finally responded. In June 1949, the New Canadian reported that the first Japanese Canadian woman to vote in a school board election had cast her ballot in Greenwood, British Columbia, and Japanese Canadians voted and acted as scrutineers in the provincial election of that month.

First Nations in British Columbia also remained provincially disenfranchised until the late 1940s. They could not vote unless they were formally enfranchised by the federal government, an assimilation process that required them to surrender their Indian status and treaty rights. Additionally, First Nations were not considered British subjects, which meant that they could not access state-funded social programs. Indigenous organizations, especially the Allied Tribes of British Columbia (1916–27) and the Native Brotherhood of British Columbia (established 1931), pushed for political rights, access to social services, and better health care and education funding but without the loss of status or the extinguishment of Aboriginal land title. The question of how to define the franchise was of key importance: throughout the 1940s, Andrew Paull, the Squamish leader of the North American Indian Brotherhood, remained suspicious of enfranchisement because of the potential for assimilation and loss of status.

Through the 1930s and 1940s, the Native Brotherhood of British Columbia emerged as a leading organization for Indigenous rights. Founded in northern coastal communities, it represented fishers and cannery employees on the northwest coast and later the interior. It championed economic autonomy, land title and fishing rights, improved health and education, the closure of residential schools, and full citizenship and voting rights. It did not perceive winning the vote as an end goal but as one key tool in the realignment of the unequal power relations between Indigenous communities and the state. In leading the campaign for voting rights, the brotherhood drew on post-war discourses of anti-racism, human rights, and equality of opportunity, linking Indigenous people with other "minority" groups that had also experienced racism, specifically blacks, Jews, Italians, and Irish.

The brotherhood found support among non-Indigenous activists such as Maisie Armytage-Moore Hurley, who embraced the liberal post-war language of justice, equality, and opportunity. Her interest in political citizenship may have been influenced by her suffragist mother, Amy Campbell-Johnson. But she was introduced to the reality of racism when she took a job as secretary in

1935 for the Irish-born criminal lawyer Tom Hurley, who often represented First Nations clients. By 1946, she was publishing the *Native Voice*, the official brotherhood newspaper, from Hurley's office. The paper played a critical role in disseminating the platform of the brotherhood at a time when the mainstream press paid little attention to First Nations activism. It also nurtured First Nations journalists and writers, and covered developments in Indigenous rights. The *Voice* attracted support from the CBC, the Local Council of Women, and the peace group Voice of Women, all of which called for the end of racial discrimination in voting rights and for equity in educational funding.

Indigenous women also played important roles in the post-war Indigenous rights campaign. Jane Constance Cook was the only woman who sat on the Allied Tribes executive committee, where she worked closely with Squamish leader Andrew Paull and Haida Methodist minister Peter Kelly. It is likely that Cook's concern for the welfare of women and children shaped certain demands of the Allied Tribes, which included access to mothers' pensions. Similarly, though Peter Kelly, Bill Mussell, Guy Williams, William Scow, and Alfred Adams were the most visible leaders of the brotherhood, women in the auxiliary Native Sisterhood were politically active. The sisterhood was organized in Masset in 1933, and its first president was Brenda Campbell, from the Heiltsuk Nation. Its members raised funds for the brotherhood and cooked for its meetings. They also fought for better wages and working conditions in canneries. For example, several Heiltsuk members of the sisterhood formed the Namu Cannery Plant Committee, and Brenda Campbell, Kitty Carpenter, and Mary Hall led negotiations with BC Packers for higher pay and improved working conditions. Women's participation meant that the brotherhood added a range of women's and family issues to its platform, pressing for access to mothers' pensions, family allowances, and old-age pensions. As early as 1947, President William Scow demanded that individual bands be given the power to reinstate women who had lost their

Indian status when they married non-Indigenous men – an issue that Ottawa would not address until the 1980s.

Although women did not take on the high-profile roles in the brotherhood, they were no less engaged. Genevieve Mussell, wife of Bill Mussell, was part of a 1947 delegation that lobbied Premier Hart for better education funding and more teachers. Genevieve was of Ukrainian descent, but under the terms of the Indian Act, she took on her husband's status when she married him in 1937. In 1959, she was elected chief of the Skwah Band (near Chilliwack) and remained an activist on Indigenous rights issues until well into the 1960s. Ruth Smith, who was born in Yale and attended the Coqualeetza residential school, became the editor of the *Native Voice* shortly after it was founded and wrote about poor education funding for Indigenous children, racism in public schools, and government failure to reform the Indian Act. President of the sisterhood and associate editor of the *Native Voice* (1953), Kitty Carpenter helped lead the successful fight against racially segregated washrooms at the Namu fish cannery in 1954. The sisterhood also protested its secondary status within the male-dominated brotherhood, which did not allow women to vote at conventions. Until this policy was changed in 1951, the only woman who could vote was Maisie Hurley, who had been granted a life membership in 1944. She supported the sisterhood's fight, telling the men to "quit passing the buck" when it came to women's equality within the organization.

The fight for Indigenous enfranchisement was bound up in a constellation of rights issues that organizations and activists placed before governments in the form of petitions and delegations. At the annual brotherhood convention in Alert Bay in 1944, delegates angrily pointed out that "many of their number are serving Canada in the armed forces, and yet the race lacks the right to vote." As the federal government conscripted First Nations men into the military, introduced income taxation, and signed the Declaration of Human Rights, the lack of the vote seemed particularly

The celebratory cover of the *Native Voice* newspaper in 1949.

regressive. In 1947, the brotherhood sent a delegation to Ottawa to present its case for reforms to the "anachronistic" Indian Act, which included demands for an unconditional federal franchise. A motion in the House of Commons to do just that failed to pass, however, leading Peter Kelly to express his "keen disappointment" and state, "Whatever else Parliament didn't do, that is the thing they should have done. For once the Indian gets the vote, his wishes will be ascertained by politicians as it is with other groups of voters." In 1947, when British Columbia was planning to enfranchise Chinese and South Asian Canadians, but not First Nations people, William Scow similarly expressed the brotherhood's displeasure to premier John Hart. Galvanized by the enfranchisement of these groups, the brotherhood increased its pressure on the province, and in 1949 Victoria finally complied.

Political citizenship in the form of the provincial franchise was articulated by Indigenous activists in the language of modernity and progress. William Scow and Herbert Cook (son of Jane Constance Cook) argued that the post-war era was a "modern age of atomic progress" and that Canada should embody such progress in its relationship with First Nations. The brotherhood took a similar tone: winning the franchise was a "step forward," an important "advancement," and a new "beginning." But it was not the end of the journey. As the editors of the *Voice* pointed out in 1949, provincial voting rights did not undo racism, reverse the chronic underfunding of education and health care, or confer the federal vote. While keeping its focus on these larger issues, the brotherhood immediately embarked on voter education campaigns. Maisie Hurley and her interpreter, Constance Cox (of Tlingit maternal ancestry), took up the challenge and travelled throughout northern British Columbia, visiting nine towns and villages between March and May of 1949. At its annual convention, the brotherhood decided to send eight deputy registrars to help people sign up for the vote. Peter and Gertrude Kelly, along with their son Horace (a war veteran and assistant editor of the *Voice*), travelled together to register voters and encourage them to participate in the upcoming provincial election.

This outreach was designed to inform First Nations people about what casting a ballot could achieve. At a March 1949 meeting at the Pemberton reserve, for example, Maisie Hurley, Chief Paul Dick, and local Native Sisterhood president Elizabeth Wallace told their listeners that the vote could be used to "carry on the fight for their other rights," especially for the "same benefits as the white people." When Peter and Gertrude Kelly were honoured in the village of Kispiox in northwestern British Columbia, the community turned out in full force to register for the vote and listen to the Kellys speak about citizenship. As Peter Kelly stated, we have "a strong lever in our hands and we are going to throw all our weight against it to move Ottawa to action."

And in 1949, when Frank Calder of the Nisga'a Nation was elected to the provincial legislature, it seemed that the lever had been pulled. A worker at the Sunnyside BC Packers Canning Factory on the Skeena River and a member of both the Native Brotherhood and the Fisherman's Union, Calder was thirty-three. Running for the CCF, he was supported by party leader Harold Winch, and he won his seat in the Atlin riding by just six votes, following a recount. Of the 1,260 registered voters in Atlin, 350 were First Nations men and women. Born in Nass Harbour, Calder came from a community that had been fighting for land title in the Nass Valley since the 1880s, eventually playing an important role in a Supreme Court case that affirmed Aboriginal title. Indigenous voters soundly supported Calder, but like enfranchised women thirty years earlier, they knew that the deep issues of poverty and inequality remained unresolved. The *Native Voice* was full of celebratory stories about both Calder's victory and the support he received from the CCF, but Calder himself told the legislature in 1950 that the vote was no "Magna Carta" and that First Nations in British Columbia were still "second-hand citizens" who were regulated by the Indian Act. Indigenous people, the brotherhood charged in 1950, remained in a "legislative concentration camp."

The struggle for a vote that was not restricted by race and gender was long and arduous, reaching forward until 1949, when the provincial government finally bowed to pressure and removed the last remaining racial barriers. But achieving the franchise, though important in many ways, did not undo economic and legal inequalities or resolve the political under-representation of women and racialized groups. White women found it extremely difficult to win provincial office, and the numbers of both female candidates and MLAs remained woefully small until the early 1990s. First Nations women were not permitted to vote or run in band council elections until the Indian Act was amended in 1951, and neither they nor First Nations men could vote federally until 1960. The under-representation of racialized men and women in provincial and federal politics remains a problem to this day.

CONCLUSION

ALTHOUGH THIS BOOK ends in 1949, the issues that suffragists grappled with remain relevant today. Achieving the right to vote was necessary for full democratic participation, symbolic reasons of belonging, and access to better-paid professions. At times, those who campaigned for suffrage invested it with a kind of transformative power that it could not possibly deliver. The right to vote was never the full solution to inequality and exploitation. It is more useful to situate suffrage over a longer period when the vote was understood as one way among many to achieve social, political, and economic change. Removing gender and racial restrictions on the vote did not solve the problems of poverty, unequal pay, lack of affordable child care, domestic violence, racism, and discrimination.

What might we learn from the suffrage campaigns of the previous century? Feminist historians challenge us to be honest about the limitations and failures of suffrage and of women's organizations more broadly. Suffragists prioritized white settler women's family and working lives, rarely reaching out to racially marginalized women. Indigenous, Chinese, Japanese, and South Asian Canadian women were denied the provincial franchise until the late 1940s – a reality grounded in deep structures of racial discrimination that went largely unacknowledged among suffragists. The refusal to grapple with the inequalities between women, the tendency to see immigration as a problem to be controlled, and the failure to acknowledge the harms done by colonization speak to long-standing hierarchies within feminism, an issue that persists today.

Many of the reforms advocated by suffragists would later be understood as reactionary rather than progressive. Their efforts to address issues of concern to women – such as sexual exploitation, wage inequality, and vulnerability to violence – were vitally important. But these concerns often rested on preserving women's role as mothers and caregivers. The idea that the state should intervene in individual lives to prevent harm to future generations was used to justify legislation that coerced sterilization or criminalized "promiscuous" sexual behaviour. The cause of prohibition inspired enormous reserves of activism but was a short-lived policy soon dismissed as unenforceable. Although alcohol abuse had a real material cost for many women and children, the regulatory impulse in prohibition blamed individuals for deeper problems of poverty, sexism, and violence, and may have stalled more successful ways of dealing with addiction. Suffragists' response to sex work was also a failure. Their critiques did address the sexual double standard, but their solutions echoed later "shame the john" campaigns, which focused on humiliating male buyers of sexual services. The attempt to abolish prostitution probably made it more dangerous for the women who engaged in it.

Suffragists themselves often wondered if women had failed to use their new power to transform the world. The limitations of the movement and the aftermath of the enfranchisement campaigns remind us that there were always significant differences *between* women, as much as similarity among them. Gender – even the experience of motherhood – could bind them together but could not overcome profound power differentials rooted in race. Furthermore, idealistic expectations that women could vote together to transform society – and anti-feminist fears that they would do exactly this and thus harm male interests – never came to pass. Women's assessments of an ideal society differed, and they disagreed on the root causes of societal inequalities. They worked together across differences, but they never acted solely on the basis of their gender.

That the suffrage movement had serious shortcomings does not mean that it has nothing to teach us or that we must judge it a failure. Taking suffrage activism seriously challenges the way in which we assess the choices, arguments, and priorities of people in the past. Some historians are highly critical of the suffragist emphasis on motherhood and have assumed that maternal feminists were "conservative," whereas those who advocated direct action were "radical." But these categories do not hold up. Suffragists may have placed differing degrees of emphasis on motherhood, individual rights, and economic independence, but they all believed to some extent that women and men differed from one another and that this difference gave women a unique perspective on politics. And though historians disagree on whether militancy was more or less successful (or necessary), we should not judge one or the other within an outmoded binary of radical versus conservative. Feminists have challenged these models of activism, insisting on intersectional approaches that take seriously the interconnections of gender with race, religion, ethnicity, sexuality, and class.

Suffragist attempts to make alliances and to link political enfranchisement to larger social improvements represent an expansive understanding of social change rather than a narrow one. The willingness to co-operate across differences of class and ideology and to partner on specific pieces of legislation produced material benefits for many women in the province. Instead of interpreting women's inability to vote in unison as a failure, it is more useful to understand their ability to work together on campaigns of common interest as prefiguring the alliance-based politics that emerged later, with third-wave feminism.

The movement also reminds us that it was – and is still – impossible to undertake social change alone. Sometimes, the focus on suffragist leaders over-represents those whose voices were the loudest, who were the most literate, or who were the most prominent people in their organizations. But intimate relationships of all kinds built the movement. There are numerous instances of entire families in British Columbia who were committed to reform and suffrage. The Pollards of Victoria are an excellent example of multigenerational activism. Maria Grant, one of the most prominent suffragists in the province, worked alongside her mother, Maria Pollard, and her daughter Frances Willard Grant. Parent-child partnerships were quite common: Dorothy (Parr) Darlington was active in the Mount Pleasant Suffrage League, along with her socialist mother, Louisa Parr. Vancouver socialist Nora Aileen Tutty, her mother, and her sister were all active in suffrage, as was Victoria socialist Helen Christopher and her daughter Dora. Traditions of Indigenous activism were passed on from Jane Constance Cook to her son Herbert and her niece Ellen Neel. The Tolmies and the Finlaysons – cousins who shared Indigenous ancestry – were involved in numerous social reform and women's groups in Victoria. Gordon Cumyow's activism was probably inspired by that of his parents: his father, Won Alexander, was a long-time community activist, and his mother, Eva, was the daughter of Methodist and suffragist Kate Chan. Kin and community relationships built on shared political activism spanned generations.

Many married couples also shared social and political values, working together as intimate and political partners. This ideal of companionate and co-operative marriage characterizes the relationships of many famous reformers and suffragists around the world: Lord and Lady Aberdeen, Emmeline and Richard Pankhurst, and Emmeline and Frederick Pethick-Lawrence. In British Columbia, Florence and William Lashley Hall shared political values rooted in their social gospel faith. Stephen and Jane Constance Cook's commitment to the Anglican Church and Indigenous rights activism was sustained over their long marriage. Socialists Bertha and Ernest Burns, and Dora and R.B. Kerr, had companionate and politically committed marriages. Methodists Mary Ann and James Cunningham shared similar values: as an MLA for New Westminster, he supported suffrage bills in the legislature, and she told the press, "We are inclined to think that men and women who love and confide in each other and who agree in most other respects, would generally arrive at the same conclusions upon political questions." Mary Ellen Smith supposedly helped her husband, Ralph, write his speeches, and she supported all of his political campaigns. When she debated anti-suffragist Father William O'Boyle in 1913, he sat next to her on the stage. Hundreds of husbands around the province attended suffrage meetings, spoke at events, helped with fundraising, and voted in the referendum. There is no doubt that this support sustained suffragists' political vision over long periods of disappointment.

Friendships between women were also foundational to the movement's success. The emphasis on engaging with people who held differing opinions produced many co-operative friendships. Suffragists spoke on platforms together, encouraged each other, and argued with each other. Bertha Merrill Burns urged women to "lift up those about you to the highest plane of your own thoughts." Helena Gutteridge and Lily Laverock, though from very different class backgrounds, forged a friendship that was sparked by activism but that outlasted the movement. But Gutteridge's friendship with Ida Douglas-Fearn dissolved under the strain of her marriage to and subsequent divorce from Ida's younger son Ollie. Cecilia Spofford and Maria Grant were long-time friends who also disagreed on a range of issues and whose activism in Victoria spanned the many years of the women's movement. Women joined together to celebrate major life events, and bonds of affection and care shone through their gatherings. A 1918 going-away party for the well-off suffragist Elizabeth Arnett was held at the home of working-class Rose Taylor, which suggests that women in Vancouver had breached some of the city's class divides. Attending her party were high-status women such as Eva Cotton and Helen

Gregory MacGill, socialist Nora Tutty, and labour activists Helen Gutteridge and Susie Lane Clark. The working-class Annie Wilson composed and read a poem in Arnett's honour. Suffragists had friendships that crossed the lines of gender as well. Due to their involvement in labour and socialist politics, both Gutteridge and Bertha Merrill Burns developed close working relationships with the male leaders of those movements, even if their interaction was often fraught and marked by an unequal power dynamic.

Studying the history of the suffrage movement shows us that efforts to make political, social, and economic change are long and ongoing. Historians have sometimes assessed women's activism though the metaphor of the wave. This captures the unique way in which feminists have organized to challenge gender inequality over different periods of time. Clearly, second- and third-wave feminists conceived of new ways to think about sexual pleasure, reproductive justice, colonialism, racism, and gender identity. Some observers have argued that we are now in a period of fourth-wave feminism, characterized by social media activism that has amplified the voices of marginalized communities, as they challenge race, gender, and sexual oppression. But the notion of separate waves misses the fact that feminist successes, failures, and hopes have remained an ongoing conversation. Movements for social change are always partial and incomplete. Feminist approaches to solving inequality remain ongoing projects, partly because our understanding of gender is always changing in response to the world around us. And the world around us is always changing by how we interact, in a gendered way, with it.

Feminists in the twenty-first century still struggle with fundamental political questions that would not be unfamiliar to suffragists more than a hundred years ago. They would be disappointed by the feminization of poverty and the failure of political parties to make women and children central to their platforms. They would be profoundly disappointed by low voter turnout and democratic disengagement, especially since they resisted the assumption that women would not bother to vote. They would be frustrated by the persistent under-representation of women in provincial and federal legislatures. And questions about political representation on the basis of gender have not been resolved. Should feminists support female candidates regardless of their partisan affiliation? North American political scientists argue that women are more likely than men to support state intervention in the economy and the provision of social welfare. Such scholars suggest that this is best understood as a gender gap that warrants attempts to create a more diverse political system. But the gender gap is shaped by race, regionalism, voter turnout, and the distribution of votes and seats in any given political system. And the most influential female politicians are deeply embedded in both partisan politics and relationships of power.

In some ways, women's political citizenship has made great strides in British Columbia. Feminists have pushed the promise of women's activism in new directions. Suffragists challenged the limited possibilities open to women, but many current feminists are attempting to reimagine the concept of gender itself. Trends in feminist theory include undoing the once assured relationship among gender identity, sex, and sexuality. These are not simply theoretical issues: they have implications for the way in which women's groups organize and provide services, how school systems treat transgender children, or how medical authorities respond to children who are born intersex.

Currently, 39 percent of BC MLAs are female, a percentage that has steadily increased since the late 1980s and especially after the 1991 election, in which women won a quarter of the seats. But as much as white women have made gains in electoral politics, racialized women have not enjoyed the same success. The first South Asian MLA (Judi Tyabji) was elected only in 1991. In 2016, Melanie Mark became the first First Nations woman to win a seat in the legislature. Women also remain significantly under-represented at the federal level. When Port Alberni–born Kim Campbell won

Rosemary Brown (1930–2003) was born in Jamaica and moved
to Montreal in 1951. She studied social work at McGill University
and the University of British Columbia. In 1972, she became the
first black woman to win a seat in the provincial legislature,
which she held until 1986. She was the Ruth Wynn Woodward
Chair in women's studies at Simon Fraser University, was chief
commissioner of the Ontario Human Rights Commission
(1993–96), and received the Order of Canada in 1996.

the leadership of the Progressive Conservative Party in 1993, she
succeeded Brian Mulroney to become the first female prime minister of Canada. More than twenty-five years have elapsed since
then, but her achievement has not been duplicated.

Despite historic and significant difficulties in getting nominated for and winning office, women have persisted. In 1972,
Rosemary Brown made history when she became the first black

woman to win a seat in a provincial legislature in Canada. She was only the second woman in the country to contest the leadership of a major federal party, and she played an important role in advancing human rights in Ontario and British Columbia. In April 1973, she gave a keynote address at the inaugural meeting of the National Congress of Black Women in Toronto. Speaking to an audience of feminist activists, Brown imagined a world in which the women's movement, the black liberation movement, and social democracy would liberate all Canadians. Echoing Bertha Merrill Burns's pledge that women should lift each other up until everyone was free of exploitation, Brown passionately expressed her commitment to the emancipation of everyone regardless of gender, race, class, or age:

> The wisdom that I have learned ... is that all people depend on all people and that unless all of us are free, none of us will be free. And that, indeed, when I fight for your freedom I am also fighting for my own and when I am fighting for my freedom I am also fighting for my sisters and my brothers and for all of our children.

Brown's hopeful, inclusive, and expansive vision of liberation and equality remains a work in progress to this day.

ACKNOWLEDGMENTS

BOOK PROJECTS LIKE this get completed only with the aid of countless people. It has been an honour to work with Veronica Strong-Boag, whose vision for this project and support for each author in the series has never wavered. Thank you to my fellow authors who have shared their research stories and advice: Denyse Baillargeon, Tarah Brookfield, Sarah Carter, Lianne Leddy, Heidi MacDonald, and Joan Sangster. The team at UBC Press provided invaluable support and is a true pleasure to work with. A special thank you to Darcy Cullen for her encouragement. Thank you also to Cathy English, curator at the Revelstoke Museum and Archives. Somayeh Bahrami, Brooklyn Fowler, Terri Lucas, Carl Mandy, and Eryk Martin all provided valuable research assistance. I am thankful for the company of the BC Pub Night folks, all of whom patiently listened to me talk about this project and answered endless questions about British Columbia history and politics. Special thanks to Allen Seager, who always shares sources and newspaper clippings, Bob McDonald, who enthusiastically answered my detailed questions about BC politics, and Laura Ishiguro and Eryk Martin, whose support has been considerable.

I am also grateful for dear friends and family whose kindness and encouragement sustained me over the last few years, especially Helen Hok-Sze Leung and Willeen Keough. I cannot thank Eric Wredenhagen enough for the time he spent reading the numerous drafts and offering generous feedback and editing advice throughout the entire process. I had the privilege of completing the first and final draft of this book on Saltspring Island, where the beauty of the Gulf Islands is a reminder of the importance of region and place in our lives and our work.

This book is dedicated to Robert A.J. McDonald (1944–2019). Bob's knowledge of the political, economic, and social history of British Columbia seemed limitless, and his profound love for the history of this province was inspiring. He was endlessly generous with his support and feedback, and his willingness to share his own manuscript in progress on the history of politics in British Columbia made this a better book. He is deeply missed.

SOURCES AND
FURTHER READING

THE REFERENCES below include material on the history of suffrage and British Columbia more generally. While writing this book, I consulted wide-ranging primary sources, including local, labour, socialist, religious, and provincial newspapers; pamphlets and posters; records of women's organizations; magazines and periodicals; government documents; and petitions and letters to politicians. Biographical and census data can be found through the digital database at http://www.ancestry.ca. Most major BC newspapers are digitized and available through the subscription database at https://www.newspapers.com/. The open-source BC Historical Newspapers database at https://open.library.ubc.ca/collections/bcnewspapers has a collection of papers from across the province. The *Colonist* (known variously as the *Daily British Colonist* and the *Daily Colonist*) is available for free at http://www.britishcolonist.ca. The primary sources quoted in the main text are cited below. Most secondary sources listed below are cited only once to minimize repetition.

INTRODUCTION

For assessments of suffrage in Canada, see Catherine L. Cleverdon, *The Woman Suffrage Movement in Canada*, 2nd ed. (Toronto: University of Toronto Press, 1974); Carol Bacchi, *Liberation Deferred? The Ideas of the English-Canadian Suffragists* (Toronto: University of Toronto Press, 1983); Kim Byrd, *Redressing the Past: The Politics of Early English-Canadian Women's Drama, 1880–1920* (Montreal and Kingston: McGill-Queen's University Press, 2004); Janice Fiamengo, "A Legacy of Ambivalence: Responses to Nellie McClung," in *Rethinking Canada*, 4th ed., ed. Veronica Strong-Boag, Mona Gleason, and Adele Perry (Don Mills: Oxford University Press, 2002), 149–63; Nancy Forestell, "Historical Feminisms in Canada to 1940: Further Reflections on the So-Called First Wave," in *Reading Canadian*

Women's and Gender History, ed. Nancy Janovicek and Carmen Nielson (Toronto: University of Toronto Press, 2019), 171–202; Veronica Strong-Boag, "Taking Stock of Suffragists: Personal Reflections on Feminist Appraisals," *Journal of the Canadian Historical Association* 21, 2 (2010): 76–89; and Joan Sangster, *One Hundred Years of Struggle: The History of Women and the Vote in Canada* (Vancouver: UBC Press, 2018). On suffrage internationalism in Canada, see Nancy Forestell and Maureen Moynagh, eds., *Documenting First Wave Feminisms,* vol. 2, *Canada – National and Transnational Contexts* (Toronto: University of Toronto Press, 2014); and Nancy Forestell, "Mrs Canada Goes Global," *Atlantis* 30, 1 (2005): 7–20. On the importance of region, see Ernest Forbes, "The Ideas of Carol Bacchi and the Suffragists of Halifax," *Atlantis* 10, 2 (Spring 1985): 119–26. For an exhaustive range of topics on women's political citizenship, consult Women Suffrage and Beyond: Confronting the Democratic Deficit, http://www.womensuffrage.org.

Although there is no published synthesis on the BC suffrage movement, a number of graduate dissertations and essays were crucial for establishing the history of suffrage in this book. See Linda Hale, "The British Columbia Woman Suffrage Movement, 1890–1917" (master's thesis, University of British Columbia, 1977); Melanie Ihmels, "The Mischiefmakers: Woman's Movement Development in Victoria, British Columbia" (master's thesis, University of Victoria, 2013); and Doreen Weppler, "Early Forms of Political Activity among White Women in British Columbia, 1880–1925" (master's thesis, Simon Fraser University, 1971). For essays on provincial suffrage politics, see Michael H. Cramer, "Public and Political: Documents of the Woman's Suffrage Campaign in British Columbia, 1871–1917: The View from Victoria," in *In Her Own Right: Selected Essays on Women's History of B.C.,* ed. Barbara Latham and Cathy Kess (Victoria: Camosun College, 1980), 79–100; Gloria Whelan, "Maria Grant, 1854–1937: The Life and Times of an Early Twentieth Century Christian," in Latham and Kess, *In Her Own Right,* 125–46; and Melanie Ihmels, "The New Chewing Gum," *Okanagan History* (Seventy-Second Report of the Okanagan Historical Society, 2008), 27–36. For books that substantively engage with the BC suffrage movement, see Irene Howard, *The Struggle for Social Justice in British Columbia: Helena Gutteridge, the Unknown Reformer* (Vancouver: UBC Press, 1992); and Veronica Strong-Boag, *The Last Suffragist Standing: The Life and Times of Laura Marshall Jamieson* (Vancouver: UBC Press, 2018).

On difference and sameness in feminism, see Ann Snitow, *The Feminism of Uncertainty: A Gender Diary* (Durham: Duke University Press, 2015); and Joan Scott, *Gender and the Politics of History* (New York: Columbia University Press, 1988). For influences on feminist thought, see Barbara Taylor, *Eve and the New Jerusalem: Socialism and Feminism in the Nineteenth Century* (Cambridge, MA: Harvard University Press, 1993); and Barbara Taylor, *Mary Wollstonecraft and the Feminist Imagination* (Cambridge: Cambridge University Press, 2003). On liberalism in Canada, consult Jean-François Constant and Michel Ducharme, eds., *Liberalism and Hegemony: Debating the Canadian Liberal Revolution* (Toronto: University of Toronto Press, 2009).

Scholars initially used "maternalism" to analyze welfare state policies that focused on women and children. But the term expanded to include the motherhood-based activism of individual women and women's organizations. I have used the terms "maternalism" and "maternal feminism" interchangeably, but for those who are interested in reading further, see Rebecca Jo Plant and Marian van der Klein, "Introduction: A New Generation of Scholars on Maternalism," in *Maternalism Reconsidered: Motherhood, Welfare and Social Policy in the Twentieth Century,* ed. Marian van der Klein et al. (New York: Berghahn Books, 2012), 1–37; Seth Koven and Sonya Michel, eds., *Mothers of a New World: Maternalist Politics and the Origins of Welfare States* (New York: Routledge, 1993); and Molly Ladd-Taylor, *Mother-Work: Women, Child Welfare, and the State, 1890–1930* (Urbana: University of Illinois Press, 1994).

Extensive historical work on the colonial, political, social, economic, and immigration history of the province informs this book. See Jean Barman, *The West beyond the West: A History of British Columbia* (Toronto: University of Toronto Press, 2007); John Belshaw, *Becoming British Columbia: A Population History* (Vancouver: UBC Press, 2009); Michael Dawson, *Selling British Columbia: Tourism and Consumer Culture, 1890–1970* (Vancouver: UBC Press, 2005); Hugh Johnston, ed., *The Pacific Province: A History of British Columbia* (Vancouver: Douglas and McIntyre, 1996); Cole Harris, *Making Native Space: Colonialism, Resistance, and Reserves in British Columbia* (Vancouver: UBC Press, 2003); Cole Harris, *The Resettlement of British Columbia: Essays on Colonialism and Geographical Change* (Vancouver: UBC Press, 1997); Lynne Marks, *Infidels and the Damn Churches: Irreligion and Religion in Settler British Columbia* (Vancouver: UBC Press, 2017); Cecilia Morgan, *Building Better Britains: Settler Societies in the British World, 1783–1920* (Toronto: University of Toronto Press, 2016); Adele Perry, *On the Edge of Empire: Gender, Race, and the Making of British Columbia, 1849–1871* (Toronto: University of Toronto Press, 2001); Adele Perry, *Colonial Relations: The Douglas-Connolly Family and the Nineteenth-Century Imperial World* (Cambridge: Cambridge University Press, 2015); Robert A.J. McDonald, *Making Vancouver: Class, Status, and Social Boundaries, 1863–1913* (Vancouver: UBC Press, 1996); Robert A.J. McDonald, *"A Long Way to Paradise": British Columbia Provincial Politics, 1870s to 1970s* (Vancouver: UBC Press, forthcoming); Martin Robin, *The Rush for Spoils: The Company Province, 1871–1933* (Toronto: McClelland and Stewart, 1972); and Patricia Roy, *Boundless Optimism: Richard McBride's British Columbia* (Vancouver: UBC Press, 2012). For a detailed overview of the electoral history of the province, see Elections British Columbia, *Electoral History of British Columbia, 1871–1986,* https://elections.bc.ca/docs/rpt/1871-1986_ElectoralHistoryofBC.pdf.

Page 3   **"A great revolutionary wave":** *B.C. Federationist,* 12 December 1913, 7.

Page 9   **"Guardian Angels":** Victoria *Daily British Colonist,* 17 February 1885, 3.

Page 9   **"Simple justice":** Victoria *Daily Colonist,* 28 May 1895, 5.

Page 11   **"The extension":** Quoted in Jonathan Beecher, *Charles Fourier: The Visionary and His World* (Berkeley: University of California Press, 1990), 208.

Page 12   **"A white man's province":** Quoted in Patricia Roy, *A White Man's Province: British Columbia Politicians and Chinese and Japanese Immigrants, 1858–1914* (Vancouver: UBC Press, 1989), viii.

ONE: SUFFRAGE AND REFORM

For the names of signatories, see the petitions in the *Journals of the Legislative Assembly*. The names of LCW members are from the Vancouver Social Directory, Local Council of Women membership list, 1914.

The *Dictionary of Canadian Biography (DCB)* is an excellent resource for biographical information on leading figures. See the following: Lyn Gough, entry on Pollard, Maria Heathfield (Grant); Lyn Gough, entry on McNaughton, Anne Cecilia (Spofford); Melanie Buddle, entry on Townsend, Margaret (Fox; Jenkins); and Susan Johnston, entry on Hussey, Florence Sarah (Hall). For biographical information on J.S. Cowper, see *Windsor Daily Star,* 14 July 1947, 5; on William Lashley Hall, see *Vancouver Western Call,* 30 May 1913, 1; on Florence Hall, see *Vancouver Daily World,* 24 March 1906, 18. See Lyn Gough, *As Wise as Serpents: Five Women and an Organization That Changed British Columbia, 1883–1939* (Victoria: Swan Lake, 1988), for details of the main figures in the WCTU.

On religion, see Lynne Marks, *Infidels and the Damn Churches: Irreligion and Religion in Settler British Columbia* (Vancouver: UBC Press, 2017); and Lynne Marks, "'Not Being Religious Didn't Take Away from Their Jewishness': The Complexities of Lived Religion among Late 19th and Early 20th Century B.C. Jews," *BC Studies* 181 (Spring 2014): 63–83. On the social gospel, see Richard Allen, *The Social Passion: Religion and Social Reform in Canada, 1914–28,* 2nd ed. (Toronto: University of Toronto Press, 1990); Ramsay Cook, *The Regenerators: Social Criticism in Late Victorian English Canada* (Toronto: University of Toronto Press, 1985); and Phyllis Airhart, *Serving the Present Age: Revivalism, Progressivism, and the Methodist Tradition in Canada* (Kingston and Montreal: McGill-Queen's University Press, 1992). On progress and perfection, see Barbara Taylor, *Mary Wollstonecraft and the Feminist Imagination* (Cambridge: Cambridge University Press, 2003); and Barbara Taylor and Sarah Knott, eds., *Women, Gender, and Enlightenment* (New York: Palgrave Macmillan, 2005).

On temperance, see Carolyn DeSwarte Gifford and Amy R. Slagell, *Let Something Good Be Said: Speeches and Writings of Frances E. Willard* (Urbana: University of Illinois Press, 2007); Sharon Anne Cook, *Through Sunshine and Shadow: The Woman's Christian Temperance Union, Evangelicalism, and Reform in Ontario, 1874–1930* (Montreal and Kingston: McGill-Queen's University Press, 1995); *Silver Anniversary of the Provincial Woman's Christian Temperance Union of British Columbia, 1883–1908*

(Victoria, 1908); Wendy Mitchinson, "The W.C.T.U.: 'For God, Home, and Native Land': A Study in Nineteenth Century Feminism," in *A Not Unreasonable Claim*, ed. Linda Kealey (Toronto: Canadian Women's Educational Press, 1979), 143–56; Albert John Hiebert, "Prohibition in North America" (master's thesis, Simon Fraser University, 1969); and Ivan E. Antak, "John Robson and His Faith: Church and State in Late Nineteenth Century British Columbia" (master's thesis, Simon Fraser University, 2012). On responses to temperance, see Janice Newton, *The Feminist Challenge to the Canadian Left, 1900–1918* (Montreal and Kingston: McGill-Queen's University Press, 1995), 23–24; and John D. Belshaw, *Colonization and Community: The Vancouver Island Coalfield and the Making of the British Columbian Working Class* (Montreal and Kingston: McGill-Queen's University Press, 2002), 178–79.

On women's organizations, see Veronica Strong-Boag, *Liberal Hearts and Coronets: The Lives and Times of Ishbel Marjoribanks and John Campbell Gordon, the Aberdeens* (Toronto: University of Toronto Press, 2015); Cyril E. Leonoff, "The Hebrew Ladies of Victoria, Vancouver Island," *Scribe: The Journal of the Jewish Historical Society of BC Jewish Museum and Archives* 24, 1–2 (2004): 3–57; Sylvie McClean, *A Woman of Influence: Evlyn Fenwick Farris* (Victoria: Sono Nis Press, 1997); Tami Adelman, "Evlyn Farris and the University Women's Club," in Latham and Kess, *In Her Own Right*, 147–66; Marjory Lang, *Women Who Made the News: Female Journalists in Canada, 1880–1945* (Montreal and Kingston: McGill-Queen's University Press, 1999); Linda Hale and Marjory Lang, "Women of *The World* and Other Dailies: The Lives and Times of Vancouver Newspaperwomen in the First Quarter of the Twentieth Century," *BC Studies* 85 (Spring 1990): 3–23; and Alexandria Zacharias, "British Columbia Women's Institute in the Early Years: Time to Remember," in Latham and Kess, *In Her Own Right*, 55–78.

On women in education, see Cathy Converse, *Against the Current: The Remarkable Life of Agnes Deans Cameron* (Victoria: Touchwood Editions, 2018); Barbara Latham and Roberta Pazdro, "A Simple Matter of Justice: Agnes Deans Cameron and the British Columbia Department of Education, 1906–1908," *Atlantis* 10, 1 (October 1984): 111–15; Jean Barman, *Sojourning Sisters: The Lives and Letters of Jessie and Annie McQueen* (Toronto: University of Toronto Press, 2003); Patrick Duane, "Home Economics, 1900–50," The Homeroom: British Columbia's History of Education, http://curric.library.uvic.ca/homeroom/content/topics/programs/homecon.htm; and Lee Stewart, *It's Up to You: Women at UBC in the Early Years* (Vancouver: UBC Press, 1990).

On women and the law, see Christopher Clarkson, "Property Law and Family Regulation in Pacific British North America, 1862–1873," *Histoire sociale/Social History* 30, 60 (1997): 386–416; Christopher Clarkson, *Domestic Reforms: Political Visions and Family Regulation in British Columbia, 1862–1940* (Vancouver: UBC Press, 2007); James Snell, *In the Shadow of the Law: Divorce in Canada, 1900–39* (Toronto: University of Toronto Press, 1991); Lori Chambers, *Married Women and Property Law in Victorian Ontario* (Toronto: Osgoode Society and University of Toronto Press, 1997); Annalee Lepp, "Constructing Normality and Confronting Deviance: Familial Ideologies, Household Structures, and 'Divorce' in the 1901 Census," in *Household Counts: Canadian Households and Families in 1901,* ed. Eric Sager and Peter Baskerville (Toronto: University of Toronto Press, 2007), 441–76; Helen Gregory MacGill, *Daughters, Wives and Mothers in British Columbia: Some Laws regarding Them* (Vancouver: Privately printed, 1913); and Elsie Gregory MacGill, *My Mother the Judge: A Biography of Helen Gregory MacGill* (Toronto: Ryerson Press, 1955).

On the history of sex work, see Patrick Dunae, "Sex, Charades, and Census Records: Locating Female Sex Trade Workers in a Victorian City," *Histoire sociale/Social History* 42, 84 (November 2009): 267–97; Shelly D. Ikebuchi, *From Slave Girls to Salvation: Gender, Race, and Victoria's Chinese Rescue Home, 1886–1923* (Vancouver: UBC Press, 2016); Yuen-Foon Woon, "Between South China and British Columbia: Life Trajectories of Chinese Women," *BC Studies* 156–57 (Winter-Spring 2007–08): 83–107; Deborah Nilson, "The Social Evil: Prostitution in Vancouver 1900–1920," in Latham and Kess, *In Her Own Right,* 205–28; Mariana Valverde, *Age of Light, Soap and Water: Moral Reform in English Canada, 1885–1925* (Toronto: University of Toronto Press, 2008); and Cecily Devereux, "'The Maiden Tribute' and the Rise of the White Slave in the Nineteenth Century: The Making of an Imperial Construct," *Victorian Review* 26, 2 (2000): 1–23. On socialism and sex work, see Janice Newton, "From Wage Slave to White Slave: The Prostitution Controversy and the Early Canadian Left," *in Beyond the Vote: Canadian Women and Politics,* ed. Linda Kealey and Joan Sangster (Toronto: University of Toronto Press, 1989), 217–36; and Linda Kealey, *Enlisting Women for the Cause: Women, Labour and the Left in Canada, 1890–1920* (Toronto: University of Toronto Press, 1998). On current feminist approaches to sex work, see Elya M. Durisin, Emily van der Meulen, and Chris Bruckert, eds., *Red Light Labour: Sex Work Regulation, Agency, and Resistance* (Vancouver: UBC Press, 2018); and Colette Parent et al., *Sex Work: Rethinking the Job, Respecting the Workers* (Vancouver: UBC Press, 2013).

For information on women's low wages, see Ivan Drury, "No Class, No Family: Women's Resistance and the Occasional Structure of Reproduction in Vancouver's Last Brothel District, 1911–1914" (master's thesis, Simon Fraser University, 2019); Jenea Tallentire, "'The Ordinary Needs of Life': Strategies of Survival for Single Women in 1901 Victoria," *BC Studies* 159 (2008): 45–80; and Robert A.J. McDonald, "Working Class Vancouver, 1886–1914: Urbanism and Class in British Columbia," *BC Studies* 69–70 (Spring-Summer 1986): 33–69.

Page 22   **"Greatly aid":** *Western Methodist Recorder,* June 1913, 5.

Page 23   **"Man and woman" . . . "eternal justice":** *Western Methodist Recorder,* February 1914, 17.

Page 23   **"Precious lives":** *Western Methodist Recorder,* April 1914, 20–21.

Page 23   **"Fight of spiritual":** *Vancouver Daily World,* 21 January 1913, 13.

Page 23   **"Necessity of spiritual":** *Vancouver Daily World,* 25 August 1913, 3.

Page 23   **"World mind":** *B.C. Federationist,* 22 November 1912, 6.

Page 23   **"Great propeller":** *Champion,* September 1913, 14–15.

Page 25   **"Despised and forsaken" ... "love one another":** *Western Clarion,* 24 July 1903, 3; 26 June 1903, 3.

Page 25   **"Some day":** *Western Clarion,* 15 October 1903, 3.

Page 25   **"The outcome" ... "of their way":** *Champion,* December 1912, 20.

Page 26   **"Possessing that occult":** Susan B. Anthony, quoted in Carolyn DeSwarte Gifford and Amy R. Slagell, *Let Something Good Be Said: Speeches and Writings of Frances E. Willard* (Urbana: University of Illinois Press, 2007), xxvii.

Page 26   **"Ladies of this Province":** *Victoria Daily British Colonist,* 4 July 1883, 1. For the establishment of the WCTU branch, see *Daily British Colonist,* 4 July 1883, 3; and WCTU of British Columbia, Minute book, 1883–86, MS 2227, British Columbia Archives (BCA).

Page 27   **"As woman is":** *Daily British Colonist,* 6 July 1883, 3.

Page 28   **"To grant to woman":** WCTU Minutes, 25 June 1884, BCA.

Page 28   **"Call on the legislators":** WCTU Minutes, 12 July 1884, BCA.

Page 29   **"WCTU woman must possess":** *Vancouver Daily World,* 30 November 1893, 5.

Page 29   **"The right to express":** *Nanaimo Daily News,* 9 June 1894, 3.

Page 30   **"Irresponsible men":** *Victoria Daily Colonist,* 21 March 1897, 7.

Page 31   **"Beer and tobacco":** *Canadian Socialist,* 13 September 1902, 3. The *Canadian Socialist* was published in Vancouver.

Page 32   **"The woman's age":** *Daily Colonist,* 28 May 1895, 4.

Page 32   **"Knight errants" ... "simple justice":** *Greater Vancouver Chinook,* 25 April 1914, 3.

Page 37   **"Getting a good ticket":** *Champion,* June 1913, 9–10.

Page 38   **"Brutal" marriages:** *Champion,* October 1912, 14–15. On Jamieson's participation, see Vancouver LCW minutes, 3 April 1911, Vancouver Council of Women records, box 6, University of British Columbia Special Collections.

Page 40   **"Best and fairest" ... "ignorant foreigners":** Alice Ashworth Townley, *Points in the Laws of BC regarding the Legal Status of Women* (Vancouver: BC Political Equality League, 1911).

Page 40   **"Barter":** *Vancouver Daily World,* 2 July 1913, 7.

Page 41   **"Sweetest word":** *Vancouver Daily World,* 19 January 1914, 14.

Page 42   **"Single standard":** *Western Methodist Recorder,* June 1913, 5.

Page 43   **"It was not by choice":** *Western Methodist Recorder,* October 1912, 10–11.

Page 43   **Low wages and international capital:** *B.C. Federationist,* 17 October 1913, 5.

Page 44   **"Traffic in women":** *Toronto Globe and Mail,* 22 June 1909, 4.

Page 44   **"Starvation or shame":** Quoted in Linda Hale, "The British Columbia Woman Suffrage Movement, 1890–1917" (master's thesis, University of British Columbia, 1977), 66.

Page 44   **"Every merchant on earth":** *Western Clarion,* 27 August 1904, 2.

TWO: BUILDING A MOVEMENT

Names of local women and organizations can be found in the Vancouver Social Directory, 1914. Records of suffrage petitions are in *Journals of the Legislative Assembly.* The *Champion* and papers from the BC Historical Newspapers database are excellent sources on the expansion of the PEL into the interior; see also Melanie Ihmels, "The New Chewing Gum," *Okanagan History* (Seventy-Second Report of the Okanagan Historical Society, 2008), 27–36. All motions to amend legislation are listed in the *Journals of the Legislative Assembly* at http://archives. leg.bc.ca. For biographical information, see the following *Dictionary of Canadian Biography* (*DCB*) entries: W. Kaye Lamb, entry on Tolmie, William Fraser; Sylvia Van Kirk, entry on Legacé, Josette (Work): 1809–1896; Michael F.H. Halleran, entry on Humphrey, Thomas Basil.

On politicians in this period, see Robert A.J. McDonald, "*A Long Way to Paradise":* *British Columbia Provincial Politics, 1870s to 1970s* (Vancouver: UBC Press, forthcoming); Martin Robin, *The Rush for Spoils: The Company Province, 1871–1933* (Toronto: McClelland and Stewart, 1972); and *DCB* entry on Hawthornthwaite, James Hurst, by Allen Seager. For the Douglas-Connolly family, see Adele Perry, *Colonial Relations: The Douglas-Connolly Family and the Nineteenth-Century Imperial World* (Cambridge: Cambridge University Press, 2015).

On municipal and school board voting, see Gillian Weiss, "As Women and as Citizens: Clubwomen in Vancouver, 1910–1928" (PhD diss., University of British Columbia, 1983); Doreen Weppler, "Early Forms of Political Activity among White Women in British Columbia, 1880–1925" (master's thesis, Simon Fraser University, 1971), 55–68; and Linda Hale, "The British Columbia Woman Suffrage Movement, 1890–1917" (master's thesis, University of British Columbia, 1977). On municipal voting restrictions, see Joan Sangster, *One Hundred Years of Struggle: The History of Women and the Vote in Canada* (Vancouver: UBC Press, 2018); Bettina Bradbury,

"Widows at the Hustings: Gender, Citizenship, and the Montreal By-Election of 1832," in *Rethinking Canada: The Promise of Women's History,* 5th ed., ed. Mona Gleason and Adele Perry (Don Mills: Oxford University Press, 2006), 73–94; and Gail Campbell, "The Most Restrictive Franchise in British North America?" *Canadian Historical Review* 71, 2 (June 1990): 159–88.

Page 48   **"Stronger moral"** ... **"valve tied down":** *Victoria Daily Colonist,* 24 March 1907, 2; *Victoria Daily Times,* 25 March 1907, 2; *Daily Colonist,* 25 March 1907, 2; 27 March 1907, 7.

Page 51   **"Tantamount to an assertion":** *Victoria Daily British Colonist and Morning Chronicle,* 10 April 1872, 3.

Page 51   **"Female"** ... **"for the ladies":** *Daily British Colonist,* 12 February 1873, 3.

Page 52   **Municipal office:** *Daily Colonist,* 15 March 1889, 4.

Page 52   **"Public expectation":** *Daily British Colonist,* 14 January 1874, 3.

Page 53   **First three voters:** *Daily British Colonist,* 13 January, 1875, 3.

Page 53   **"Swarms of Chinamen":** *Daily British Colonist,* 14 January 1875, 2.

Page 54   **"Woman's domain":** C.L. Davie, "Woman's Municipal Vote," *Daily Colonist,* 28 May 1895, 5.

Page 54   **"Big national or provincial issues":** *B.C. Federationist,* 7 November 1913, 5.

Page 54   **"Watch" over city politics:** *Daily Colonist,* 28 May 1895, 5.

Page 54   **"Enlightened world":** *Vancouver Daily World,* 8 February 1910, 5.

Page 54   **Address to city council:** Alice Ashworth Townley, *Points in the Laws of British Columbia regarding Legal Status of Women* (Vancouver: BC Political Equality League, 1911); Vancouver City Council Minutes, 14 November 1910, series S31 , City of Vancouver Archives.

Page 54   **"Property values ahead of life":** *Vancouver Daily World,* 21 October 1913, 3.

Page 55   **"Let us learn":** *Vancouver Daily World,* 21 October 1913, 3.

Page 55   **Women's Forum numbers:** *Vancouver Daily World,* 21 October 1913, 3.

Page 56   **"Immoral women":** *Daily Colonist,* 26 March 1907, 4.

Page 56   **"Seems to have been some fear"** ... **"only moral men vote":** *Daily Colonist,* 24 March 1907, 2.

Page 57   **"The members":** *Victoria Daily Times,* 8 February 1908, 2.

Page 57   **Jenkins and Grant:** Margaret Jenkins and Maria Grant to Richard McBride, 1 February 1908, 3 February 1908, 20 February 1908, 10 March

1908, GR 0441, Premier's Records, Official Correspondence Inward, vol. 31, file 64, British Columbia Archives (BCA).

Page 58　**"Dragged":** *Daily British Colonist,* 18 January 1884, 3.

Page 58　**"They are deeply":** *Daily British Colonist,* 19 June 1884, 2.

Page 58　**"Dignity" and "womanliness":** *Daily British Colonist,* 18 June 1884, 2.

Page 58　**"Rude and ungentlemanly":** *Daily British Colonist,* 18 June 1884, 2.

Page 58　**"Were more directly concerned":** *Daily Colonist,* 9 November 1895, 3.

Page 59　**"Progressive cities" and LCW campaign:** *Vancouver Daily World,* 22 November 1895, 4; 8 December 1896, 2; 17 December 1896, 4; 30 January 1897, 5; *Vancouver Province,* 6 February 1897, 3; 6 March 1897, 2; *Vancouver Daily World,* 29 January 1898, 2.

Page 59　**"One or two sensible":** *Vancouver Daily World,* 19 January 1898, 2.

Page 59　**"Don't vote for the ladies":** *Daily Colonist,* 19 January 1896, 2.

Page 60　**"Every person" ... "old-time prejudice":** *Daily British Colonist,* 10 April 1875, 3.

Page 60　**"Transforthanus":** *Daily British Colonist,* 27 and 28 March 1875, 3; 4 April 1875, 3.

Page 62　**"There was no possibility":** *Daily Colonist,* 13 June 1902, 7.

Page 63　**"Ancient prejudice" ... "should suffer":** *Daily Colonist,* 25 February 1899, 6.

Page 63　**"Revolutionary":** *Daily Colonist,* 2 March 1899, 4.

Page 64　**"For They Are Jolly":** *Abbotsford Post,* 6 June 1913, 3; *Champion,* July 1913, 7.

Page 65　**"All planks":** *Vancouver Daily World,* 11 August 1913, 8.

Page 66　**"Keenly interested" ... "their favour":** D. Davis to Richard McBride, 13 February 1913, GR 0441, Premier's Records, Official Correspondence Inward, vol. 49, file 97, BCA.

Page 66　**"That the present":** Quoted in Michael H. Cramer, "Public and Political: Documents of the Woman's Suffrage Campaign in British Columbia, 1871–1917: The View from Victoria," in *In Her Own Right: Selected Essays on Women's History of B.C.,* ed. Barbara Latham and Cathy Kess (Victoria: Camosun College, 1980), 83.

Page 67　**"Men say we are" ... "without their consent":** *Daily Colonist,* 15 December 1910, 21.

Page 68　**"Establishment of the Political":** Constitution and By-Laws of the Vancouver Branch of the British Columbia Political Equality League, NWp971.5B862, BCA.

Page 68   **Population data:** Jean Barman, *The West beyond the West: A History of British Columbia* (Toronto: University of Toronto Press, 2007), Table 14, 436.

Page 69   **Complaints:** *Champion*, February 1913, 14.

Page 71   **"Give the long-haired darlings":** *Champion*, January 1913, 11.

Page 71   **"The Government needs":** Rose Winstead to Richard McBride, 7 February 1913, GR 0441, Premier's Records, Official Correspondence Inward, vol. 49, file 97, BC

Page 71   **"Bank boys giggling":** Enderby Political Equality League to Richard McBride, 2 February 1913, GR 0441, Premier's Records, Official Correspondence Inward, vol. 49, file 97, BCA.

Page 71   **"Sore feeling and rivalry":** *Champion*, June 1913, 5–6.

Page 72   **"Responsibility" ..."status":** *Champion*, June 1913, 5–6.

Page 73   **"Suffrage Vitality" ..."contain legions":** *Champion*, December 1913, 4.

THREE: THE ANTI-SUFFRAGISTS

For biographical references, see the *Dictionary of Canadian Biography* entries by Zane H. Lewis on Davie, Alexander Edmund Batson; Jacqueline Gresko on Holbrook, Henry; Marianne Gosztonyi Ainley on Henderson, Julia Willmothe (Henshaw). Records of votes in the legislature can be found in *Journals of the Legislative Assembly*. Many local newspapers printed verbatim coverage of the debates.

On anti-suffrage movements more generally, see Veronica Strong-Boag, "Independent Women, Problematic Men: First- and Second-Wave Anti-Feminism in Canada from Goldwin Smith to Betty Steele," *Histoire sociale/Social History* 29, 57 (May 1996): 1–22; Veronica Strong-Boag, "The Opponents of Woman Suffrage," Women Suffrage and Beyond, 22 February 2012, http://womensuffrage.org/ ?designsentry_portf=the-opponents-of-woman-suffrage; Kenneth Florey, *American Woman Suffrage Postcards: A Study and Catalog* (Jefferson, IA: McFarland, 2005); Julia Bush, *Women against the Vote: Female Anti-Suffragism in Britain* (Oxford: Oxford University Press, 2007); Julia Bush, "British Women's Anti-Suffragism and the Forward Policy, 1908–14," *Women's History Review* 11, 3 (2002): 431–54; and Michael Kluckner, *Julia* (Vancouver: Midtown Press, 2018). For anti-suffrage iconography, see Lisa Tickner, "Representation," *The Spectacle of Women: Imagery of the Suffrage Campaign, 1907–14* (London: Chatto and Windus, 1987).

Page 76   **"Through the streets" ..."And why not?":** *Victoria Daily Times*, 1 March 1913, 3.

Page 77   **"With so much levity":** *Victoria Daily British Colonist*, 7 April 1875, 3.

Page 78   **"Politics is no sphere":** *Vancouver Province,* 4 September 1912, 12.

Page 79   **"Soured old spinster[s]":** *Vancouver Daily World,* 15 September 1913, 2.

Page 79   **Holbrook's joke:** *Daily British Colonist,* 10 April 1875, 3.

Page 79   **"Serious doubts":** *Vancouver Daily World,* 22 March 1911, 21.

Page 80   **"A Woman Who Admires":** Anonymous writer to Richard McBride, 31 March 1913, GR 0441, Premier's Papers, Official Correspondence Inward, vol. 49, file 97, British Columbia Archives (BCA).

Page 80   **"Acrimonies":** *Daily British Colonist,* 18 February 1885, 2; 17 February 1884, 3.

Page 80   **"Disarrange the whole":** *Daily British Colonist,* 7 April 1875, 3.

Page 81   **"Sooner put my hand":** Quoted in Michael Kluckner, *Julia* (Vancouver: Midtown Press, 2018), 70.

Page 81   **"Men were strong":** *Victoria Daily Times,* 7 December 1909, 6.

Page 81   **"Are no less public":** *Greater Vancouver Chinook,* 14 November 1914, 1.

Page 82   **"Noticeable turmoil":** *Daily British Colonist,* 7 February 1884, 3.

Page 82   **"The contentions":** *Daily British Colonist,* 17 February 1881, 3.

Page 82   **"Too much respect" . . . "dragged into politics":** *Daily British Colonist,* 18 February 1885, 3.

Page 82   **"Repugnant":** Letter to the editor from Publicola, *Daily British Colonist,* 27 February 1886, 2.

Page 82   **"Strong minded women":** *Colonist,* 7 April 1875, 3.

Page 82   **"Fossilized":** *Daily British Colonist,* 18 February 1885, 3.

Page 83   **"Lawyers, soldiers":** *Daily British Colonist,* 10 April 1875, 3.

Page 83   **"Merely [have] the power":** *Daily British Colonist,* 7 February 1884, 4.

Page 83   **"Woman's Party":** *B.C. Federationist,* 12 December 1913, 1.

Page 83   **"Had too much respect":** *Daily Colonist,* 22 April 1898, 6.

Page 84   **"Too refined and delicate":** *Vancouver Daily World,* 13 April 1894, 1.

Page 84   **"Get on with legislative":** *Victoria Daily British Colonist and Morning Chronicle,* 26 October 1871, 2.

Page 84   **"Mixed up":** *Vancouver Province,* 2 June 1913, 22.

Page 84   **"The woman made the man":** *Daily British Colonist,* 7 February 1884, 3.

Page 84   **"Parliament was":** *Victoria Daily Times,* 1 March 1913, 3.

Page 85   **"Faces like the engraving":** *Daily Colonist,* 3 March 1899, 4.

Page 86   **"Unladylike" … "into account":** *Vancouver Daily World,* 18 January 1913,
              1; *New Westminster News,* 6 February 1914, 4.

Page 86   **Double their political clout:** *Vancouver Daily World,* 13 April 1894, 1.

Page 86   **"Excellent decision" … "give them more":** Elenor W. Johnson to
              Richard McBride, 29 February 1913, GR 0441, Premier's Papers, Official
              Correspondence Inward, vol. 49, file 97, BCA.

Page 87   **"All progressive countries":** *Daily British Colonist,* 7 February 1884, 3.

Page 87   **Fraudulent petition:** *Daily British Colonist,* 18 February 1885, 3.

Page 87   **"Opposed the granting":** *Victoria Daily Times,* 16 May 1916, 7.

Page 87   **"Dumb as oysters":** *Daily Colonist,* 5 March 1899, 8.

Page 88   **"Lowering":** *Daily Colonist,* 13 April 1894, 1.

Page 88   **"Publicola":** *Daily British Colonist,* 10 March 1886, 2.

Page 89   **"Who can't subdue":** *Greater Vancouver Chinook,* 14 November 1914, 1.

Page 89   **"Shackles":** *Daily Colonist,* 3 March 1899, 4.

Page 89   **"Seductive arguments":** *Daily Colonist,* 3 March 1899, 4.

Page 89   **Birds:** *Western Clarion,* 11 May 1907, 4; **"shrewish":** *Daily British Colonist,*
              27 October 1871, 3; **"magpies":** *Vancouver Province,* 2 June 1913, 22.

Page 90   **"Disgusting":** *Daily Colonist,* 26 March 1907, 4.

Page 91   **"Unfit":** *Daily Colonist,* 2 March 1899, 4.

Page 91   **"Political power from":** *Daily Colonist,* 5 March 1899, 8.

FOUR: PERFORMING POLITICS

For biographical references, see the following entries in the *Dictionary of Canadian
Biography*: Vincent J. McNally, entry on Casey, Timothy; Linda Hale, entry on
Maclure, Sara Anne (McLagan). On Father William O'Boyle, see Vincent J. McNally,
*The Lord's Distant Vineyard: A History of the Oblates and the Catholic Community in
British Columbia* (Edmonton: University of Alberta Press, 2000).

On the role of petitions, see Janice Potter-Mackinnon, *While the Women Only Wept:
Loyalist Refugee Women* (Montreal and Kingston: McGill-Queen's University Press,
1993). On petitions and deputations, see Catherine L. Cleverdon, *The Woman
Suffrage Movement in Canada,* 2nd ed. (Toronto: University of Toronto Press, 1974);
Irene Howard, *The Struggle for Social Justice in British Columbia: Helena Gutteridge, the
Unknown Reformer* (Vancouver: UBC Press, 1992); and Gloria Whelan, "Maria Grant,
1854–1937: The Life and Times of an Early Twentieth Century Christian," in *In Her
Own Right: Selected Essays on Women's History of B.C.,* ed. Barbara Latham and Cathy
Kess (Victoria: Camosun College, 1980), 125–46.

On women authors, see Carole Gerson, *Canadian Women in Print, 1750–1918* (Waterloo: Wilfrid Laurier University Press, 2011); Janice Fiamengo, *The Woman's Page: Journalism and Rhetoric in Early Canada* (Toronto: University of Toronto Press, 2008); Cecily Devereux, *Growing a Race: Nellie McClung and the Fiction of Eugenic Feminism* (Montreal and Kingston: McGill-Queen's University Press, 2005); Mary Chapman, *Making Noise, Making News: US Suffrage Print Culture in Modernism* (New York: Oxford University Press, 2014), 28–58; Maria Dicenzo with Lucy Delap and Leila Ryan, *Feminist Media History: Suffrage, Periodicals, and the Public Sphere* (New York: Palgrave Macmillan, 2011). On building a sense of larger community, see Benedict Anderson, *Imagined Communities: Reflections on the Origin and Spread of Nationalism* (London: Verso, 2006).

Page 94 **"Supreme in the care" . . . "a little mothering":** *Vancouver Province,* 18 November 1913, 21.

Page 95 **Open to everyone:** *Champion,* August 1912, 1.

Page 96 **"Babies and children":** Helen Gregory MacGill, "History of Women Suffrage in BC," unpublished manuscript, n.d., Helen Gregory MacGill fonds, MSS 270, box 517-c-3, folder 5, City of Vancouver Archives.

Page 96 **"It is the intention":** *Champion,* November 1912, 1.

Page 97 **"Quite content":** *Champion,* September 1912, 6.

Page 97 **"In the public":** *Champion,* March 1913, 5–6. For newspaper coverage of speeches, see *Victoria Daily Times,* 17 February 1913, 24; *Vancouver Province,* 15 February 1913, 16.

Page 97 **"Some of these members":** *Champion,* March 1914, 6.

Page 99 **"Vice Versa" . . . "itself obnoxious":** *Daily Colonist,* 1 June 1910, 5. On the Vancouver University Women's Club performance, see University Women's Club of Vancouver, Minutes, 1911–17, AM 872, City of Vancouver Archives.

Page 99 **Mock Parliaments in Chilliwack:** *Chilliwack Progress,* 4 February 1903, 4; 11 February 1903, 5; 18 February 1903, 4.

Page 100 **"With some of Nelson's":** *Nelson Miner,* 21 January 1893, 1; 28 January 1893, 9. For other debates, see *Vancouver Daily World,* 9 January 1890, 2; 17 January 1894, 4; *Nanaimo Daily News,* 13 April 1894, 1.

Page 100 **"Women are human" . . . "chew gum properly":** *B.C. Federationist,* 24 July 1914, 6.

Page 100 **Kelowna PEL:** *Kelowna Record,* 6 March 1913, 1.

Page 100 **"Really in favor":** *Vancouver Daily World,* 16 October 1913, 18.

Page 100   **"Ardent" . . . "her own arguments":** *Vancouver Daily World,* 6 October 1913, 8.

Page 101   **"Ardent suffragists":** *Champion,* April 1914, 6.

Page 101   **"Extinguished":** *Vancouver Daily World,* 29 September 1913, 11. On the Kitsilano debate, see *Vancouver Daily World,* 30 November 1915, 5.

Page 101   **"He shall not talk":** *Vancouver Daily World,* 14 July 1913, 11.

Page 101   **"A man of such prominence":** *Vancouver Daily World,* 12 November 1913, 2.

Page 101   **"First step" . . . "Which is it?":** *Vancouver Daily World,* 18 November 1913, 5.

Page 102   **"We'll send him":** *Vancouver Daily World,* 18 November 1913, 5.

Page 102   **"Does the Reverend Father":** Quoted in Irene Howard, *The Struggle for Social Justice in British Columbia: Helena Gutteridge, the Unknown Reformer* (Vancouver: UBC Press, 1992), 76.

Page 103   **"Witty" . . . "symptoms of fear":** *Vancouver Daily World,* 6 May 1911, 5.

Page 104   **"Almost an ovation" . . . "good will":** *Vancouver Daily World,* 8 September 1913, 8.

Page 104   **"On a pedestal stood Liberty":** *Champion,* September 1913, 4.

Page 104   **Made-in-Canada fair:** *Vancouver Daily World,* 3 June 1911, 5; 10 June 1911, 17.

Page 105   **"Man's Suffrage" . . . "delight of the crowd":** *Champion,* November 1913, 13.

Page 105   **"Sunbeams from Summerland":** *Champion,* October 1912, 13.

Page 106   **"Nerve":** *Vancouver Daily World,* 14 July 1913, 11; *Vancouver Province,* 11 June 1913, 24.

Page 106   **"Silent, sweeping condemnation":** *Vancouver Daily World,* 15 September 1913, 2.

Page 106   **"Many Reasons Why Women":** *New Westminster Daily News,* 22 July 1912, 5.

Page 106   **Picnic and "suffrage hymn":** *Greater Vancouver Chinook,* 25 July 1914, 2; 19 September 1914, 1.

Page 106   **"Suffragette" convention:** *Chilliwack Progress,* 4 February 1915, 7; 18 February 1915, 1.

Page 107   **"Home-made candy":** *Greater Vancouver Chinook,* 24 April 1915, 4. On performances of the play, see *Vancouver Daily World,* 10 June 1915, 5; 30 March 1914, 5.

Page 107   **"Original burlesque":** *Champion,* October 1912, 11.

Page 107   **"New woman is" . . . "led an army?":** Alice Ashworth Townley, *Opinions of Mary* (Toronto: William Briggs, 1909), 57, 207, 208, 226.

Page 110   **"Is opposed to woman suffrage"** ... **"our political life":** *Daily Colonist,* 2 March 1899, 4; 15 June 1902, 4.

Page 111   **"Place themselves" . . . "a livelihood":** *Daily Colonist,* 28 May 1895, 4, 6; *Victoria Daily Times,* 27 May 1895, 6.

Page 111   **"Simple justice" . . . "should vote":** *Daily Colonist,* 28 May 1895, 4.

Page 111   **"Man in political matters":** *Victoria Daily Times,* 27 May 1895, 8.

Page 112   **"Enfranchisement of women":** *Vancouver Daily World,* 7 February 1891, 4.

Page 112   **"The only thing we ask":** *Vancouver Daily World,* 2 July 1913, 7; **reaching out to anti-suffragists:** *Vancouver Daily World,* 24 June 1913, 13.

Page 112   **"In many homes 'Papa'":** *Vancouver Daily World,* 27 October 1913, 15.

Page 113   **"In harmony with":** *Champion,* December 1912, 20.

Page 113   **"Absurdity":** *Champion,* August 1912, 15.

Page 114   **"To make a common plea":** *Champion,* May 1913, 14.

Page 114   **"Hinder [this] evolution":** *Vancouver Daily World,* 24 June 1913, 13.

Page 115   **"Our Men's Cosy Corner" . . . "Real Estate Transactions":** *Champion,* August 1913, 14; July 1913, 15; October 1913, 5.

FIVE: THE POLITICS OF RACE

On race in the Canadian suffrage movement, see Jennifer Henderson, *Settler Feminism and Race Making in Canada* (Toronto: University of Toronto Press, 2003); Janice Fiamengo, "Rediscovering Our Foremothers Again: Racial Ideas of Canada's Early Feminists, 1885–1945," in *Rethinking Canada: The Promise of Women's History,* 5th ed., ed. Mona Gleason and Adele Perry (Don Mills: Oxford University Press, 2006), 144–62; Mariana Valverde, "When the Mother of the Race Is Free: Race, Reproduction, and Sexuality in First-Wave Feminism," in *Gender Conflicts: New Essays in Women's History,* ed. Franca Iacovetta and Mariana Valverde (Toronto: University of Toronto Press, 1992), 3–26; and Lykke de la Cour, "Eugenics, Race and Canada's First-Wave Feminists: Dis/Abling the Debates," *Atlantis* 38, 2 (2017): 176–90.

On immigration and xenophobia, see Donald H. Avery, *Reluctant Host: Canada's Response to Immigrant Workers, 1896–1994* (Toronto: McClelland and Stewart, 1995); Donald Avery, *"Dangerous Foreigners": European Immigrant Workers and Labour Radicalism in Canada, 1896–1932* (Toronto: McClelland and Stewart, 1979); David Goutor, *Guarding the Gates: The Canadian Labour Movement and Immigration, 1872–1934* (Vancouver: UBC Press, 2007); and Robert A.J. McDonald, "The Immigrant

Section," in *Making Vancouver: Class, Status, and Social Boundaries, 1863–1913* (Vancouver: UBC Press, 1996), 201–29. On anti-Asian racism in British Columbia, see Patricia Roy, *A White Man's Province: British Columbia Politicians and Chinese and Japanese Immigrants, 1858–1914* (Vancouver: UBC Press, 1989); Patricia Roy, *The Oriental Question: Consolidating a White Man's Province, 1914–41* (Vancouver: UBC Press, 2003); John Price, "'Orienting' the Empire: Mackenzie King and the Aftermath of the 1907 Race Riots," *BC Studies* 156 (Winter 2007–08): 533–81; Peter Ward, *White Canada Forever: Popular Attitudes and Public Policy toward Orientals in British Columbia* (Montreal and Kingston: McGill-Queen's University Press, 2002); and Joan Brockman, "Exclusionary Tactics: The History of Women and Visible Minorities in the Legal Profession in British Columbia," in *Essays in the History of Canadian Law: British Columbia and the Yukon,* ed. Hamar Foster and John McLaren (Toronto: Osgoode Society and University of Toronto Press, 1995), 508–62.

On South Asian immigration and communities, see Peter Campbell, "East Meets Left: South Asian Militants and the Socialist Party of Canada in British Columbia, 1904–1914," *International Journal of Canadian Studies* 20 (Fall 1999): 35–65; Nilum Panesar, Yolande Pottie-Sherman, and Rima Wilkes, "The Komagata Maru through a Media Lens: Racial, Economic, and Political Threat in Newspaper Coverage of the 1914 Komagata Maru Affair," *Canadian Ethnic Studies* 49, 1 (2017): 85–101; Enakshi Dua, "Exclusion through Inclusion: Female Asian Migration in the Making of Canada as a White Settler Nation," *Gender, Place and Culture* 14, 4 (2007): 445–66; Enakshi Dua, "The Hindu Woman's Question: Canadian Nation Building and the Social Construction of Gender for South Asian Women," in *Anti-Racist Feminism: Critical Race and Gender Studies,* ed. Agnes Calliste and George Sefa Dei (Halifax: Fernwood, 2000), 55–72 ; Norman Buchignani, Doreen M. Indra, and Ram Srivastiva, *Continuous Journey: A Social History of South Asians in Canada* (Toronto: McClelland and Stewart, 1985); and Hugh J.M. Johnston, *Jewels of the Qila: The Remarkable Story of an Indo-Canadian Family* (Vancouver: UBC Press, 2012).

On Chinese immigration and communities, see Haiming Liu, "The Social Origins of Early Chinese Immigrants: A Revisionist Perspective," in *The Chinese in America: A History from Gold Mountain to the New Millennium,* ed. Susie Lan Cassel (Walnut Creek: AltaMira Press, 2002), 21–36; Wing Chung Ng, *The Chinese in Vancouver, 1945– 80: The Pursuit of Identity and Power* (Vancouver: UBC Press, 1999); Yuen-Foon Woon, "Between South China and British Columbia: Life Trajectories of Chinese Women," *BC Studies* 156–57 (Winter-Spring 2007–08): 83–107; and Patrick Dunae et al., "Making the Inscrutable Scrutable: Race and Space in Victoria's Chinatown, 1891," *BC Studies* 169 (Spring 2011): 51–80.

On Japanese immigration and communities, see Michiko Midge Ayukawa, "Good Wives and Wise Mothers: Japanese Picture Brides in Early Twentieth-Century British Columbia," *BC Studies* 105–6 (Spring-Summer 1995): 103–18; Michiko Midge Ayukawa, *Hiroshima Immigrants in Canada, 1891–1941* (Vancouver: UBC Press, 2008);

and Mona Oikawa, *Cartographies of Violence: Japanese Canadian Women, Memory, and the Subjects of the Internment* (Toronto: University of Toronto Press, 2012).

On race and myths of the West, see Sarah Carter, *Imperial Plots: Women, Land, and the Spadework of British Colonialism on the Canadian Prairies* (Winnipeg: University of Manitoba Press, 2016); Rebecca J. Mead, *How the West Was Won: Woman Suffrage in the Western United States* (New York: New York University Press, 2004); T. Kulba and V. Lamont, "The Periodical Press and Western Women's Suffrage Movements in Canada and the United States: A Comparative Study," *Women's Studies International Forum* 29, 3 (May-June 2006): 265–78; Kathryn McPherson, "Was the 'Frontier' Good for Women? Historical Approaches to Women and Agricultural Settlement in the Prairie West, 1870–1925," *Atlantis* 25, 1 (Fall-Winter 2000): 75–86; Tiffany Lewis, "Winning Women's Suffrage in the Masculine West: Abigail Scott Duniway's Frontier Myth," *Western Journal of Communication* 75, 2 (March-April 2011): 127–47; Holly J. McCammon and Karen E. Campbell, "Winning the Vote in the West: The Political Successes of the Women's Suffrage Movements, 1866–1919," *Gender and Society* 15, 1 (February 2001): 55–82; Sarah Carter, "Britishness, 'Foreignness,' Women and Land in Western Canada, 1890s–1920s," *Humanities Research* 13, 1 (2006): 43–60; Adele Perry, *On the Edge of Empire: Gender, Race, and the Making of British Columbia, 1849–1871* (Toronto: University of Toronto Press, 2001); and Adele Perry, "Oh I'm Just Sick of the Faces of Men: Gender Imbalance, Race, Sexuality, and Sociability in Nineteenth-Century British Columbia," *BC Studies* 105–6 (Spring-Summer 1995): 27–43.

On black communities, see Sherry Edmunds Flett, "'Abundant Faith': Nineteenth-Century African-Canadian Women on Vancouver Island," in *Telling Tales: Essays in Western Women's History,* ed. Catherine A. Cavanaugh and Randi Warne (Vancouver: UBC Press, 2000), 261–80; Crawford Kilian, *Go Do Some Great Thing: The Black Pioneers of British Columbia* (Burnaby: Commodore Books, 2008); Crawford Kilian, "BC's Black Pioneer Women," *Tyee,* 6 February 2009, https://thetyee.ca/Books/2009/02/06/BlackPioneerWomen/; Carla Marano, "Rising Strongly and Rapidly: The Universal Negro Improvement Association in Canada, 1919–1940," *Canadian Historical Review* 91, 2 (June 2010): 233–59; Eli Yahri, "Order-in-Council P.C. 1911-1324: The Proposed Ban on Black Immigration to Canada," *Canadian Encyclopedia,* 30 September 2016, https://www.thecanadianencyclopedia.ca/en/article/order-in-council-pc-1911-1324-the-proposed-ban-on-black-immigration-to-canada; and Jane Rhodes, *Mary Ann Shadd Cary: The Black Press and Protest in the 19th Century* (Bloomington: Indiana University Press, 1998).

On Indigenous women, see Jan Hare and Jean Barman, *Good Intentions Gone Awry: Emma Crosby and the Methodist Mission on the Northwest Coast* (Vancouver: UBC Press, 2006); Sylvia Van Kirk, "Colonized Lives: The Native Wives and Daughters of Five Founding Families of Victoria," in *In the Days of Our Grandmothers: A Reader in Aboriginal Women's History in Canada,* ed. Mary-Ellen Kelm and Lorna Townsend

(Toronto: University of Toronto Press, 2006), 170–99; Sylvia Van Kirk, *Many Tender Ties: Women in Fur-Trade Society, 1670–1870* (Winnipeg: Watson and Dwyer, reprint 1999); Leslie A. Robertson with the Kwagu'L Gix̱sa̱m Clan, *Standing Up with G̱a'ax̱sta'las: Jane Constance Cook and the Politics of Memory, Church, and Custom* (Vancouver: UBC Press, 2012); Peggy Brock, *The Many Voyages of Arthur Wellington Clah: A Tsimshian Man of the Pacific Northwest Coast* (Vancouver: UBC Press, 2011); Susan Neylan, *The Heavens Are Changing: Nineteenth-Century Protestant Missions and Tsimshian Christianity* (Montreal and Kingston: McGill-Queen's University Press, 2003); John Lutz, "Gender and Work in Lewammen Families, 1843–1970," in Kelm and Townsend, *In the Days of Our Grandmothers*, 216–50; Mary-Ellen Kelm and Keith D. Smith, *Talking Back to the Indian Act: Critical Readings in Settler Colonial Histories* (Toronto: University of Toronto Press, 2018); Margaret B. Blackman, *During My Time: Florence Edenshaw Davidson: A Haida Woman* (Seattle: University of Washington Press, 1982); and Martine J. Reid and Daisy Sewid-Smith, *Paddling to Where I Stand: Agnes Alfred, Qwiqwasutinuxw Noblewoman* (Vancouver: UBC Press, 2004).

On progress and civilization, see Ann Towns, "The Status of Women as a Standard of 'Civilization,'" *European Journal of International Relations* 15, 4 (2009): 681–706; Ian Angus, "Marx and Engels ... and Darwin? The Essential Connection between Historical Materialism and Natural Selection," *International Socialist Review* 65 (May 2009): https://isreview.org/issue/65/marx-and-engelsand-darwin; Jeannette E. Jones et al., eds., *Darwin in Atlantic Cultures: Evolutionary Visions of Race, Gender, and Sexuality* (New York: Routledge, 2009); and Peter Campbell, *Canadian Marxists and the Search for a Third Way* (Montreal and Kingston: McGill-Queen's University Press, 2000). On utopian socialism, see Jonathan Beecher, *Charles Fourier: The Visionary and His World* (Berkeley: University of California Press, 1990); and Barbara Taylor, *Eve and the New Jerusalem: Socialism and Feminism in the Nineteenth Century* (Cambridge, MA: Harvard University Press, 1993). On connections of mothering to citizenship and global nation building, see Nichole Saunders, "Protecting Mothers in Order to Protect Children: Maternalism and the 1935 Pan-American Child Congress," 148–67, and Yoshie Mitsuyoshi, "Maternalism, Soviet Style: The Working 'Mothers with Many Children' in Post-War Western Ukraine," 205–26, both in *Maternalism Reconsidered: Motherhood, Welfare and Social Policy in the Twentieth Century*, ed. Marian van der Klein et al. (New York: Berghahn Books, 2012); and Firoozeh Kashani-Sabet, *Conceiving Citizens: Women and the Politics of Motherhood in Iran* (New York: Oxford University Press, 2011).

Page 118 **"In this wonderful land":** Speech by Maria Grant to Richard McBride, 14 February 1913, GR 0441, Premier's Papers, Official Correspondence Inward, vol. 49, file 97, British Columbia Archives (BCA).

Page 121 **"Can neither read or write":** WCTU Report, 1888, quoted in Linda Hale, "The British Columbia Woman Suffrage Movement, 1890–1917" (master's thesis, University of British Columbia, 1977), 15.

Page 121   **"Deny their countrywomen":** *Kelowna Record,* 26 September 1912, 2.

Page 121   **"Ignorant foreign immigrants"** ... **"valuable citizens":** *Champion,* April 1914, 11.

Page 122   **"Aliens":** *Greater Vancouver Chinook,* 5 May 1916, 3; **"Anglo Saxon women":** *Vancouver Western Call,* 3 March 1916, 5.

Page 122   **"The mother, the wives":** *Victoria Daily Colonist,* 25 April 1897, 6.

Page 122   **"Do not consider":** *Nanaimo Daily News,* 9 June 1895, 3.

Page 122   **"Mother wit":** *Western Clarion,* 20 August 1904, 4.

Page 123   **"Concerns the mothers":** *Champion,* October 1913, 7.

Page 124   **"Rapid influx":** *Creston Review,* 25 October 1912, 5. See similar language in the PEL Petition, 1913, GR 0441, Premier's Records, Official Correspondence Inward, vol. 49, file 97, 1913, BCA.

Page 125   **"Indians and Hindoos":** *Western Clarion,* 7 July 1906, 4.

Page 125   **"Occupation of these shores":** *B.C. Federationist,* 3 July 1914, 2.

Page 125   **"Against Asiatics":** Quoted in Susan Wade, "Helena Gutteridge: Votes for Women and Trade Unions," in *In Her Own Right: Selected Essays on Women's History in B.C.,* ed. Barbara Latham and Cathy Kess (Victoria: Camosun College, 1980), 196; and see Ivan Drury, "No Class, No Family: Women's Resistance and the Occasional Structure of Reproduction in Vancouver's Last Brothel District, 1911–1914" (master's thesis, Simon Fraser University, 2019), 74.

Page 126   **"Universal brotherhood"** ... **"liquor, immorality":** *Western Methodist Recorder,* July 1911, 17.

Page 127   **Right to family life:** "India and Canada, 1915," *Woman's Century,* October 1915, quoted in Nancy Forestell and Maureen Moynagh, eds., *Documenting First Wave Feminisms,* vol. 2, *Canada – National and Transnational Contexts* (Toronto: University of Toronto Press, 2014), 51–52.

Page 127   **"Irresponsible":** *Vancouver Daily World,* 29 January 1912, 6.

Page 128   **"Dumping":** *Vancouver Daily World,* 12 April 1912, 33.

Page 128   **"Hindu wives" debate:** *Daily Colonist,* 23 January 1912, 7; 10 February 1912, 18, 29 May 1912, 1.

Page 128   **"Barbarism":** *Vancouver Daily World,* 2 July 1913, 7.

Page 128   **"The educated women"** ... **"of the world":** *Nanaimo Daily News,* 9 June 1894, 3.

Page 129   **"Ghosts and ghouls":** *Vancouver Daily World,* 2 July 1913, 7.

Page 129   **"Has always meant":** *Vancouver Daily World,* 18 August 1913, 8.

Page 129 **Examples of women's history:** *Daily Colonist,* 28 May 1895, 4–7; *Champion,* September 1913, 14.

Page 129 **"Harems":** *Champion,* August 1912, 19.

Page 129 **"Today women have" … "women in BC":** *Vancouver Daily World,* 29 September 1913, 11.

Page 130 **"Even in China":** *Champion,* October 1912, 11.

Page 130 **"We hope that":** *Champion,* September 1912, 7.

Page 130 **"Pioneering":** See T. Kulba and V. Lamont, "The Periodical Press and Western Women's Suffrage Movements in Canada and the United States: A Comparative Study," *Women's Studies International Forum* 29, 3 (May–June 2006): 265.

Page 130 **"Broadest vision":** *Vancouver Western Call,* 24 March 1911, 8.

Page 131 **"Pacific Slope" … "custard beneath":** *Prince Rupert Journal,* 2 May 1911, 2.

Page 131 **"Tireless efforts" … "wonderful reading":** Blanche Murison, "Women of the West in Clubland: The Athenaeum Club, Vancouver BC," *British Columbia Magazine,* March 1911, 188–90.

Page 131 **"The men of the West":** *Vancouver Daily World,* 2 July 1913, 7.

Page 131 **"Broad-minded enough":** *Daily Colonist,* 6 March 1914, 11.

Page 131 **"Splendid type":** *Champion,* December 1912, 11.

Page 132 **"Woman suffragist":** *Vancouver Daily World,* 6 May 1911, 5.

Page 132 **"Boasts of political equality":** *Vancouver Daily World,* 16 June 1913, 5.

Page 132 **"The suffragists' trusting":** *Vancouver Daily World,* 2 July 1913, 7.

Page 132 **"Strongest" leader:** Dorothy Davis and PEL Executive to Richard McBride, 29 January 1913, GR 0441, Premier's Records, Official Correspondence Inward, vol. 49, file 97, BCA.

Page 132 **"The Men" … "political freedom?":** *Champion,* February 1913, 4.

Page 132 **"Progressive west":** *B.C. Federationist,* 12 December 1913, 1.

Page 135 **"The Negro race":** Order-in-Council P.C. 1323, 12 August 1911, quoted in Eli Yarhi, "Order-in-Council P.C. 1911–1324 – the Proposed Ban on Black Immigration to Canada," *Canadian Encyclopedia,* 30 September 2016, https://www.thecanadianencyclopedia.ca/en/article/order-in-council-pc-1911-1324-the-proposed-ban-on-black-immigration-to-canada.

Page 135 **"Moral, social and general":** *Vancouver Daily World,* 20 July 1911, 8.

Page 135 **Negro Christian Alliance protest:** *Vancouver Daily World,* 18 December 1915, 15.

Page 135   **"A benefit to humanity":** *Vancouver Daily World,* 17 February 1914, 12.

Page 135   **Negro Christian Alliance:** *Vancouver Daily World,* 4 November 1915, 16; *Vancouver Province,* 4 July 1915, 11.

Page 135   **"Foolish" ... "outrages":** *Edmonton Capital,* 27 March 1911, 1.

SIX: LABOURING WOMEN

Biographical information from the Brantford City Directory 1894 (on Bertha Merrill Burns). For information in the *Dictionary of Canadian Biography,* see Mark Leier, entry on Smith, Ralph Smith; Lyn Gough, entry on McNaughton, Anne Cecilia. On L.D Taylor, see Mary Rawson, "L.D. Taylor: The Man Who Made Vancouver," *American Journal of Economics and Sociology* 75, 1 (January 2016): 217–45; and Daniel Francis, *LD: Mayor Louis Taylor and the Rise of Vancouver* (Vancouver: Arsenal Pulp Press, 2004).

On the labour movement and socialism, see Bryan Palmer, *Working-Class Experience: Rethinking the History of Canadian Labour, 1880–1991* (Toronto: McClelland and Stewart, 1992); Mark Leier, *Red Flags and Red Tape: The Making of a Labour Bureaucracy* (Toronto: University of Toronto Press, 1995); David Buchanan, "Yours for the Revolution: Communication and Identity in the *Western Clarion,*" *ESC: English Studies in Canada* 41, 2–3 (2015): 133–64; Allen Seager, "Socialists and Workers: The Western Canadian Coal Miners, 1900–21," *Labour/Le travail* 16 (Fall 1985): 23–59; John Belshaw, "The British Collier in British Columbia: Another Archetype Reconsidered," *Labour/Le travail* 34 (Fall 1994): 11–36; Allen Seager and Adele Perry, "Mining the Connections: Class, Community, Ethnicity and Gender and Nanaimo, B.C., 1891," *Histoire sociale/Social History* 30, 59 (1997): 58–59; Ross McCormack, "The Emergence of the Socialist Movement in British Columbia," *BC Studies* 21 (Spring 1974): 3–27; Ross A. McCormack, *Reformers, Rebels, and Revolutionaries: The Western Canadian Radical Movement, 1899–1919* (Toronto: University of Toronto Press, 1977); and Rod Mickleburgh, *On the Line: A History of the British Columbia Labour Movement* (Madeira Park, BC: Harbour, 2018). On labour in Vancouver, see Working Lives Collective, *Working Lives: Vancouver, 1886–1986* (Vancouver: New Star Books, 1985); and Robert A.J. McDonald, *Making Vancouver: Class, Status, and Social Boundaries, 1863–1913* (Vancouver: UBC Press, 1996), 175–200.

On women and the left, see Joan Sangster, *Dreams of Equality: Women on the Canadian Left, 1920–1950* (Toronto: McClelland and Stewart, 1989); Linda Kealey, "Canadian Socialism and the Woman Question, 1900–14," *Labour/Le travail* 13 (Spring 1984): 77–100; Linda Kealey, *Enlisting Women for the Cause: Women, Labour, and the Left in Canada, 1880–1920* (Toronto: University of Toronto Press, 1998); Janice Newton, *The Feminist Challenge to the Canadian Left, 1900–1918* (Montreal and Kingston: McGill-Queen's University Press, 1995); Marie Campbell, "Sexism in Trade Unions, 1900–1920," in *In Her Own Right: Selected Essays on Women's History of B.C.,* ed. Barbara Latham and Cathy Kess (Victoria: Camosun College, 1980), 167–86;

and Susan Wade, "Helena Gutteridge: Votes for Women and Trade Unions," in *In Her Own Right,* 187–201. On the family wage, see Lara Campbell, *Respectable Citizens: Gender, Family, and Unemployment in Ontario's Great Depression* (Toronto: University of Toronto Press, 2009).

On women in the paid labour force, see Star Rosenthal, "Union Maids: Organized Women Workers in Vancouver, 1900–1915," *BC Studies* 41 (Spring 1979): 36–55; Roberta J. Pazdro, "Agnes Deans Cameron: Against the Current," in Latham and Kess, *In Her Own Right,* 101–21; Melanie Buddle, *The Business of Women: Marriage, Family, and Entrepreneurship in British Columbia, 1901–51* (Vancouver: UBC Press, 2011); John Sutton Lutz, *Makúk: A New History of Aboriginal-White Relations* (Vancouver: UBC Press, 2009); and Alicia Muszynksi, *Cheap Wage Labour: Race and Gender in the Fisheries of British Columbia* (Montreal and Kingston: McGill-Queen's University Press, 1996).

On infant mortality rates, see R.D. Fraser, "Section B: Vital Statistics and Health," Table B 51-58, *Historical Statistics of Canada* (Ottawa: Statistics Canada, 1983), 195; and Cynthia Commachio, *Nations Are Built of Babies: Saving Ontario's Mothers and Children, 1900–1940* (Montreal and Kingston: McGill-Queen's University Press, 1993).

On Vancouver Island coal-mining communities, see Jeremy Mouat, "The Politics of Coal: A Study of the Wellington Miners' Strike of 1890–1," *BC Studies* 77 (Spring 1988): 3–29; John Douglas Belshaw, *Colonization and Community: The Vancouver Island Coalfield and the Making of the British Columbian Working Class* (Montreal and Kingston: McGill-Queen's University Press, 2002); John R. Hinde, "'Stout Ladies and Amazons': Women in the British Columbia Coal-Mining Community of Ladysmith, 1912–14," *BC Studies* 114 (Summer 1997): 33–57; John R. Hinde, *When Coal Was King: Ladysmith and the Coal-Mining Industry on Vancouver Island* (Vancouver: UBC Press, 2003); and Lyn Bowen, *Three Dollar Dreams* (Lantzville: Oolichan Books, 1987).

Page 144   **"Sex war" ... "widest liberty":** *B.C. Federationist,* 31 October 1913, 5.

Page 146   **Gutteridge and equal pay:** *Vancouver Daily World,* 25 September 1915, 2.

Page 148   **Grant estate:** Grant Probate file, 1939, GR 2083.2795, BC Supreme Court, British Columbia Archives.

Page 148   **"The experience of life":** Quoted in Janice Newton, *The Feminist Challenge to the Canadian Left, 1900–1918* (Montreal and Kingston: McGill-Queen's University Press, 1995), 105.

Page 148   **"Why self-supporting women":** *Champion,* August 1912, 14.

Page 149   **"Voice":** *Champion,* February 1914, 4.

Page 150   **"Loud applause":** *Western Socialist,* 23 May 1903, 1.

Page 150   **Irene Smith:** *Western Clarion,* 17 September 1903, 1, 4.

Page 151   **"Not a woman delegate":** *Western Socialist,* 25 October 1902, 3.

Page 151   **"She is supposed to be":** *Western Clarion,* 5 November 1903, 1.

Page 151   **Imported from England:** *Western Clarion,* 13 May 1905, 4.

Page 151   **"Pillars and props":** *Western Clarion,* 9 June 1906, 1.

Page 151   **"Striking resemblance":** *Western Clarion,* 11 May 1907, 4.

Page 151   **Not "violently opposed":** Quoted in Newton, *Feminist Challenge,* 140.

Page 152   **"Civilizing force":** *Western Clarion,* 7 July 1906, 4.

Page 152   **"Most oppressed" . . . "purity and simplicity":** *Western Clarion,* 10 February 1906, 1.

Page 152   **"Keep your eyes":** *Western Clarion,* 22 January 1910, 1.

Page 152   **Talks by Burns and Parr:** *Vancouver Daily World,* 30 November 1907, 7; 25 January 1908, 10.

Page 153   **"Votes for Women":** *Vancouver Daily World,* 26 October 1912, 4.

Page 153   **"When the working class":** *B.C. Federationist,* 31 October 1913, 5.

Page 154   **"Rapid aging":** *Vancouver Sun,* 12 December 1914, 8.

Page 154   **Gutteridge to BC Federation of Labour:** Quoted in Irene Howard, *The Struggle for Social Justice in British Columbia: Helena Gutteridge, the Unknown Reformer* (Vancouver: UBC Press, 1992), 82.

Page 154   **"Support and expand":** BC Federation of Labour, 1914, quoted in Linda Hale, "The British Columbia Woman Suffrage Movement, 1890–1917" (master's thesis, University of British Columbia, 1977), 113.

Page 155   **"Noisy advocates" . . . "industrial life":** *B.C. Federationist,* 14 April 1916, 2; 11 August 1916, 1.

Page 157   **The emergence of the WSL:** *Vancouver Daily World,* 10 July 1913, 9.

Page 158   **"Women of leisure":** *Vancouver Province,* 7 April 1916, 7.

Page 158   **Bernice Panagopolous's talk:** *Vancouver Daily World,* 8 September 1913, 8; 2 September 1913, 11.

Page 159   **"A class of helpers":** *Champion,* October 1912, 6.

Page 159   **"Touch[ed] their own pockets":** *Vancouver B.C. Federationist,* 28 March 1913, 3, quoted in Star Rosenthal, "Union Maids: Organized Women Workers in Vancouver, 1900–1915," *BC Studies* 41 (Spring 1979): 52.

Page 159   **On WSL and unions:** See *B.C. Federationist* from October to December 1913.

Page 160   **"Issues that relate":** *Vancouver B.C. Federationist,* 3 October 1913, 8.

Page 160   **"Secure this tool" . . . "but your chains":** *Vancouver Daily World,* 2 July 1913, 7.

Page 160   **"She is the bottom dog":** *B.C. Federationist,* 19 December 1913, 5.

Page 160   **"The woman and the worker":** *B.C. Federationist,* 12 December 1913, 7.

Page 161   **"Altar of mammon":** *Vancouver Daily World,* 15 September 1913, 2.

Page 161   **"Money interests":** *Vancouver Daily World,* 16 June 1915, 5.

Page 161   **Douglas-Fearn:** *Vancouver Daily World,* 16 June 1913, 14.

Page 161   **Monopoly capital:** *Vancouver Daily World,* 20 September 1913, 11.

Page 161   **"A woman buys" . . . "mercantile world":** Quoted in Newton, *Feminist Challenge,* 57.

Page 161   **"Everything is made":** *Vancouver Daily World,* 14 July 1913, 11.

Page 162   **"If mothers were awake":** *B.C. Federationist,* 10 July 1914, 2.

Page 162   **"Man was so liable":** *Champion,* November 1912, 7.

Page 163   **"Need for political power":** *B.C. Federationist,* 3 October 1913, 8.

Page 163   **"Relieving pressure":** *B.C. Federationist,* 10 October 1913, 5.

Page 163   **Socialist disruption:** *Vancouver Daily World,* 27 October 1913, 15.

Page 163   **"Palliative":** *Vancouver Daily World,* 13 October 1913, 14.

Page 164   **"Independent":** *Nanaimo Daily News,* 9 June 1894, 3. On the platform itself, see *Vancouver Daily World,* 9 March 1894, 4.

Page 164   **Miners' march:** *Nanaimo Daily News,* 13 March 1891, 1, 4.

Page 165   **Gutteridge and Crosfield:** *Vancouver Province,* 15 November 1913, 7.

Page 165   **"Taxpaying women":** *Vancouver Daily World,* 25 August 1913, 3.

Page 166   **"The miners of Nanaimo":** *B.C. Federationist,* 17 October 1913, 5.

Page 166   **"Awakened":** *B.C. Federationist,* 7 November 1913, 5.

SEVEN: A GLOBAL MOVEMENT

For biographical information on Kate Chan, see Boxer Indemnity Scholars, "The Chan Family," 1 December 2015, https://boxerindemnityscholars.wordpress.com/2015/12/01/the-chan-陳-family/; on Kang Tongbi, see Lily Xiao Hong Lee, "Kang Tongbi," in *Biographical Dictionary of Chinese Women: The Twentieth Century, 1912–2000,* ed. Lily Xiao Hong Lee and A.D. Stefanowska (New York: Routledge, 2003), 272–74; on Mrs. Creasy Smith, see *113th Report of the Baptist Missionary Society* (London: Baptist Missionary Society, 1905), 126; on Dr. Ernest Hall, see Mary-Ellen

Kelm, "'The Only Place Likely to Do Her Any Good': The Admission of Women to British Columbia's Provincial Hospital for the Insane," *BC Studies* 96 (Winter 1992–93): 66–89. For information on CELRA members, see "Chinese Women in the Northwest," Chinese in Northwest America Research Committee (CINARC), https://www.cinarc.org/Women.html. For detailed biographies of British suffragists and suffragettes, see Elizabeth Crawford, *The Women's Suffrage Movement: A Reference Guide, 1866–1928* (London: UCL Press, 1999).

On suffrage and militancy in Canada, see Katja Thieme, "Uptake and Genre: The Canadian Reception of Suffrage Militancy," *Women's Studies International Forum* 29 (2006): 279–88; Deborah Gorham, "English Militancy and the Canadian Suffrage Movement," *Atlantis* 1, 1 (1975): 83–112; and Joan Sangster, "Exporting Suffrage: British Influences on the Canadian Suffrage Movement," *Women's History Review* 28, 4 (2019): 566–86. On the WSPU, see Jane Purvis, *Emmeline Pankhurst: A Biography* (New York: Routledge, 2002); and Jane Chapman, "The Argument of the Broken Pane: Suffragette Consumerism and Newspapers," *Media History* 21, 3 (2015): 238–51. On WSPU colours, see Lisa Tickner, *The Spectacle of Women: Imagery of the Suffrage Campaign, 1907–14* (London: Chatto and Windus, 1987), 93, 265.

On Kang Tongbi, CERA, and CELRA, see Jane Leung Larson, "The Kang Tongbi Collection of South Windsor, Connecticut" (paper presented to New England Association of Asian Studies, University of Connecticut, Storrs, 4 October 2014), https://drive.google.com/file/d/0By7Ajg4xYgVqOEEyM2R0eXpieVk/view; Jane Leung Larson, "The United States as a Site for Baohuanghui Activism" (paper presented to Fifth International Conference of Institutes and Libraries in Chinese Overseas Studies, Vancouver, 17 May 2012); Jane Leung Larson, "The Chinese Empire Reform Association (Baohuanghui) and the 1905 Anti-American Boycott: The Power of a Voluntary Association," in *The Chinese in America: A History from Gold Mountain to the New Millennium*, ed. Susie Lan Cassel (Walnut Creek, CA: AltaMira Press, 2002), 195–238; and Zhongping Chen, "Kang Youwei's Activities in Canada and the Reformist Movement among the Global Chinese Diaspora," *Twentieth-Century China* 39, 1 (2014): 3–23. On activism in Chinese Canadian communities, see Patricia Owen and Jim Wolf, *Yi Fao: Speaking through Memory – A History of New Westminster's Chinese Community, 1858–1980* (Victoria: Heritage House, 2008); and Timothy Stanley, *Contesting White Supremacy: School Segregation, Anti-Racism, and the Making of Chinese Canadians* (Vancouver: UBC Press, 2011).

On the Chinese women's movement and New Women, see Louise Edwards, *Gender, Politics, and Democracy: Women's Suffrage in China* (Stanford: Stanford University Press, 2008); Louise Edwards, "Narratives of Race and Nation in China: Women's Suffrage in the Early Twentieth Century," *Women's Studies International Forum* 25, 6 (November–December 2002): 619–30; Louise Edwards and Mina Roces, eds., *Women's Suffrage in Asia: Gender, Nationalism, Democracy* (London: Routledge, 2004);

Mary Chapman, "Edith Eaton/Sui Sin Far's 'Revolutions in Ink': Print Cultural Alternatives to U.S. Suffrage Discourse," in *Making Noise, Making News: US Suffrage Print Culture in Modernism* (New York: Oxford University Press, 2014), 174–205; Judy Yung, *Unbound Feet: A Social History of Chinese Women in San Francisco* (Berkeley: University of California Press, 1995); and Kazuko Ono, *Chinese Women in a Century of Revolution, 1850-1950,* ed. Joshua A. Fogel (Stanford: Stanford University Press, 1978).

On transnational suffrage, see Maureen Moynagh and Nancy Forestell, eds., *Documenting First Wave Feminisms,* vol. 1, *Transnational Collaborations and Cross-currents* (Toronto: University of Toronto Press, 2012); Jad Adams, *Women and the Vote: A World History* (Oxford: Oxford University Press, 2014); and Christine Bolt, *The Women's Movements in the United States and Britain from the 1790s to the 1920s* (Amherst: University of Massachusetts Press, 1993). On Susan B. Anthony's tour, see G. Thomas Edwards, *Sowing Good Seeds: The Northwest Suffrage Campaigns of Susan B. Anthony* (Portland: Oregon Historical Society Press, 1990).

Page 170   **"We are at war":** *Vancouver Daily World,* 18 January 1913, 1.

Page 170   **"If window breaking":** *Vancouver Daily World,* 18 January 1913, 2.

Page 172   **"In force":** Quoted in G. Thomas Edwards, *Sowing Good Seeds: The Northwest Suffrage Campaigns of Susan B. Anthony* (Portland: Oregon Historical Society Press, 1990), 42.

Page 172   **"There was no town":** *Victoria Daily British Colonist and Morning Chronicle,* 26 October 1871, 2.

Page 172   **"Victoria: A City":** *Daily British Colonist,* 26 October 1871, 3.

Page 172   **"Submitting herself"** ... **"would be upset":** *Daily British Colonist,* 27 October 1871, 3.

Page 173   **"Old maid"**..."**I ever saw":** Quoted in Edwards, *Sowing Good Seeds,* 74.

Page 173   **"Calculated to destroy"** ... **"'hear, hear'":** *Daily British Colonist,* 28 January 1872, 2.

Page 173   **"Causing many women":** *Daily British Colonist,* 24 January 1872, 3.

Page 173   **Frost theft:** Edwards, *Sowing Good Seeds,* 112; *Vancouver Daily World,* 2 February 1906, 4.

Page 174   **"Let those who oppose":** *Victoria Daily Colonist,* 6 November 1909, 2 (insert); see also *Colonist,* 4 July 1909, 8.

Page 175   **Coverage of events:** *Vancouver Daily World,* 12 July 1909, 1, 9, 22 May 1909, 5; 22 June 1909, 11.

Page 175   **"Tall and muscular"** ... **"and misrepresentation":** *Daily Colonist,* 13 July 1909, 1–2.

Page 175   **Pethick's talk sold out:** *Vancouver Daily World,* 9 June 1914, 11.

Page 176   **"Western movement":** *B.C. Federationist,* 27 June 1913, 4.

Page 179   **"Surrender":** *Champion,* September 1912, 13, 16.

Page 179   **"Ripe":** Quoted in Jane Purvis, *Emmeline Pankhurst: A Biography* (London: Routledge, 2002), 175.

Page 179   **"The Militant Methods" ... "Great Britain":** *Daily Colonist,* 20 December 1911, 18; 21 December 1911, 16.

Page 180   **"Hysterical suffragette":** *Phoenix Pioneer and Boundary Mining Journal,* 28 September 1912, 2.

Page 180   **"Moral suasion" ... "militant methods":** *Vancouver Daily World,* 18 January 1913, 1–2; 21 January 1913, 13; 22 January 1913, 19; 5 February 1913, 8; *Delta Times,* 8 February 1913, 4; *New Westminster News,* 6 February 1913, 1, 4.

Page 181   **"Aroused a good deal":** *Champion,* February 1913, 11.

Page 181   **"Brutality" ... "even heroic":** *Western Methodist Recorder,* March 1914, 20.

Page 181   **"Redeem[ed] the womanhood":** *Champion,* April 1913, 16.

Page 181   **"Action of":** *New Westminster News,* 9 June 1913, 8.

Page 181   **"Can we condemn":** *Champion,* August 1912, 10.

Page 182   **"Enduring a great deal":** *Champion,* November 1912, 8.

Page 182   **"I stand":** *Champion,* May 1913, 10.

Page 182   **"Our saints":** *Vancouver Daily World,* 29 September 1913, 11.

Page 182   **"Necessary":** *Kelowna Record,* 26 December 1912, 1.

Page 182   **"Ingenious and tactical":** *Kelowna Record,* 7 May 1914, 5.

Page 182   **"Persons deprived":** *Vancouver Daily World,* 14 July 1913, 11.

Page 183   **"The limelight":** *Vancouver Daily World,* 24 June 1913, 13.

Page 183   **Burning tree and theatre:** *Vancouver Daily World,* 14 July 1913, 11; *Revelstoke Mail-Herald,* 17 May 1913, 8.

Page 183   **"The one fly":** *Vancouver Daily World,* 29 September 1913, 11.

Page 183   **PEL meeting:** *Daily Colonist,* 8 May 1914, 13.

Page 183   **"If many of them":** Maria Grant to Richard McBride, 23 February 1913, GR 0441, Premier's Records, Official Correspondence Inward, vol. 49, file 97, British Columbia Archives.

Page 183   **"Never again" ... "tactics of militancy":** *Victoria Daily Times,* 17 February 1913, 24; *Vancouver Province,* 15 February 1913, 16.

Page 183 **Blackmore's boycott:** *Victoria Week,* 19 April 1913, 2.

Page 185 **Kang Tongbi in Victoria:** *Daily Colonist,* 23 May 1903, 5.

Page 185 **"Ladies":** *Daily Colonist,* 18 October 1903, 3.

Page 187 **"With considerable" ... "public questions":** *Daily Colonist,* 5 December 1905, 5.

Page 187 **"New woman" Sieh King King:** *Daily Colonist,* 7 November 1902, 5.

Page 187 **"New woman" Mrs. Loo Lin and Li Sum Sing:** *Daily Colonist,* 10 June 1903, 5; 5 November 1908, 8.

Page 187 **"My dear sisters":** Quoted in Judy Yung, *Unbound Voices: A Documentary History of Chinese Women in San Francisco* (Berkeley: University of California Press, 1999), 193.

Page 188 **"First occasion":** *Daily Colonist,* 23 May 1903, 5.

Page 188 **"In the rise of the country":** See translation at Baohuanghui Scholarship, "The Chinese Ladies Empire Reform Association in Victoria, BC," 6 September 2014, https://baohuanghui.blogspot.com/2014/09/the-chinese-ladies-empire-reform.html.

Page 188 **"Even China is ahead":** *Champion,* October 1912, 12.

Page 189 **"Celestial Empire":** *Daily Colonist,* 31 May 1907, 11.

EIGHT: ACHIEVING THE VOTE

For information on Isaac Rubinowitz, see *Vancouver Daily World,* 1 October 1913, 2; 21 May 1919, 11. On Harlan Brewster, see entry in *Dictionary of Canadian Biography,* Patricia E. Roy, "Brewster, Harlan Carey."

On referendums, see J. Patrick Boyer, *Direct Democracy in Canada: The History and Future of Referendums* (Toronto: Dundurn Press, 1992). On municipal referendums, see Tarah Brookfield, *Our Voices Must Be Heard: Women and the Vote in Ontario* (Vancouver: UBC Press, 2018). On the representation of women and gender in editorial cartoons, see Carmen Nielson, "Caricaturing Colonial Space: Indigenous Feminized Bodies and Anglo-American Identity, 1873–94," *Canadian Historical Review* 96, 4 (December 2015): 473–506; and G. Bruce Retallack, "Drawing the Lines: Gender, Class, Race and Nation in Canadian Editorial Cartoons, 1840–1926" (PhD diss., University of Toronto, 2006).

On women, suffrage, and the First World War, see Tarah Brookfield, "Divided by the Ballot Box," *Canadian Historical Review* 89, 4 (December 2008): 473–501; Gloria Geller, "The Wartime Elections Act of 1917 and the Canadian Women's Movement," *Atlantis* 2, 1 (1976): 88–106; Barbara Roberts, "Women's Peace Activism in Canada," in *Beyond the Vote: Canadian Women and Politics,* ed. Linda Kealey and Joan Sangster (Toronto: University of Toronto Press, 1989), 276–308; John R. English, "War Time

Elections Act," *Canadian Encyclopedia;* and Philip Girard, "Married Women, Race, Ethnicity and Suffrage," in *Women Suffrage and Beyond: Confronting the Democratic Deficit,* http://womensuffrage.org/?p=22636%20C.

On running for office, see Linda Hale, "The British Columbia Woman Suffrage Movement, 1890–1917" (master's thesis, University of British Columbia, 1977); Legislative Assembly of British Columbia, "100 Years of Women and the Vote," https://www.leg.bc.ca/wotv; Susan Walsh, "The Peacock and the Guinea Hen: Political Profiles of Dorothy Gretchen Steeves and Grace MacInnis," in *Not Just Pin Money: Selected Essays on the History of Women's Work in British Columbia,* ed. Barbara Latham and Roberta Pazdro (Victoria: Camosun College, 1984), 365–79; and Connie Carter and Eileen Daoust, "From Home to House: Women in the BC Legislature," in Latham and Pazdro, *Not Just Pin Money,* 389–405. On the National Council of Women, see Naomi Griffiths, *The Splendid Vision: Centennial History of the National Council of Women of Canada* (Ottawa: Carleton University Press, 1997); and Veronica Strong-Boag, *Parliament of Women: The National Council of Women of Canada, 1893–1929* (Ottawa: National Museum of Man, 1976).

Page 192   **"If the men":** *Vancouver Daily World,* 4 March 1916, 5.

Page 192   **"Took three days":** *Victoria Daily Times,* 14 April 1917, 15.

Page 193   **"Wise to this war" ... "her son's hand":** *Vancouver Daily World,* 24 June 1913, 13.

Page 193   **"We firmly believe":** *Western Methodist Recorder,* February 1915, 6.

Page 194   **"Subject of the war":** *Creston Review,* 12 November 1915, 1; 6 November 1914, 8; *Revelstoke Mail-Herald,* 13 February 1915, 5.

Page 194   **"Relegated to the background":** *B.C. Federationist,* 21 August 1914, 2.

Page 194   **"Which so vitally affect them":** *B.C. Federationist,* 21 August 1914, 2.

Page 196   **"Had a long way to go":** *Vancouver Daily World,* 26 April 1916, 10.

Page 197   **"Stated that their organizations":** *Vancouver Western Call,* 19 May 1916, 4.

Page 198   **"All over the Lower Mainland":** Transcript of interview with Leon J. Ladner, 26 April 1973, R.R.A.S. Oral History Programme, Vancouver Cultural Communities Series, PR 1993, Item AAA B0202, Reynoldston Research and Studies Oral History Collection, British Columbia Archives (BCA).

Page 198   **"Purifying power" ... "heroes at home":** Ibid.

Page 198   **Flyers to soldiers:** *Vancouver Daily World,* 23 September 1916, 15.

Page 198   **"The ladies cannot make":** *Hedley Gazette,* 31 August 1916, 8.

Page 199   **"We do not claim":** *To the Electors* (Victoria, BC: Women's Suffrage Referendum Association, 1 August 1916), NWp 324.3 W872, BCA.

Page 199 **On Tupper:** Ladner interview, 26 April 1973, BCA. See also *Vancouver Province*, 20 June 1916, 3.

Page 199 **"Show the whole civilized":** *Vancouver Daily World*, 26 July 1916, 5.

Page 200 **"Splendid":** *Vancouver Daily World*, 28 June 1916, 5.

Page 200 **Candidate debates:** *Vancouver Daily World*, 6 July 1916, 11; 29 July 1916, 15; *New Westminster Pacific Canadian*, 11 August 1916, 3.

Page 200 **Kelowna heckling:** *Victoria Daily Colonist*, 3 August 1916, 5; *Kelowna Record*, 24 August 1916, 1.

Page 200 **"Is the vote of a drunken":** *Cranbrook Herald*, 20 July 1916, 2.

Page 201 **"Our women are":** *Daily Colonist*, 14 July 1916, 7.

Page 201 **"So few ladies":** *Daily Colonist*, 30 August 1916, 8.

Page 201 **"At present occupied":** *Daily Colonist*, 3 September 1916, 8.

Page 202 **Address to Miners' Union:** *Cumberland Islander*, 26 August 1916, 1.

Page 202 **"Brought a change":** *Daily Colonist*, 3 September 1916, 2, 5.

Page 202 **"Beside her men folk":** *Daily Colonist*, 29 August 1916, 9.

Page 202 **Smith's talks:** *New Westminster Pacific Canadian*, 21 July 1916, 1; *Vancouver Standard*, 19 August 1916, 3.

Page 202 **"One party was":** *Vancouver Daily World*, 29 July 1916, 15.

Page 202 **"Public interest":** *Daily Colonist*, 14 July 1916, 4.

Page 203 **"Unbounded confidence" ... "the outcome":** *Vancouver Daily World*, 29 July 1916, 15.

Page 203 **"Sanguine":** Quoted in Irene Howard, *The Struggle for Social Justice in British Columbia: Helena Gutteridge, the Unknown Reformer* (Vancouver: UBC Press, 1992), 96.

Page 203 **Numbers of scrutineers:** *Vancouver Daily World*, 14 September 1916, 5; 18 September 1916, 5.

Page 203 **"Marched in formation":** Quoted in Howard, *The Struggle for Social Justice*, 96.

Page 203 **Referendum results:** *Colonist*, 17 September 1916, 1; *Cumberland Islander*, 16 September 1916, 1; *Grand Forks and Kettle Valley Orchardist*, 15 September 1916, 1.

Page 204 **"Speed":** *Vancouver Daily World*, 9 February 1917, 1; 14 February 1917, 10.

Page 205 **"Never been an active":** *Vancouver Province*, 24 March 1917, 13.

Page 205 **Grant's assessment:** Lyn Gough, *As Wise as Serpents: Five Women and an Organization That Changed British Columbia, 1883–1939* (Victoria: Swan Lake, 1988), 178.

Page 205   **"Beneficent influence and power":** *Victoria Daily Times,* 14 April 1917, 15.

Page 205   **Schooling women:** *Daily Colonist,* 17 September 1916, 4.

Page 206   **"Contrary in its spirit":** Gough, *As Wise as Serpents,* 181–82.

Page 206   **"Back and forth" ... "fallen down":** *Vancouver Daily World,* 29 September 1917, 5.

Page 206   **"Gross, flagrant injustice":** *Vancouver Daily World,* 8 September 1917, 5.

Page 207   **"Her willing workers":** *Vancouver Daily World,* 1 February 1918, 5.

Page 207   **"Second in importance" ... "their standards":** *Victoria Daily Times,* 8 February 1918, 9; *Vancouver Daily World,* 11 February 1918, 5.

Page 208   **"I have been":** Quoted in Doreen Weppler, "Early Forms of Political Activity among White Women in British Columbia, 1880–1925" (master's thesis, Simon Fraser University, 1971), 120–21.

NINE: EXTENDING SUFFRAGE

For biographical information on Foon Sien, see Larry Wong, "The Life and Times of Foon Sien," Vancouverhistory.ca, https://www.vancouverhistory.ca/archives_foon_sien.htm. On Tomekichi Homma, see John Price and Grace Eiko Thomson, "Remembering a BC Civil Rights Leader," *Times Colonist,* 10 December 2017, https://www.timescolonist.com/islander/remembering-a-b-c-civil-rights-leader-1.23118215. On Won Alexander Cumyow, see Janet Mary Nicol, "Canadian First: The Life of Won Alexander Cumyow (1861–1955)," *BC Booklook,* 28 December 2016, https://bcbooklook.com/2016/12/28/won-alexander-cumyow-pure-canadian/. On Peter and Gertrude Kelly, see *Dictionary of Canadian Biography* entry on Russ, Amos, by Hamar Foster and Megan Harvey; and J.H. Van Den Brink, *The Haida Indian: Cultural Change, Mainly between 1876–1970* (Leiden: Brill, 1974). On Frank Calder, see entry in the *Canadian Encyclopedia,* by Bennett McCardle (October 2007); and *Vancouver Sun,* 8 July 1949, 5. On Genevieve Mussell, see *Indian Record,* May 1959, 3. On Ruth Smith and the Women's International League for Peace and Freedom, see *Vancouver Sun,* 30 April 1948, 20.

On post-suffrage reforms, see Diane Crossley, "The BC Liberal Party and Women's Reforms, 1916–1928," in *In Her Own Right: Selected Essays on Women's History of B.C.,* ed. Barbara Latham and Cathy Kess (Victoria: Camosun College, 1980), 229–53. On mothers' pensions, see Margaret Little, "Claiming a Unique Place: The Introduction of Mothers' Pension in B.C.," *BC Studies* 105–6 (Spring-Summer 1995): 80–102; Lisa Pasolli, *Working Mothers and the Child Care Dilemma: A History of British Columbia's Social Policy* (Vancouver: UBC Press, 2015); and Veronica Strong-Boag, "Wages for Housework: Mothers' Allowances and the Beginnings of Social Security in Canada," *Journal of Canadian Studies* 14, 1 (Spring 1979): 24–34. On policies related to eugenics, see Erika Dyck, *Facing Eugenics: Reproduction, Sterilization, and the Politics of Choice* (Toronto: University of Toronto Press, 2013); Sarah Carter, "'Develop a Great Imperial Race': Emmeline Pankhurst, Emily Murphy, and Their Promotion of 'Race Betterment' in Western Canada in the 1920s," in *Finding Directions West: Readings That Locate and Dislocate Western Canada's Past,* ed. George Colpitts and Heather Devine (Calgary: University of Calgary Press, 2017), 133–50; Angus McLaren, *Our Own Master Race: Eugenics in Canada, 1885–1945* (Toronto: University of Toronto Press, 1990); Joan Sangster, *Girl Trouble: Female Delinquency in Canada* (Toronto: Between the Lines, 2002); Joan Sangster, *Regulating Girls and Women: Sexuality, Family and the Law in Ontario, 1920–1960* (Don Mills: Oxford University Press, 2001); Scott Kerwin, "The Janet Smith Bill of 1924 and the Language of Race and Nation in British Columbia," *BC Studies* 121 (Spring 1999): 83–114; and Nic Clarke, "Sacred Daemons: Exploring British Columbia Society's Perception of 'Mentally Deficient' Children, 1870–1930," *BC Studies* 144 (Winter 2004–05): 61–89. On the influenza epidemic, see Janice Dickin, Patricia G. Bailey, and Erin James-Abra, "Influenza (Flu)," *Canadian Encyclopedia.* On income tax, see Shirley Tillotson, *"Give and Take": The Citizen-Taxpayer and the Rise of Canadian Democracy* (Vancouver: UBC Press, 2019).

On post-suffrage politics and women's organizations, see Margaret Lang Hastings and Lorraine Ellenwood, *Blue Bows and the Golden Rule: Provincial Council of Women of BC: An Historical Account* (Burnaby: Provincial Council of Women of BC, 1984); Barb Schober, "'Put Up or Shut Up': Women's Volunteer Groups in Canadian Jewish History," *The Scribe: The Journal of the Jewish Historical Society of British Columbia* 31 (2011): 21–42; Irene Howard, "The Mothers' Council of Vancouver: Holding the Fort for the Unemployed, 1935–1938," *BC Studies* 69–70 (Spring-Summer 1986): 249–87; Linda Kealey and Joan Sangster, eds., *Beyond the Vote: Canadian Women and Politics* (Toronto: University of Toronto Press, 1989); and Sylvie McClean, *A Woman of Influence: Evlyn Fenwick Farris* (Victoria: Sono Nis Press, 1997). On the principle of less eligibility, see James Struthers, *No Fault of Their Own: Unemployment and the Canadian Welfare State, 1914–1941* (Toronto: University of Toronto Press, 1983). On Chinese women and naturalization, see Kate Bagnall, "Were Chinese Women Naturalized in British Columbia?" 26 January 2019, Tiger's Mouth, http://chinese australia.org/tag/naturalization/.

On Chinese Canadian communities, see Timothy Stanley, "'By the Side of Other Canadians': The Locally Born and the Invention of Chinese Canadians," *BC Studies* 156 (Winter 2007–08): 109–39; Paul Yee, *Saltwater City: Story of Vancouver's Chinese Community* (Vancouver: Douglas and McIntyre, 2006); Lisa Mar, "Beyond Being Others: Chinese Canadians as National History," *BC Studies* 156 (Winter 2007–08): 13–34; and Tony P.K. Law, "Anti-Orientalism, Communities of Chinese Canadians and Leadership of Chinese Voluntary Associations," *SFU Communications* 499 (Spring 1980): 1–118.

On Japanese Canadian communities, see Stephanie Bangarth, *Voices Raised in Protest* (Vancouver: UBC Press, 2008); Patricia Roy, *The Triumph of Citizenship: The Japanese and Chinese in Canada, 1941–67* (Vancouver: UBC Press, 2007); Perry Kwok, "Commemorating with (In)Visibility: The Case of the Japanese Canadian War Memorial," Report for the Nikkei National Museum and Cultural Centre, n.d.; Jordan Stanger-Ross, Nicholas Blomley, and the Landscapes of Injustice Research Collective, "'My Land Is Worth a Million Dollars': How Japanese Canadians Contested Their Dispossession in the 1940s," *Law and History Review* 35, 3 (2017): 711–51; Carol F. Lee, "The Road to Enfranchisement: Chinese and Japanese in British Columbia," *BC Studies* 30 (Summer 1976): 44–76; and Andrea Geiger-Adams, "Pioneer Issei: Tomekichi Homma's Fight for the Franchise," *Nikkei Images: Japanese-Canadian National Museum Newsletter* 8, 1 (Spring 2003): 1–4. On Japanese Canadians voting in school board elections, see *New Canadian*, 30 June 1948, 1.

On Indigenous activism, see Leslie A. Robertson with the Kwagu'L Gix̱sa̱m Clan, *Standing Up with G̱a'ax̱sta'las: Jane Constance Cook and the Politics of Memory, Church, and Custom* (Vancouver: UBC Press, 2012); Arthur Ray, *An Illustrated History of Canada's Native People: I Have Lived Here Since the World Began* (Montreal and Kingston: McGill-Queen's University Press, 2011); Pamela T. Brown, "Cannery Days: A Chapter in the Lives of the Heiltsuk" (master's thesis, University of British Columbia, 1994); Philip Drucker, *The Native Brotherhoods: Modern Intertribal Organizations of the Northwest Coast* (Washington, DC: Smithsonian, 1958); Eric Jamieson, *The Native Voice: The Story of How Maisie Hurley and Canada's First Aboriginal Newspaper Changed a Nation* (Halfmoon Bay: Caitlin Press, 2016); and Sharon Fortney, "Entwined Histories: The Creation of the Maisie Hurley Collection of Native Art," *BC Studies* 167 (Autumn 2010): 71–104. On Constance Cox, see Susan Neylan, *The Heavens Are Changing: Nineteenth-Century Protestant Missions and Tsimshian Christianity* (Montreal and Kingston: McGill-Queen's University Press, 2003), 322.

On South Asian community activism, see Hugh J.M. Johnston, *Jewels of the Qila: The Remarkable Story of an Indo-Canadian Family* (Vancouver: UBC Press, 2012); Norman Buchignani, Doreen M. Indra, and Ram Srivastiva, *Continuous Journey: A Social History of South Asians in Canada* (Toronto: McClelland and Stewart, 1985); and Centre for Indo-Canadian Studies, "(Dis)Enfranchisement, 1907–1947: The Forty-Year Struggle for the Vote," catalogue and exhibit at the Sikh Heritage Museum, 2017, http://canadiansikhheritage.ca/exhibitions/dis-enfranchisement/.

Page 214 **"Oldest man" ... "dream today":** *Native Voice,* May 1949, 2.

Page 215 **"Duties arising":** *Revelstoke Mail-Herald,* 25 November 1916, 1.

Page 218 **"Adequate provision":** Quoted in Christopher Clarkson, *Domestic Reforms: Political Visions and Family Regulation in British Columbia, 1862–1940* (Vancouver: UBC Press, 2007), 172.

Page 218 **Minimum Wage League:** *Vancouver Daily World,* 13 March 1918, 5.

Page 219   **"Capital and labour":** Quoted in Irene Howard, *The Struggle for Social Justice in British Columbia: Helena Gutteridge, the Unknown Reformer* (Vancouver: UBC Press, 1992), 122.

Page 219   **"If a woman's place":** *B.C. Federationist,* 7 November 1913, 5.

Page 221   **"Comparable to those":** Quoted in Leslie A. Robertson with the Kwagu'L Gixsam Clan, *Standing Up with Ga'axsta'las: Jane Constance Cook and the Politics of Memory, Church, and Custom* (Vancouver: UBC Press, 2012), 280.

Page 223   **"Sitting back":** Quoted in Catherine L. Cleverdon, *The Woman Suffrage Movement in Canada,* 2nd ed. (Toronto: University of Toronto Press, 1974), 102.

Page 224   **"Party aloof":** *Victoria Daily Times,* 21 February 1917, 14.

Page 225   **"B.C. is being held":** *Montreal Standard,* 4 January 1946, quoted in Tony P.K. Law, "Anti-Orientalism, Communities of Chinese Canadians and Leadership of Chinese Voluntary Associations," *SFU Communications* 499 (Spring 1980): 76.

Page 226   **"By right of Birth":** Quoted in Joan Brockman, "Exclusionary Tactics: The History of Women and Visible Minorities in the Legal Profession in British Columbia," in *Essays in the History of Canadian Law: British Columbia and the Yukon,* ed. Hamar Foster and John McLaren (Toronto: Osgoode Society and University of Toronto Press, 1995), 521.

Page 226   **"Enjoy the same privileges":** Quoted in Paul Yee, *Saltwater City: Story of Vancouver's Chinese Community* (Vancouver: Douglas and McIntyre, 2006), 41.

Page 226   **"I am fighting":** *Vancouver Province,* 22 January 1945, 4.

Page 227   **"Lay down their lives":** Petition to the Governments of the Province of British Columbia and the Dominion of Canada from the Chinese Canadian Association, September 1944.

Page 227   **"Race friendship":** *Vancouver Sun,* 5 May 1945, 11; *Vancouver Province,* 5 May 1945, 30. On the YWCA, see *Vancouver Sun,* 28 September 1944, 6.

Page 228   **Delegation to Union of BC Municipalities:** *Toronto Globe and Mail,* 9 September 1948, 9.

Page 228   **"We have tried":** *Daily Colonist,* 2 March 1943, 11; *Nanaimo Daily News,* 2 March 1943, 3.

Page 228   **"Unreliable, dishonest":** Quoted in Centre for Indo-Canadian Studies, "(Dis)Enfranchisement, 1907–1947: The Forty-Year Struggle for the Vote," catalogue and exhibit at the Sikh Heritage Museum, 2017, http://canadiansikhheritage.ca/exhibitions/dis-enfranchisement/.

Page 231   **"Protect Canadian":** Quoted in Roy, *The Triumph of Citizenship: The Japanese and Chinese in Canada, 1941–67* (Vancouver: UBC Press, 2007), 144.

Page 231   **Tanaka:** *Toronto Globe and Mail,* 29 March 1948, 9.

Page 232   **"Minority":** *Native Voice,* March 1947, 4; April 1949, 14.

Page 234   **"Quit passing the buck":** Quoted in Eric Jamieson, *The Native Voice: The Story of How Maisie Hurley and Canada's First Aboriginal Newspaper Changed a Nation* (Halfmoon Bay: Caitlin Press, 2016), 114.

Page 234   **"Many of their number":** *Vancouver Sun,* 10 November 1944, 31.

Page 234   **"Anachronistic":** Quoted in Jamieson, *The Native Voice,* 81.

Page 234   **"Keen disappointment":** *Vancouver Sun,* 24 June 1948, 9.

Page 235   **"Modern age" ... "beginning":** *Native Voice,* January 1947, 4.

Page 236   **"Carry on the fight":** *Native Voice,* April 1949, 2.

Page 236   **"A strong lever":** *Native Voice,* May 1949, 2.

Page 237   **"Magna Carta":** Quoted in Jamieson, *The Native Voice,* 106; *Native Voice,* March 1950, 17.

Page 237   **"Legislative concentration camp":** *Nanaimo Daily News,* 23 October 1950, 3.

CONCLUSION

On women and political participation, see Brenda O'Neill, "Unpacking Gender's Role in Political Representation in Canada," *Canadian Parliamentary Review* 38, 2 (Summer 2015): 22–30; Lynda Erickson and Brenda O'Neill, "The Gender Gap and the Changing Woman Voter in Canada," *International Political Science Review/Revue Internationale de science politique* 23, 4 (October 2002): 373–92; Kelly Dittmar, "The Gender Gap: Gender Differences on Vote Choice and Political Orientations," Rutgers, State University of New Jersey, Center for American Women and Politics, http://www.cawp.rutgers.edu/sites/default/files/resources/closerlook_gender -gap-07-15-14.pdf; Jocelyne Praud, "When Numerical Gains Are Not Enough: Women in British Columbia Politics," in *Stalled: The Representation of Women in Canadian Governments,* ed. Linda Trimble, Jane Arscott, and Manon Tremblay (Vancouver: UBC Press, 2013), 55–74.

On gender, sexuality, and feminism, see Anne Fausto-Sterling, *Sexing the Body: Gender Politics and the Construction of Sexuality* (New York: Basic Books, 2000); and Susan Stryker and Stephen Whittle, *The Transgender Studies Reader* (New York: Routledge, 2006).

On friendship and relationships, see Veronica Strong-Boag, "Mary Ellen Spear Smith," 23 January 2013, Women Suffrage and Beyond, http://womensuffrage. org/?p=21014; Veronica Strong-Boag, *Liberal Hearts and Coronets: The Lives and Times of Ishbel Marjoribanks and John Campbell Gordon, the Aberdeens* (Toronto: University of Toronto Press, 2015); Anne Toews, "For Liberty, Bread, and Love: Annie Buller, Beckie Buhay, and the Forging of Communist Militant Femininity in Canada, 1918–1939" (master's thesis, Simon Fraser University, 2009); and J. Balshaw, "Sharing the Burden: The Pethick Lawrences and Women's Suffrage," in *The Men's Share? Masculinities, Male Support and Women's Suffrage in Britain, 1890– 1920*, ed. Angela V. John and Claire Eustace (London: Routledge, 1997), 135–57.

Page 242   **"We are inclined":** *Nanaimo Daily News,* 9 June 1894, 3.

Page 242   **"Lift up those":** Bertha Merrill Burns, writing as Dorothy Drew, *Western Socialist,* 27 December 1902, 3.

Page 243   **Wilson's poem:** *Vancouver Daily World,* 2 March 1918, 7.

Page 246   **"The wisdom":** Rosemary Brown, speech to the founding convention of the National Congress of Black Women in Canada, April 1973, Rise Up! A Digital Archive of Feminist Activism, https://riseupfeministarchive.ca/ activism/organizations/congress-of-black-women-of-canada-cbwc/ cwbc-1973-speechrosemary-brown/.

PHOTO CREDITS

Page 2:   *The Champion*, December 1913. Image courtesy of the Royal British Columbia Museum and Archives.

Page 10:   "A Very Good Idea," *Vancouver Sun*, 10 December 1913.

Page 19:   Courtesy Royal BC Museum and Archives, Item I-51701.

Page 27:   Courtesy Royal BC Museum and Archives, Item C-06485.

Page 39:   Courtesy Vancouver Public Library, Special Collections, Acc. 22341.

Page 47:   Courtesy Royal BC Museum and Archives, Item F-02309.

Page 61:   Courtesy Royal BC Museum and Archives, Item G-04990.

Page 70:   Courtesy Royal BC Museum and Archives, Item H-03690.

Page 75:   "To Proud to Speak," *Vancouver Sun*, 24 February 1913.

Page 85:   "More Trouble for R.L.," *Victoria Daily Times*, 25 September 1912.

Page 88:   "Miss Debutante Will Vote This Year," *Vancouver Daily World*, 21 November 1921.

Page 93:   Courtesy Vancouver Public Library, Special Collections, Acc. 35220.

Page 105:   Courtesy Royal BC Museum and Archives, Item E-02929.

Page 108:   Courtesy City of Vancouver Archives, AM 54-S4-: PortP726.

Page 117:   Courtesy Chief Wedłidi Speck.

Page 123:   "One Argument for Woman Suffrage," *Vancouver Daily World*, 20 December 1911.

Page 134:   Courtesy Royal BC Museum and Archives, Item A-09464.

Page 137:   Courtesy Royal BC Museum and Archives, Item F-07285.

Page 138:   "As It Should Be," *Vancouver Daily Sun*, 30 March 1917.

Page 143:   Courtesy UBC Library, Rare Books and Special Collections, Angus MacInnis Memorial Collection, BC 1485/20, Box 69, File 8.

Page 147:   Courtesy City of Vancouver Archives, AM54-S4-: CVA 371-2693.

Page 156:   Courtesy City of Vancouver Archives, AM54-S4-: CVA 371-1234.

Page 169: Courtesy Barnard Archives and Special Collections, Mortarboard 1909, Volume 8.

Page 177: "Votes for Women a Success: North America Proves It," National Woman Suffrage Publishing Company, 1917, Cornell University, PJ Mode Collection of Persuasive Cartography.

Page 186: Courtesy Harvard-Yenching Library.

Page 191: Courtesy Royal BC Museum and Archives, "Vote for Woman's Freedom," NWP. 324.623 V971.

Page 210: Courtesy Royal BC Museum and Archives, Image E-00045.

Page 213: Postmedia Network, *Vancouver Sun,* staff photo.

Page 230: Courtesy Nikkei National Museum & Cultural Centre, Isami (Sam) Okamoto fonds, 2000.14.1.1.1.

Page 235: Front page, *Native Voice* 3, 2 (March 1949).

Page 245: From website of Department of Gender, Sexuality and Women's Studies at Simon Fraser University; photographer unknown.

INDEX

Note: Page numbers with (f) refer to illustrations.

102, 122–23, 163; moral superiority of women, 9–11, 10(f), 48, 60, 62, 123(f); "mothers of the race," 9, 119, 122–24; political rights, 9, 12, 29, 42, 48, 67; progress and modernity, 8–12, 62, 82–83, 128–32; referendum (1916), 191(f), 198–201; removal of degradation, 48, 62; white female settlers, 15, 60. *See also* anti-suffragist rationale; enfranchisement of women; maternal feminism; progress and modernity

entertainment. *See* performance of politics

Equal Franchise Association, 7, 72, 108, 197

Equal Franchise League, Kelowna, 69, 190

equal pay, 7, 146–48, 154

equality ideals. *See* enfranchisement of women, rationale

eugenics movement, 222–23, 239

European immigrants (non-British): about, 119–22; anti-immigrant sentiment, 30, 40; enfranchisement of European men vs Canadian women, 40, 62, 97, 119–22, 124; patriarchy, 121–22; stereotypes, 30. *See also* race and national origin

Evans, Alys, 70

Evening Work Committee (PPEL), 16, 105, 113, 145, 157. *See also* WSL (Woman's Suffrage League)

exhibitions, 104–5

family law: about, 37–42; divorce, 40–42; guardianship of children, 37–38, 40–41, 217–18; ideal family model, 37, 78; inheritance rights, 37–38, 42; legal reform activism, 38; property rights, 37–38, 42, 130–31, 217–18; provincial jurisdiction, 13; reforms vs patriarchy, 21; sources and further

reading, 253–54; women judges, 39(f), 56, 222; women lawyers and judges, 34, 39(f), 56, 222. *See also* marriage and families

Farris, Evlyn Fenwick, 34–35, 64, 80–81, 196, 205, 217–18

Farris, J. Wallace, 34, 205, 208

federal franchise: about, 4, 13–14, 193, 206–7; division of powers under BNA Act, 13; Indigenous peoples, 3, 214–15, 224–25, 231–32, 234–35, 237; legislation (1917), 122, 206–7; military status, 3–4, 193, 206, 234; provincial jurisdiction over federal franchise, 4, 13–14, 206–7, 215; timelines, 122, 193, 206–7. *See also* candidates and elected officials, women; enfranchisement; race and national origin, exclusion from suffrage ideals

Federation of Labour, BC, 112, 153–55, 202, 218. *See also* labour movement

feminism: about, 243–44; gender difference and sameness, 9–12, 10(f); intersectional approaches, 240; limitations, 238–40, 243–44; recent trends, 243–44; socialist alliances, 150; sources and further reading, 250–51, 284; waves in, 3, 7–8, 243. *See also* enfranchisement of women; enfranchisement of women, rationale; gender; maternal feminism; suffrage movement; women's movement

Fernie, 69

Finlayson family, 28, 136, 241

First Nations: citizenship and treaty status, 225–26; enfranchisement, 3–4, 215, 225, 231–32, 237; exclusion from suffrage ideals, 3–4, 12, 119, 141; municipal franchise, 54. *See also* Indigenous peoples; Indigenous women; race and national origin

First World War: anti-immigrant sentiment, 122; anti-suffragists, 202–3;

early marriage, 140; employment, 145, 233, 234; enfranchisement, 237; exclusion from suffrage ideals, 3–4, 12, 42, 137–39, 138(f), 141, 238; fur trade marriages, 136–37, 139; marriage and status, 15, 42, 139, 225, 233–34; MLAs, 244; Native Sisterhood of BC, 214, 233–34, 236; sources and further reading, 266–67, 282; suffrage movement role, 139–40. *See also* Cook, Jane Constance Gilbert (Ga'axsta'las)

Indo-Canadians. *See* South Asian Canadians

International Council of Women, 33, 36, 44, 174

international networks. *See* global networks

interwar period, 217–24. *See also* post-suffrage reforms

Inuit, enfranchisement, 225

IODE (Imperial Order Daughters of the Empire), 80–81, 127

Jacobs, Laura, 166

Jamieson, John Stuart (Jack), 32, 38, 56

Jamieson, Laura: about, 56, 148, 210(f); CCF member, 56, 209, 210(f); family members, 32, 162; judge, 56, 222; MLA, 56, 209, 210(f); municipal franchise, 55; peace movement, 56, 216; socialist, 144–45; views of, 34, 223–24

Japanese Canadians: about, 229–31, 230(f); alliances, 229; community organizations, 229–31; demographics, 124; employment, 124, 145, 230(f); enfranchisement, 3–4, 215, 225, 229–31, 237; exclusion from suffrage ideals, 3–4, 12–13; internment, 224, 229–31; post-suffrage activism, 224–25, 229–30; racism, 124; sources and further reading,

265–66, 280, 282; veterans, 229. *See also* immigrants

Jenkins, Margaret, 27–28, 35, 47(f), 57–59, 162, 175

Jews, 15, 28, 32, 199–200, 216

Johnson, Elenor W., 86

journalists. *See* media and print culture

judges, women, 39(f), 56, 222

justice ideals. *See* enfranchisement of women, rationale

Kamloops, 69, 96

Kang Tongbi, 169(f), 185–89, 186(f)

Kang Tongwei, 185

Kang Youwei, 169, 184–85, 186(f)

Kaslo, 69, 71, 96, 208

Kelly, Gertrude, 236

Kelly, Peter, 117(f), 233, 234–35, 236

Kelowna, 6, 68–70, 100, 190, 197, 200. *See also* Kerr, Dora Forster; Kerr, Robert B.

Kemp, Janet, 54–55, 64, 72, 97

Kerr, Dora Forster, 69–70, 100, 130, 144–45, 148, 152, 175, 197, 241–42

Kerr, Robert B., 38, 69–70, 130, 152, 175, 241–42

Khalsa Diwan Society, 126, 228

Kobayashi, Minoru, 230(f)

Komagata Maru incident, 125

labour force. *See* professions and higher education; working women

labour movement: about, 144–45, 153–55, 218–19; anti-immigrant sentiment, 125, 226; anti-suffragist rationale, 83, 145, 202; exploitation of labour, 64, 159, 166–67; Indigenous activism, 232, 233; labour standards jurisdiction, 13; male domination, 145, 153–54; media, 112–13; minimum wage, 154, 218–19; mining communities, 163–67, 271; post-suffrage reforms, 154–55, 218–19;

referendum (1916), 202–3; skilled working-class families, 15–16, 155–58; socialist alliances, 149–50, 155, 163; sources and further reading, 270; suffragist alliances, 7, 16, 63, 153–55, 158–63, 166–67, 243; WCTU alliances, 29; WSL alliances, 7, 16, 158–63. *See also* BC Federation of Labour; *B.C. Federationist* (newspaper); capitalism; labour unions; working women

labour unions: about, 153–55, 163–64; coal miners, 164–65, 200; domestic servants, 159; racial exclusions, 226; suffragist alliances, 153–55, 159–60, 163; Trades and Labour Councils, 16, 125, 153–54, 202, 218. *See also* labour movement

Ladner, Leon, 198, 199

Lang, Marjory, 34

Laverock, Lily, 35, 110, 242

law. *See* family law

LCWs (Local Councils of Women): about, 32–33, 47(f); anti-immigrant sentiment, 127–28; interior branches, 32; labour activism, 154, 218; male allies, 38; Mock Parliament, 99; municipal and school board franchise, 54–55, 58; New Woman ideal, 32; post-suffrage activism, 216; research by, 32, 38; Vancouver branches, 32–33, 54, 59; Victoria branch, 5, 19, 32–33, 47(f), 56–59, 99, 128, 139; women's legal rights, 38. *See also* NCW (National Council of Women of Canada)

legal issues. *See* family law

legislature: anti-suffrage sentiment, 76–77; lobbying and deputations, 7, 47(f), 95–98; Mock or Model Parliaments, 98–99; political theatre of suffragists, 96. *See also* MLAs (Members of the Legislative Assembly); political parties

LeSueur, Evelyn, 146, 217

Liang Qichao, 184, 186(f)

Liberal Party of BC: about, 64–65, 196–200; debates, 100; election win (1916), 4, 196, 217; legislation on women's enfranchisement (1917), 4, 204–5; mainstream media, 112; post-suffrage reforms, 217; referendum (1916), 196–201, 204–5; suffragist alliances, 64–65, 112, 155, 196–200, 204–5; women MLAs, 207–9; women's associations, 35, 64, 93, 196–97. *See also* Brewster, Harlan; government (1916–18); Hart, John; non-partisanship; political parties

lobbying and deputations: about, 7, 95–98; McBride government, 71, 80, 97, 183; PEL members, 95–96; sponsors, 47(f); temperance movement, 28; women's legal rights, 38. *See also* MLAs (Members of the Legislative Assembly); petitions

Local Councils of Women. *See* LCWs (Local Councils of Women)

local franchise. *See* municipal franchise; school board franchise

Macdonald, John A., 13

MacGill, Helen Gregory: about, 39, 39(f), 148; family law, 38–39, 217–18, 222; journalist, 35, 39, 146; lobbying, 96, 195–96; political career, 64, 204–5, 218, 221; views of, 34, 223, 229, 243; Women's Forum, 55

MacGill, James, 39

MacInnis, Grace, 208, 209–10, 210(f), 278

Macmillan, Chrystal, 175

Macphail, Agnes, 208

Macphail, Andrew, 77

male allies: about, 17, 49–50, 240–42; Christians, 22, 50; companionate marriages, 32, 34, 241–42; debates

Mussell, Genevieve and Bill, 233–34, 280

Mutter, James, 83–84

Nanaimo, 52, 100, 152, 164–66. *See also* Smith, Mary Ellen Spear

national origin. *See* race and national origin, enfranchisement; race and national origin, enfranchisement; race and national origin, exclusion from suffrage ideals

Native Brotherhood of BC, 214, 232–36, 282

Native Sisterhood of BC, 214, 233–34, 236

Native Voice (periodical), 232–37, 235(f), 282

NCW (National Council of Women of Canada), 32–33, 127–28, 174, 196, 209, 216, 223. *See also* LCWs (Local Councils of Women)

Negro Christian Alliance, 135–36. *See also* black Canadians

Nelson, 32, 65, 100

New Brunswick, 205–6

New Era League, 41, 206, 215, 218

New Man ideal, 32, 131–32

New Westminster: municipal and school board franchise, 52, 59; referendum (1916), 197, 200; suffragists, 30, 32, 72, 105–6, 181. *See also* Cunningham, Mary Ann Woodman

New Woman ideal, 31–32, 81–82, 107–8, 111, 131

newspapers. *See* media and print culture

Nielson, Carmen, 138

Nisga'a people, 213(f), 236–37

non-partisanship: about, 50, 64–66, 95; Independent candidates, 209; journalists, 112; male allies, 50; political parties as alliances, 64–66; post-suffrage activism, 215–16;

referendum (1916) allies, 196, 201–2, 204–5; women's organizations, 55, 95, 209. *See also* political parties

North Vancouver, 72

Norton, Mary, 144–45, 217

novels, 107–9, 108(f)

O'Boyle, William, 84, 89, 94–95, 101–2, 242

open-air events, 95, 104–6, 158

Opinions of Mary (Townley), 107–9

opponents of suffrage. *See* anti-suffragists

Oregon, 132, 170, 195

organized labour. *See* labour unions

Osterhout, Mildred, 209–10

Panagopolous, Bernice, 100, 104, 157–58

Pandora Street Methodist Church, Victoria, 26–27, 27(f)

Pankhurst, Emmeline, 11, 37, 70, 171, 175, 176, 179, 182, 194, 223, 241

parades, 103–4, 105(f), 158

Parker, Adela, 131, 176

Parkhurst, Miss, 70

Parliaments, Model or Mock, 98–99

Parr, Dorothy, 152, 157, 241

Parr, Frank, 143(f), 152

Parr, Louisa, 54, 143(f), 152, 157, 161–62, 241

partisan politics. *See* non-partisanship; political parties

patriarchy, 8–9, 37, 129. *See also* gender; marriage and families; men and masculinity

Paull, Andrew, 232, 233

peace movement, 193, 216–17

Peachland, 208

Pearson, George, 228

PEL (Political Equality League): about, 6–7, 66–73, 205; *Champion* (journal), 1–2, 2(f), 14, 71–72, 109, 113–15, 129,

204–5. *See also* candidates and elected officials, women; enfranchisement of women; federal franchise; municipal franchise; race and national origin, enfranchisement; race and national origin, exclusion from suffrage ideals

Punjab, 124, 126, 127. *See also* South Asian Canadians

Qichao, Liang, 184, 186(f)
Quebec, 194, 206

race and national origin: about, 118–19, 141, 224–25, 238; anti-immigrant sentiment, 119–28; community vs suffragist activism, 135–36; eugenics movement, 222–23; hierarchies in, 119; human rights, 224–25, 231; intersectional approaches, 240; legal rights of women, 41–42; mixed-race relationships, 126–27; "mothers of the race," 122–24; mothers' pensions, 221; political under-representation, 193, 210–11, 244–46, 245(f); power relations, 239; primitive vs civilized society, 8; professions, 224, 226, 230; "race" as non-British and non-Christian immigrants, 119; segregation, 133, 136; social welfare eligibility, 221; sources and further reading, 264–67; South Asian women, 125–28; WCTU members, 28; white entitlement assumptions, 12–14, 118–20, 122. *See also* black Canadians; Chinese Canadians; European immigrants (non-British); immigrants; Indigenous peoples; Indigenous women; Japanese Canadians; South Asian Canadians; white settlers
race and national origin, enfranchisement: about, 3–4, 214–15, 237; British subjects, 126–27, 225–26,

228; candidates and elected officials, 193, 209–11, 213(f), 236–37; municipal franchise, 51–54, 228; provincial jurisdiction over enfranchisement, 4, 13–14, 206–7, 214–15, 237; provincial restrictions, 214–15, 237; rationale for, 225–30
race and national origin, exclusion from suffrage ideals: about, 3–4, 118–19, 141, 238; Asian Canadians, 3–4, 12–13, 118–19, 141, 188, 238; European immigrant men vs Canadian women's enfranchisement, 40, 62, 97, 119–22; Indigenous peoples, 42, 119, 137–41; "mothers of the race" as white, 123–24; referendum (1916) aftermath, 205–6; South Asian Canadians, 4, 126–28
Rahim, Husain, 126
Rankin, Jeannette, 171, 175–76
referendum (1916): about, 4, 14–15, 90–91, 191–95; aftermath, 4, 193–94, 204–11; Bowser's government, 192, 195–97, 200; election results, 4, 192, 203–4; enfranchisement rationale, 90–91, 97, 191(f), 198–201; historical context, 192–95; media, 191(f), 198–203; non-partisanship, 201–2, 205; opposition to, 195, 197, 202–3; political alliances, 194–205; prohibition issue, 31, 204; sources and further reading, 277; SRA activism, 191(f), 197–203, 206
reform movement. *See* social reform movements
reforms, post-suffrage. *See* postsuffrage reforms
religion and spirituality: about, 21–26; allies for referendum (1916), 199; anti-suffragist rationale, 77, 83–85; global networks, 114; "irreligion," 21; Jews, 15, 28, 32, 199–200, 216; media, 112–14; Muslims, 129; opposition to

weeklies. *See* media and print culture
Western Clarion (periodical), 25, 44, 65, 69, 113, 150–52
Western Methodist Recorder (periodical), 23, 112–13
Western Socialist (periodical), 150
Western women, 130–31
white settlers: demographics, 6, 12, 20; domestic science in rural areas, 36; entitlement assumptions, 12–14, 118–20, 122, 126; male allies, 49–50; "mothers of the race," 122–24; suffrage movement, 6–7, 12–13, 49–50, 132, 135. *See also* progress and modernity; race and national origin
Willard, Frances, 26–27, 29
Williams, Parker, 149–50, 152, 165, 181
Wilson, Belle, 34, 146
Winch, Harold, 228, 237
Winstead, Rose, 71
Wollstonecraft, Mary, 7–8
Women's Canadian Clubs, 70(f), 81, 108, 182
Women's Employment League, 125
women's enfranchisement. *See* candidates and elected officials, women; enfranchisement; enfranchisement of women; enfranchisement of women, rationale; marital status and enfranchisement; race and national origin, enfranchisement
Women's Forum, 55, 56, 70, 215, 218
Women's Freedom Union (Go-Aheads), 7, 68, 72
Women's Institutes, 36
Women's International League for Peace and Freedom, 56, 216–17
Women's Liberal Association, 35, 64, 93, 196, 197
women's movement: about, 6–8, 20–21, 44–45, 72–73; education on women's legal rights, 38–40; interconnection of issues, 29; New Woman

ideal, 31–32, 81–82, 107–8, 111, 131; research on policy and law, 32, 37, 43; sex work reforms, 42–44, 239; social services, 20; sources and further reading, 253, 254, 281, 284; suffragist alliances, 21, 114–15; Western woman, 130–31. *See also* family law; feminism; global networks; male allies; marriage and families; maternal feminism; motherhood; professions and higher education; suffrage movement; temperance movement
women's movement organizations: about, 20–21, 31–36, 72–73, 253. *See also* International Council of Women; LCWs (Local Councils of Women); NCW (National Council of Women of Canada); Vancouver; Victoria; WCTU (Woman's Christian Temperance Union); WSL (Woman's Suffrage League)
Women's Parliament, 98–99
Women's Press Club, 34–35
Women's Social and Political Union (WSPU) (UK), 15, 84–86, 85(f), 175–82
work. *See* capitalism; labour movement; labour unions; professions and higher education; working women; working-class women
working women: about, 111, 144–49, 153–55; anti-immigrant sentiment, 125; demographics, 145–46; equal pay, 7, 146–48, 154; labour programs, 125, 153–54; low pay, 145, 153–54; media coverage, 111; sources and further reading, 254, 271; suffrage alliances, 153–54. *See also* labour movement; professions and higher education; working-class women
working-class women: about, 15–16, 144–49, 155–63, 166–67; Christian congregations, 21; competition with men, 155, 220; demographics, 146,